Contemporary Police Organization and Management
Issues and Trends

Edited by

William G. Doerner, Ph.D.
School of Criminology and Criminal Justice,
Florida State University

and

M. L. Dantzker, Ph.D.
Department of Criminal Justice,
University of Texas—Pan American

BUTTERWORTH
HEINEMANN

Boston Oxford Auckland Johannesburg Melbourne New Delhi

Recognizing the importance of preserving what has been written, Butterworth–Heinemann prints its books on acid-free paper whenever possible.

 Butterworth–Heinemann supports the efforts of American Forests and the Global ReLeaf program in its campaign for the betterment of trees, forests, and our environment.

Library of Congress Cataloging-in-Publication Data

Contemporary police organization and management : issues and trends / edited by William G. Doerner, M.L. Dantzker.
    p.   cm.
    Includes bibliographical references and index.
    ISBN 0-7506-7137-8 (alk. paper)
    1. Police administration—United States. 2. Police chiefs—United States. 3. Leadership—United States. 4. Communication in police administration—United States. 5. Police ethics—United States. 6. Police—United States—Personnel management. I. Doerner, William G., 1949– . II. Dantzker, Mark L., 1958– .
    HV7935.C63   1999
    363.2'068—dc21   99-17481
                                                                    CIP

British Library Cataloguing-in-Publication Data
A catalogue record for this book is available from the British Library.

The publisher offers special discounts on bulk orders of this book.
For information, please contact:
Manager of Special Sales
Butterworth-Heinemann
225 Wildwood Avenue
Woburn, MA 01801-2041
Tel: 781-904-2500
Fax: 781-904-2620

For information on all Butterworth–Heinemann publications available, contact our World Wide Web home page at: http://www.bh.com

10 9 8 7 6 5 4 3 2 1

Printed in the United States of America

Contents

Illustrations

Tables

Preface

The very nature of policing and its continuous drive to keep pace with societal changes means that there always is ample room for discussion, criticism, and more research. In examining the growth of policing, both as an occupation and as a separate field of study, books that provide contemporary insights into various operational aspects continue to be in demand. Butterworth–Heinemann already has ventured into this area with *Contemporary Policing: Personnel, Issues, and Trends* (1997), edited by M. L. Dantzker. Butterworth–Heinemann is building on this start by expanding into a series of works under the general rubric of Contemporary Policing. Given the framework, this volume centers around issues of police management and organization.

A second driving force behind this project is that the book is intended to serve as a supplementary reader to *Police Organization and Management: Yesterday, Today, and Tomorrow* (1999) written by M. L. Dantzker. Special care was taken to ensure that this edited collection of readings would support other primary textbooks in undergraduate courses. At the same time, the currency of the topics included in the book, as well as the broad literature coverage, makes it suitable reading for graduate students searching for a sound orientation to the field.

A third feature of this book is that the editorial team combines a unique blend of academic and practical concerns along with a demonstrated research record. In terms of law enforcement, Professors Doerner and Dantzker have amassed considerable variations in background as sworn police officers, accumulated a wealth of experience training new and seasoned police personnel, and served as consultants to various local, state, and international organizations. On the academic side, both editors teach undergraduate and graduate criminal justice courses at the university level, are active researchers, have written numerous articles and several books, and serve as manuscript reviewers for a variety of journals and book publishers. In short, the two editors are "known commodities" in both the law enforcement and academic worlds. Combining their backgrounds with those of all the contributors provides an accumulation of experiences and knowledge that few books can match. Furthermore, because of their extensive backgrounds, readers should feel comfortable with what they digest, knowing that the information comes from real people with a firm understanding of the topics discussed. In short, this text offers more in its brevity that many more arduous books could ever hope to present.

Turning to the actual contents of this book, we offer discussion of 12 very important topics for police management and organization. Beginning with Chapter 1, "Organizing the Police Response," the foundation for police management and organization, as well as the remainder of the text, is established. Chapter 2, "The Police Executive," provides an introduction to the person that leads and manages police agencies and visits several related issues. Chapter 3, "Bumps in the Road to Advancement: A Chief's Perspective," is unique in that it is written from the perspective of a former police chief. How one behaves is extremely important, but how a leader behaves may have far more reaching implications. Chapter 4, "Ethical Leadership," looks at the concept of leader behavior from an ethical perspective. Whether an individual understands what he or she is told or how that person interacts with others is extremely important. The key is communication, a topic scrutinized in Chapter 5, "Communication: An Agency Imperative." Because police agencies do not produce easily recognized or measured products, assessing an agency or officer can be difficult. Yet, this is an important aspect for effective leadership. Therefore, Chapter 6, "Productivity and Performance Evaluation," looks at the issues related to these important topics.

In what is obviously becoming a litigation happy society, police leaders must be well-versed in civil liability. Chapter 7, "Civil Liability: Executive Preparation," provides important insights into this growing area of concern. The physical and mental health of officers are as important to individuals as they are to an organization. Chapter 8, "Wellness: A Matter of Health," steers attention to the importance of a healthy work group. Chapter 9, "Labor Relations," examines one of the more difficult aspects of being a manager or a leader.

Although the practice is almost 20 years old, Chapter 10, "Accreditation: Agency Professionalization," addresses a movement that still is in its infancy. Even though the number of accredited agencies continues to grow, much remains to be done. Another key factor, money and the economic aspects behind the police organization, occupies Chapter 11, "Financing Police Services." Finally, the book concludes by looking at an interesting and important concept, "Policing in a Multicultural Society." How difficult is it for today's police officer to do the job? This chapter helps answer that question.

Overall, the text provides insight and information about 12 important and time-tested issues. The information is presented in a manner we hope will stimulate further thought and discussion.

Acknowledgments

We would like give a special note of thanks to all the authors who contributed their thoughts to this volume. Everybody worked under very tight deadlines and responded cheerfully to the suggestions for revisions, which made the editing chores run smoothly.

The biggest contributor to this book, though, was Laurel DeWolf, our senior editor at Butterworth–Heinemann. Laurel gave us free rein on the project, helped us with the technical aspects whenever we felt uncomfortable, and created a harmonious atmosphere from beginning to end.

It also took the keen eye and incisive pen of Gnomi Gouldin, our copyeditor, to hone what we had put on paper into acceptable prose.

Finally, this project was made possible by our families, who put up with the grumbling, impatience, and frustration that accompany an undertaking such as this one.

Contributors

Damon D. Camp, Jr., has been a faculty member in the Criminal Justice Department at Georgia State University since 1982 and served as the department chair from 1982 to 1988. He holds a Ph.D. in government from Claremont Graduate School and earned a J.D. from Georgia State University. Professor Camp is a past editor of *Criminal Justice Review* and has held a variety of offices in state and regional criminal justice educational associations. During the 1988–1989 term, Dr. Camp was elected president of the Southern Criminal Justice Association. He worked closely with the Georgia Public Safety Training Center and conducted research and training for the Metropolitan Atlanta Rapid Transit Authority Police Department, the Georgia Department of Corrections, the Fulton County Sheriff's Office, the Georgia Association of Chiefs of Police, the Georgia Sheriff's Association, and the East Point, Georgia, Police Department. His research interests include domestic terrorism, civil liability, criminal justice management issues, and white-collar crime.

M. L. Dantzker currently is an associate professor and the graduate program director in the Department of Criminal Justice at the University of Texas—Pan American. He holds a Ph.D. in administration through the Institute of Urban Studies at the University of Texas at Arlington. While attending graduate school, Dr. Dantzker worked as a full-time law enforcement officer in the Terre Haute, Indiana, and Fort Worth, Texas, Police Departments. He also has been certified as a police officer in Georgia. His research interests have focused on the impact of education, stress, and job satisfaction on police officers, as well as various facets of the careers of police executives. Professor Dantzker has written textbooks on policing, statistics, and research methods. His most recent book, *Police Organization and Management: Yesterday, Today, and Tomorrow,* is published by Butterworth–Heinemann.

William G. Doerner is a professor in the School of Criminology and Criminal Justice at Florida State University. He earned a B.A. in sociology from Fairfield University, an M.A. in sociology at Emory University (1973), and a Ph.D. in sociology from the University of Tennessee (1977). He also is in his 20th year as a part-time sworn law enforcement officer with the Tallahassee Police Department, where he works as a one-person uniformed patrol unit. He has written *Introduction* *to Law Enforcement: An Insider's View* (Butterworth–Heinemann, 1998) and coauthored the second edition of *Victimology* (Anderson, 1998), as well as the *Study Guide for the Florida Corrections Officer's Certification Examination* (Pineapple Press, 1997) and the *Study Guide for the Florida Law Enforcement Officer's Certification Examination* (Pineapple Press, 1996).

James W. Golden is an associate professor in the Department of Criminal Justice at the University of Arkansas at Little Rock. He holds a B.S. in radio-television (1974), a B.A. in criminology (1981), and an M.P.A. (1985) from Arkansas State University, as well as a Ph.D. in criminal justice from Sam Houston State University (1994). Prior to assuming his present position, he was a senior research coordinator in the Criminal Justice Institute at the University of Arkansas at Little Rock. Dr. Golden also was an assistant professor of law enforcement and criminology at Arkansas State University and spent eight years as a patrol officer, traffic accident investigator, and criminal investigator with the Jonesboro, Arkansas, Police Department. He is a member of the Police and Advocacy Leadership Project Team with the Police Executive Research Forum, which is developing a leadership curriculum for police and advocacy executives in cooperation with the National Institute of Justice Community-Oriented Policing Services and the Violence Against Women's Office. He is a consultant and evaluator with both the COPS Domestic Violence Training Project and the Arkansas Violence Against Women's Act Grant to Encourage Arrest Project. He leads a project team evaluating a Community Policing Problem Solving–Residential Burglary Reduction project, was recently awarded a grant to study the effects of jail overcrowding in Pulaski County, and is working on a crime survey for the state of Arkansas.

Barbara J. Hauptman, a deputy chief of police since 1993, is a 20-year veteran of the Omaha Police Department. As a police officer, she worked assignments ranging from uniformed patrol, vice and narcotics, training, and homicide to research and planning. She earned two bachelor's degrees from the University of Nebraska at Omaha, one in education (1978) and another in criminal justice (1982). Chief Hauptman also holds master's degrees in social work (University of Nebraska at Omaha, 1986), management (Bellevue University, 1994), and leadership (Bellevue University, 1998). She also is a graduate of the Federal Bureau of Investigation's National Academy. Chief Hauptman delivered a seminar, "Organizational Ethics: A Top-Down Approach," at the Southwestern Law Enforcement Institute's Fifth Annual Ethics Conference in Plano, Texas, during 1996. She attended the Southwestern Law Enforcement Institute's Ethics: Train-the-Trainer course and conducts ethics training with the Omaha Police Department's recruit academy classes. Currently, she is assigned as the chief's executive officer and fills in as the Administrative Services Bureau commander with responsibility for the department's budget, crime laboratory, detention, evidence/property, and facilities and fleet management.

Michael J. Heidingsfield is the former chief of police and director of public safety for the city of Scottsdale, Arizona, a position he held from 1991 until 1998.

Prior to gaining that post, he moved up the ranks to become the senior deputy police chief with the Arlington, Texas, Police Department. Chief Heidingsfield earned an undergraduate degree in criminology from Florida State University, an M.A. in liberal arts with an emphasis on public policy from Texas Christian University, and now is a doctoral candidate in business administration at Andrew Jackson University. He also is a graduate of the Senior Management Institute for Police, generally considered to be the most advanced police executive training program in the country with faculty drawn primarily from the Harvard University Schools of Business and Government. In addition, he was tapped three times for gubernatorial appointments to criminal justice posts for the state of Arizona and has made presentations before the International Association of Chiefs of Police and the Police Executive Research Forum. At the present time, he is the director and faculty chair for Law Enforcement Programs at Rio Salado College and holds the rank of colonel in the U.S. Air Force Reserve.

Ronald D. Hunter is an associate professor of criminology at the State University of West Georgia in Carrollton, Georgia. He holds a bachelors degree in criminology, master's degrees in public administration and social science, and a Ph.D. in criminology, all from Florida State University. Prior to entering academia, Dr. Hunter was a sergeant with the Tallahassee, Florida, Police Department, where he held a variety of supervisory assignments within patrol, administrative services, and criminal investigations. He is the 1998 president of the Southern Criminal Justice Association and the immediate past chair of the Academy of Criminal Justice Sciences Section on Security and Crime Prevention. Dr. Hunter is a consultant and expert witness in law enforcement and crime prevention and has written several articles and books in these areas. He also is an appointed municipal judge in Cave Springs, Georgia.

Richard H. Martin is the director of the Criminal Justice and Law Enforcement Programs at Elgin Community College in Illinois. He earned an Ed.D. from Indiana University in higher education administration with concentrations in criminal justice and health sciences. Dr. Martin is the executive counselor for the Community College Section of the Academy of Criminal Justice Sciences. In addition, he is a commissioner for the Woodstock, Illinois, Police Department and the McHenry County, Illinois, Sheriff's Department. Dr. Martin also is on the Executive Board of the Midwest Region of the National Association of Academic Affairs Administrators, a delegate for the Illinois Association of Fire and Police Commissioners to the Illinois Training Board, and a member of the Illinois Police Intern Curriculum Advisory Committee. He holds a third-degree black belt and is a certified instructor in both Chung Moo Doe and Shin Nagare Karate.

Kimberly A. McCabe is an assistant professor of criminal justice at the University of South Carolina. She received her Ph.D. in sociology from the University of South Carolina in 1996. Her research interests include small-town law enforcement and rural policing. She currently is the administrator of South

Carolina's State Accreditation Program as well as a national assessor for law enforcement accreditation. Her most current works may be found in the journals of *Criminal Justice Review* and *Social Science Computer Review*. She recently received one of South Carolina's Top Ten Government Documents Awards for her report, *A National Examination of Small Police Departments, 1997*.

James B. Merritt is the director of research and training for the Southern States Police Benevolent Association, which is housed in Atlanta and covers a ten-state area. Prior to joining the PBA, he served as director of research and development at the Georgia Police Academy. There, he conducted task analyses and designed training programs for supervisors, managers, trainers, and investigators as well as acting as the legislative liaison to the Georgia Assembly. In addition to holding a bachelors degree from Diablo Valley College and a master's degree in education administration from the University of North Carolina at Greensboro, Mr. Merritt worked as the director of staff development and training with the North Carolina Department of Corrections and as a police officer with the city of Alameda, California. He is a qualified expert witness on law enforcement policies and procedures, training, and performance analysis.

David Olson is an assistant professor of criminal justice at Loyola University of Chicago. He was the recipient of the Assistant United States Attorney General's Graduate Research Fellowship and received a Ph.D. in political science and public policy analysis from the University of Illinois in 1997. Prior to his appointment at Loyola, Olson held the position of senior research scientist at the Illinois Criminal Justice Information Authority. There, he directed the Illinois Statewide Drug and Violent Crime Control Strategy Impact Evaluation Program and served on the staff of the Illinois Governor's Task Force on Crime and Corrections, the Illinois Legislative Committee on Juvenile Justice, and the Illinois Truth-in-Sentencing Commission. He has written extensively on the topic of criminal justice finance, including an analysis of justice expenditure trends and transactional costs of various criminal justice system activities for the Statistical Analysis Center in the Montana Department of Justice.

Mittie D. Southerland is a professor and coordinator of criminal justice in the Department of Political Science, Criminal Justice, and Legal Studies at Murray State University. She earned an M.S. in criminal justice at Eastern Kentucky University in 1973 and a Ph.D. in social and philosophical studies in higher education at the University of Kentucky in 1984. A former criminal justice planner and juvenile counselor, her expertise is in the areas of administration, management, and supervision, with particular emphasis on organizational environments and change in the police setting. Dr. Southerland was a consultant to a number of police agencies and is involved in field research and evaluation of community policing. Dr. Southerland is coauthor of *Police Administration* (McGraw-Hill, 1991) and *Workplace Violence: A Continuum from Threat to Death* (Anderson, 1997). She was elected president of the Southern Criminal Justice Association and has served two terms as a member of the Academy of Criminal Justice Sciences Executive Board. She currently is chair of the Academic Review Committee for ACJS and chairs the ACJS Committee on Minimum Standards for Criminal Justice Education. In 1997, she received the Educator of the Year Award from the Southern Criminal Justice Association.

Benjamin S. Wright is an associate professor of criminology, criminal justice, and social policy as well as the division chair at the University of Baltimore. He received a Ph.D. from Florida State University in criminology in 1988 after earning his undergraduate and master's degrees at the University of South Carolina. He taught on the criminal justice faculties at South Carolina State University and Louisiana State University. Dr. Wright's research and teaching emphases include law enforcement, criminal and procedural law, research methods, police organizational behavior, and affirmative action in law enforcement. His most recent work culminated in two evaluation reports for the city of Baltimore. The first project, in conjunction with the Baltimore Police Department, examined the effectiveness of a juvenile firearms reduction program. The second project, undertaken on behalf of the mayor's office, focused on the status of African-American males in Baltimore's criminal justice system.

Chapter 1

Organizing the Police Response

William G. Doerner, Florida State University

Welcome to *Contemporary Police Organization and Management: Issues and Trends*. As you leaf through the pages of this book, you might begin wondering why you are even studying the topic of police management. After all, when you graduate, you will start out in an entry-level job, at the bottom of the organization, and remain there for the next several years. A number of reasons emerge here. First of all, no matter what kind of a job you take, you will be working within an organizational environment and subject to managerial decisions. While you will have no veto power over management's promulgations, the readings assembled in this book will give you a foundation for understanding some of the things that go on around you. Second, at some point in your career, you might decide that you would like to move up in your job. While there is no sure-fire recipe for advancement through the ranks and achieving success, the discussions throughout this book will alert you to a variety of things you need to consider. Third, even if you decide not to take a position within a criminal justice organization, this book will be helpful. As a citizen and taxpayer, you will be affected in many ways by the decisions police administrators reach. This book will give you a fuller understanding of those issues and appreciation of the reasoning behind those decisions.

It is important to realize that this book is not an encyclopedia of police organization and management. However, it is more than just a collection of catchy ideas and snazzy topics. We assembled a group of experts, who have amassed a considerable background and a wide range of talents in the police world and in academia. We asked them to focus on a group of critical subjects and delve deeper into these important concerns than an average textbook might cover. The outcome is a broad array of insights that highlight a number of key issues prominent in today's arena of law enforcement. Within these pages you will find no glib solutions. Instead, the goal is to equip the reader with the necessary tools and relay essential information so that he or she can arrive at a sound conclusion pertaining to the subject matter.

This chapter serves as the gateway to the rest of the book. Its purpose is to provide you a set of fundamental building blocks. The concepts and ideas presented here will help you mold a framework for understanding what appears in the later chapters. They also will provide a backdrop that will help you recognize the complexities that surround the police world whenever you see an officer performing his or her duties. But, before we launch right into a discussion of these issues, we need to make sure we have a grasp on how the American police system is assembled, the structure within an agency, and how local law enforcement agencies are organized.

THE AMERICAN POLICE SYSTEM

When observers compare the American police system to how law enforcement is organized in other countries, one key difference becomes immediately noticeable: American policing is a highly fragmented, decentralized enterprise. For example, many countries have installed a single organization, bureau, or department that assumes responsibility for law enforcement throughout that entire nation. However, just the opposite is true here in the United States. The early American settlers were leery of concentrating unbridled power within one government entity. Their objections to a singular national security force prompted the policing mandate to be spread over a number of different agencies. These subdivisions usually parallel or correspond to geographical areas. *Fragmentation*, then, refers to this lack of concentration. Instead of housing police powers under a single umbrella, law enforcement activity in America is scattered over numerous agencies.

In a very broad sense, while some of this fragmentation is based on function, most of it is due to *geographical jurisdiction*. Local police perform their duties within city or municipal boundaries. Generally, sheriff's departments, in addition to other obligations, provide similar services in unincorporated areas or the remainder of the county. At the state level, one typically encounters a highway patrol that focuses on vehicular traffic and a state police that operates as a scaled-down version of the Federal Bureau of Investigation. Superimposed over these layers is a myriad of federal agencies, which enjoy national jurisdiction. Sandwiched in between these organizations are special police departments. These independent organizations tend to perform unique functions or serve a narrow populace. For example, they may provide security for such locations as reservations, hospitals, college and university campuses, schools, airports, transit systems, state capital complexes, and so forth. As you might guess, this labyrinth of sworn personnel dedicated to providing protective services is the modern day equivalent of the Tower of Babel.

The fragmentation and decentralization become more apparent when one tries to count the number of law enforcement agencies and sworn personnel (police officers and sheriff's deputies) in this country. Contrary to what one might assume, the federal government maintains no master list of all the police and sheriff departments in existence. The Federal Bureau of Investigation has a pretty extensive listing, as do other federal offices. However, a comparison of these lists uncovers substantial differences. After consolidating all the entries and eliminating obvious duplicates, the best estimate is that there were 17,784 local police and sheriff agencies employing 521,858 full-time sworn officers in calendar year 1993 (Maguire et al., 1998, pp. 109–110).

Perhaps a peek at some numbers will help frame this discussion. According to the most recent figures available (Reaves and Goldberg, 1998, p. 5), 62% of all local municipal agencies in this country employ fewer than ten officers. Less than 4% of all local agencies (515 agencies) have at least 100 officers on their payrolls. In 1996, the combined roster of the five largest agencies in the United States (Chicago, Houston, Los Angeles, New York, and Philadelphia) accounted for one out of every six officers in this country (Reaves and Goldberg, 1998, p. 6).

A similar picture emerges when one focuses on sheriff's departments. Almost 90% of these agencies employ fewer than 100 sworn personnel. In fact, the typical sheriff's office registers 50 full-time deputies and 34 full-time nonsworn personnel (Reaves and Goldberg, 1998, p. 8).

Given this diversity, it is next to impossible to talk about the "average" police department. Agency size dictates what an agency looks like, how a department is structured, and what specialized functions are pursued. Much of what follows throughout this book refers to larger, urban police departments. With that caveat in mind, one should realize that certain consistencies appear from one agency to the next as law enforcement administrators attempt to wrestle with the crime problem and discharge the mandate "to serve and to protect."

THE RANK STRUCTURE

Many police departments embrace and resemble a paramilitary structure. The rank structure, for example, consists of a hierarchy that takes the shape of a pyramid. Authority decreases as one descends in rank. The chief or sheriff sits at the peak or the highest point in the organization. Directly below the chief is the assistant chief or deputy chief. Similarly, the sheriff usually has an undersheriff or a similarly named position that represents the second-in-command person. Borrowing heavily from military terminology, the rank structure in a law enforcement organization may consist of colonel, major, captain, lieutenant, sergeant, corporal, and finally, officer or deputy.

This relative arrangement of roles also denotes the authority or control that each incumbent possesses over other agency members. Lieutenants, for example, supervise sergeants and other lesser-ranking officers or deputies. In turn, lieutenants are accountable to supervisors vested with a higher rank. This vertical differentiation is referred to as the *chain of command.*

The bureaucratic chain of command also determines the nature of formal interaction within an agency. Generally speaking, orders and directives flow from the top of the structure down to the bottom rungs of the organization. In a traditional department, the chief or sheriff, along with his or her inner circle of advisors, formulate policy, rules, and regulations. These expectations, in turn, make their way downward to supervisors, who are responsible for their implementation, and to employees, who are responsible for adhering to these standards.

This strategy intends to accomplish two objectives. For one thing, the top echelon usually has amassed a wide range of occupationally relevant experience and expertise. Under ideal conditions, then, the policy formulation process taps this reservoir of knowledge and draws on the best talent available. The second objective here is to ensure continuity and uniformity. In other words, the organization wants to be assured that decision making does not vary from one call to the next or from one member to another (Doerner, 1998, pp. 260–261).

This need for carefully written policy guidelines and appropriate training has not escaped outside notice. Damon Camp, a criminal justice professor who later in his career attended law school and became a lawyer, devotes attention to this facet in Chapter 7, where he deals with civil liability. He explains that the failure to draft appropriate policy guidelines does not excuse police leaders or make them immune from being responsible for employee misbehavior. In fact, Professor Camp presents a number of issues of which police executives need to be aware if they wish to avoid unnecessary litigation and costly civil lawsuits.

Another traditional feature associated with chain of command centers around the immutable channel of communication. Under a strict chain-of-command operation, formal communication between organizational layers of different ranks must follow a rigid protocol. For instance, a sergeant who wishes to bring a matter to the attention of the chief or sheriff must route the message through the lieutenant. The lieutenant then forwards the communication to the captain, who sends it up to the major. The major passes it on to the colonel, who delivers it to the assistant chief or undersheriff. After this link, the message reaches the top executive. Should a formal response be forthcoming, it will make its way down the formal chain of command through each supervisory level until it reaches the initiating member. Although this route may not be expeditious, the practice ensures that everybody in the organization is kept abreast of developments. Professor Southerland deals with the intricacies of communication within and between these layers in a later chapter.

This arrangement also allows the upper echelon to groom selected members for supervisory roles. As former Police Chief Heidingsfield explains in Chapter 3, supervisors wear two hats. Not only are they interested in delivering police services, they also must convey administrative expectations to their subordinates so as not to circumvent the leadership vision. Sometimes, differing interpretations can lead to opposite viewpoints and stagnate the organization. Deputy Chief Hauptman elaborates on this point in Chapter 4. There, she explains that ethics are of paramount importance. In other words, leadership should be sensitive to possible conflicts and help set the tone as to what is expected of individual members.

ORGANIZATIONAL STRUCTURE

Like any formal organization, size (either in terms of membership or functions) determines the structure of an agency. As the size of a law enforcement agency increases, the need to isolate the police response into smaller and more specialized units grows correspondingly. While this expansion adds more layers to the structure, the differentiation is intended to provide more effective delivery of police services. Instead of trying to be jacks of all trades, officers or units can develop particular job skills and carve out niches that are beneficial to the agency.

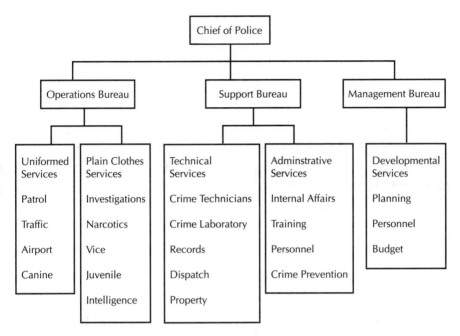

Figure 1–1 An Organizational Chart for a Hypothetical Police Agency

Many agencies divide their work into two major branches: line functions and staff functions. *Line functions* encompass units devoted to carrying out the daily function of the agency. Organizational components here include the patrol division, the detective bureau or criminal investigation division, vice and narcotics, traffic, juvenile offenders, and intelligence. *Staff functions* pertain to the operation and management of the police agency. Some departments further divide staff functions into technical services and administration. Technical services include such elements as the crime laboratory, communications, records, property and evidence, and fleet maintenance. Administrative services refer to such things as personnel recruitment, training, internal affairs, community relations, research and development, and budget.

Figure 1–1 displays an organizational chart for a hypothetical law enforcement agency. As you can imagine, the number of different possible configurations is enormous. Sheriff's offices, for example, usually carry responsibility for jails, court security, and serving civil processes. Other agencies may include such sections as aviation or underwater recovery units, units focusing on gangs or organized crime, media relations, legal affairs, victim services, a reserve or auxiliary detachment, and so forth. In any event, an organizational chart shows the interplay among all the various branches and lends a visual picture of the overall deployment of an agency's resources.

One should realize that some agencies may employ more detailed internal organizational charts to help plot responsibilities. These depictions can be based on function, form, or geographical considerations. As Figure 1–2 shows, these graphs provide an instant snapshot as to where each member of the organization belongs and

Figure 1–2   A Detailed Internal Organizational Chart for a Hypothetical Police Agency

the immediate supervisor and corresponding chain of command. These links also spell out accountability. As Professor Golden explains in Chapter 6, measuring productivity and performance helps determine whether individuals are making progress toward meeting agency goals. If shortcomings emerge, these assessments may provide a mechanism for identifying additional resources or avenues and help shore up weak spots within the agency. For example, a dramatic rise in traffic crashes or fatalities associated with motor vehicle accidents may signal a hitherto neglected area of emphasis. Astute administrators may see the need for initiating a public awareness campaign, increased in-service training for patrol officers, specialized instruction for traffic enforcement officers, the deployment of additional personnel to the traffic unit, vehicle safety inspections, the utilization of publicized driver sobriety checkpoints, driver safety education classes in local high schools, and so forth. In essence, then, these charts can go a long way in a critical self-examination.

Another organizational concept that can be illustrated in organizational charts is span of control. *Span of control* refers to the number of persons under a supervisor's direct control. One authority on police administration (Swanson, Territo, and Taylor, 1998, p. 158) recommends that supervisors have no more than seven subordinates directly under their direction. The policy guidelines of one agency, contained in Box 1–1, put that number at eight.

Box 1–1 An Example of Policy Guidelines Regarding Span of Control

III. Span of Control. It shall be the responsibility of the bureau commanders to periodically review the span of control of all supervisory personnel under their command in order to maintain the efficiency of both the supervisors and their subordinates. In doing so, a minimum of the following should be considered:

    A. The competence of both the supervisor and the subordinates.

    B. The extent to which the supervisor must carry out non-managerial responsibilities, and the demands on the supervisor's time from other people and units.

    C. The similarity or dissimilarity of the activities being supervised.

    D. The incidence of new problems in a unit.

    E. The extent of standardized procedures.

    F. The degree of interaction between the units or personnel being supervised.

    G. The degree of geographical separation of subordinates.

    H. As a general rule, span of control should not exceed eight employees unless working conditions allow a greater number or temporarily in the event of an emergency.

Source: Tallahassee [Florida] Police Department, *Manual of Written Directives.*

Later on in this book, we visit a number of issues that surround these organizational concerns. In the next chapter, for instance, Professor Dantzker talks about the backgrounds of police executives. The historical pattern was to promote insiders. In other words, most police chiefs started their law enforcement careers at the bottom rung and worked their way to the top of the agency. Today, though, that is starting to change. Many agencies are more receptive to bringing in "outsiders" to assume the leadership role. The new leader inherits an agency that has been guided by older policies and practices. The leader becomes responsible for transforming the structure into a more progressive format.

The friction bound to ensue between the new avant-garde and the encrusted dinosaurs inevitably spawns tension within the organization. The old line will dismiss any new organizational reforms as being merely fashionable. They will point to past fads like management by objectives (MBO), team policing, total quality management (TQM), and problem-oriented policing (POP), which swept police circles like wildfire only to fade into oblivion a short time later (Hunter and Barker, 1993). One way to safeguard against the charge that current changes amount to nothing more than a shell game and to implement sound managerial practices is accreditation. Professor McCabe, currently the administrator of South Carolina's accreditation efforts and also an assessor on the national scene, explains how accreditation intends to upgrade law enforcement by making administrators aware of contemporary organizational standards. She notes that much attention in the past has centered on the professionalization of individuals as they enter the police world. While this emphasis is all well and good, it has a major limitation. If the typical law enforcement career lasts 25–30 years, then it will be almost three decades before these changes take complete effect. Accreditation, by redirecting this focus onto the police organization, represents a very conscious effort to speed up the process and render agencies more capable of satisfying their mission statements and goals.

AN OVERVIEW OF THE BOOK

Some of the comments so far have given you a glimpse of what lies ahead in this book. We assembled a team of experts based on their knowledge and expertise regarding various facets of police organization and management. We asked each contributor to concentrate on a specific area and explain some of the current problems and issues that police administrators face. Our writers also probe to determine what currents underlie these matters in an effort to determine which solutions are most applicable. Each chapter ends with a series of questions that should prompt further discussion. The experience of consuming the contents of each chapter and rummaging through the discussion questions should provoke the realization that policing is a dynamic enterprise that continues to evolve to help meet society's needs.

The next chapter, written by M. L. Dantzker, who is a former police officer turned professor, provides a closer look at the police executive. Surprisingly, the top layer of policing is one of the most neglected areas of research. Rather than aligning himself with whether the police chief should be a leader or a manager, Dantzker argues that the consummate police executive is a blend of these two roles. Whether the head of the agency should come from within the ranks or from outside the organization is not as important a consideration as the skills this person brings to the office. The skills that a "law and order" chief must emphasize differ immensely from the talents a "community policing" chief needs to exercise. In fact, just employing the word *executive* instead of *chief* implies that the expectations for this position are changing dramatically. In days gone by, advertisements could spell out achievements that prospective police chiefs needed to list on their resumes. They should have a college degree, a certain number of years of experience as sworn officers, and a threshold in terms of years of police managerial experience. Today, that orientation has changed. The emphasis now is on the possession of attributes like intelligence, leadership and managerial abilities, ability to communicate with various groups, strong mental and emotional stability, and drive and motivation. Most important, though, the new police executive must be a visionary and have a plan for where he or she is taking the organization. As you can see, the recipe for what it takes to be a police executive today represents quite a shift from yesteryear.

Chapter 3, written by Chief Michael J. Heidingsfield, who recently retired after seven years at the helm of the Scottsdale, Arizona, Police Department and now chairs the law enforcement program at Rio Salado College, looks at promotion into supervisory roles. As you might well imagine, Chief Heidingsfield launched a fair number of police careers during his time. He shares that experience and reminds the reader that the promotional path is two-sided. While the individual must do certain things to prepare himself or herself for upward mobility, the agency has a vested interest in molding future police leaders. Mentoring and stewarding careers is a responsibility that current leaders cannot ignore. From Chief Heidingsfield's perspective, newly minted supervisors are walking into a minefield fraught with a wide variety of career-numbing and career-ending traps and pitfalls. With just a little patience and some gentle guidance, the organization can assure itself of a much smoother transition. As you might imagine, Chief Heidingfield's synopsis provides a realistic guide of how to succeed in the police business for aspiring contenders.

Deputy Chief Barbara J. Hauptman from the Omaha, Nebraska, Police Department lends another insider's view as she talks about ethical leadership in Chapter 4. One of the more telling maxims is the admonition that police leaders need to "walk the talk." In other words, it is important for leaders to do as they say. A leader's actions speak volumes about which values are cherished and what expectations the executive holds for others in the organization. While most people issue the usual laundry list of traits that make a good leader, Chief Hauptman emphasizes that a well-grounded moral compass allows for sound vision, especially in times of structural change, and sets the tone within the organization.

The placement of the next chapter is important because Dr. Mittie D. Southerland explores how communication is the backbone of an agency. She reminds us that police executives typically devote much time and considerable energy to hammering out an appropriate vision statement for the entire organization. However, that task is far from finished once the ink dries on the page. In fact, the real hard work has just begun. Police executives must take great care to promote their values to the membership and ensure that "hidden messages" do not subvert their intended meaning. Of course, the paramilitary structure and the one-way, trickle-down flow of directives commonly associated with rigid chain of command are just some of the more visible hazards. Misunderstandings will emerge and, if handled properly, can provide a convenient opportunity to reinforce the desired course. Disagreements, though, are much more serious. They are indicative of potential conflict and clashing values that have the potential to thwart goal attainment. Therefore, good leaders will use these opportunities to help mold an appropriate organizational culture.

James W. Golden, another former police officer who switched careers and became a university professor, takes this opportunity to visit productivity and performance issues in Chapter 6. When we think about evaluations, we move almost automatically to looking at individual officer performance. However, Professor Golden starts out on a different note. He reminds us that agencies themselves need to be evaluated periodically to see how well they are fulfilling their missions. Another poignant reminder is that personnel evaluations are intended to serve as diagnostic and corrective tools. Rather than merely pinpointing deficiencies and punishing slumping officers with inferior pay raises, a sound evaluation procedure also carries implications for remedial efforts to help achieve goals and objectives the next time around. Most important, though, the reader becomes acutely aware that the introduction of a community policing philosophy has enormous implications for both the agency and its workers. Therefore, Professor Golden warns that it is vital for agencies to revamp their employee evaluation procedures if they intend to make a firm commitment to community policing.

Professor Damon D. Camp, Jr., took a slightly different route than other contributors to this book. After establishing himself as a university professor, he used a sabbatical to attend law school and eventually became trained as a lawyer. As you will see in Chapter 7, Dr. Camp blends these two interests deftly. The lawyer side of him devours a large volume of case law, which he organizes and digests for the reader. He focuses on civil liability, the different grounds that citizens invoke when suing an agency and its executive officers, as well as the basis for employee claims against police leaders. The criminal justice side of Professor Camp shines through when he engages the reader in a discussion of how to prevent these legal issues from materializing in the first place. Little idioms like "plaintiffs don't sue loved ones" and "winning a lawsuit can be a terrible thing to do" are humorous but absolutely right on target. Such a novel approach is a pleasant relief when dealing with a heavy topic.

Professor Richard H. Martin tackles a problem that most police administrators tacitly acknowledge but prefer to avoid. As someone directly involved in training future law enforcement officers, Dr. Martin reminds us that physical fitness is not a luxury but a necessity. As he explains, most police officers are not in optimal physical health. Sure, police work takes a toll on the body. Stressors on the job can aggravate occupational pressures. The stress becomes compounded by poor dietary habits, detrimental lifestyle choices, the sedentary nature of the job, and other adverse practices. Astonishingly, many police agencies fail to hold their officers accountable to any physical fitness standards whatsoever. From Professor Martin's viewpoint, such a deliberate shortcoming borders on sheer lunacy. For one thing, criminal activity is concentrated in youthful offenders. In other words, officers deal routinely with suspects who are in much better physical shape than they. The safety implications are self-evident. For another thing, wellness concerns translate into a major employment issue. Workers compensation claims, a reduced life expectancy for law enforcement officers, morbidity or sickness patterns, fatigue, decreased productivity, and a need to resort to extreme force during physical confrontations all are affected by this major concern. In short, Dr. Martin makes a compelling argument for why administrators should reverse current standards and implement wellness programs for their members.

Professors Hunter and Merritt bring considerable talent to explaining how the needs of the organization do not always mesh with the best interests of its members. Professor Merritt is affiliated with the Southern States Police Benevolent Association, a labor organization that champions employee issues for police officers. Dr. Hunter, a former police sergeant, has sat at the bargaining table negotiating labor contracts, pension packages, and employee benefits. Their combined experience provides a springboard for introducing the topic of police labor organizations. Many law enforcement officers serve as "at-will" employees. This means that such men and women can be fired for any reason whatsoever with no due process. When viewed in this context, it is easy to see the need for adequate job protections. Of course, a number of labor groups are competing to represent law enforcement personnel. In addition to talking about the various kinds of police labor groups and what they provide, Hunter and Merritt explain the interface between police unions and management when it comes to things like contract negotiations, disciplinary concerns, job security, and pension benefits. Their discussion on these and other issues shed interesting light on a highly critical managerial component.

Chapter 10 introduces the reader to the notion of accreditation for law enforcement agencies. Professor Kimberly A. McCabe draws on her background as the administrator of South Carolina's State Accreditation Program and an assessor for the national program to provide us a glimpse of a new effort to upgrade police organizations. Traditional reform proposals tend to earmark personnel changes as the way to alter unwanted police practices. Over the years, we have seen renewed calls for more precise hiring standards, better training, college degrees for officers, and so forth. All these efforts focused on personnel improvement. Now, a recent shift emphasizes the need to revamp organizations as a more visible solution. Dr. McCabe shares her experiences and explains why agencies should involve themselves in a self-study assessment, what they have to do to become accredited, and what tangible benefits flow from being accredited. Even more telling, though, is that Professor McCabe relies on her on-site assessment visits to illuminate some problems she has seen and offers suggestions for avoiding unnecessary difficulties with the accreditation process.

Running a police agency, of course, can be very expensive. Dr. David Olson, who has amassed an extensive background in criminal justice financing while working for various state agencies, focuses on novel funding sources. Criminal justice agencies are public entities, funded mainly by local taxpayers. While residents are clamoring for more services, a corresponding allotment of dollars is not possible. Local law enforcement agencies compete with education, health, welfare, transportation, and other sectors for their fair share of the pie. Police officials, then, have to keep a watchful eye out for nontraditional funding sources to supplement meager budgets. In this chapter, Professor Olson removes some of the mystery from the budgeting maze, explains how the various portions fit together, and demonstrates how budgetary decisions affect policy decisions. Reading this chapter will provide an appreciation for the intricacies with which police managers must deal on a daily basis.

Professor Benjamin S. Wright reminds us, in the final chapter, that police agencies must be accountable to the people whom they serve. This constituency, though, is experiencing a dramatic makeover. Dr. Wright explains how the once-heralded notion of the American "melting pot" no longer is true. Instead, uniculturalism is giving way to multiculturalism or a pluralistic society. More and more, immigrants are resisting efforts to shed their ethnic identities and blend into the mainstream. Unless police administrators cultivate a greater cultural sensitivity among the rank and file, interactional barriers are bound to foster misunderstanding between officers and members of different ethnic groups. Astute police managers must lead their membership into the 21st century by embracing multicultural policing and training officers to make fundamental changes in the way in which they embrace people who are different from themselves.

CONCLUSION

As you can see, this book highlights a number of intriguing contemporary issues confronting police administrators. Promoting organizational change is not always an easy thing to accomplish. There will be internal resistance, as well as an external reluctance, against embracing efforts to transform the organization. However, if today's police leaders are to be successful, they must confront these challenging problems and search for innovative solutions. I hope this collection of original works, written and compiled by people who are well versed in their specialties, will serve as a guide for agencies that are in transition and help stimulate novel solutions.

DISCUSSION QUESTIONS

1. Suppose the county in which you live and go to college has a local police department that provides services within the city limits, a sheriff's office that provides services throughout the county, and a university police department that provides services just on the campus. Community leaders are concerned that having three separate law enforcement agencies in the area is too much fragmentation. As a result, they wonder whether it would make sense to consolidate all three departments into a single law enforcement agency. What would be some of the benefits and shortcomings of this organizational realignment?
2. Suppose that a new police chief assumes office. As one of the reforms, the new chief wants to reduce bureaucratic congestion by eliminating all ranks within the agency. What advantages and disadvantages would accompany the dissolution of this formal chain-of-command structure?
3. Continuing with the previous question, what implications does the elimination of the rank structure carry for "span of control?"
4. Every year the Federal Bureau of Investigation compiles a report that contains information about crime and law enforcement personnel. Use this data source to create a picture of local law enforcement agencies in your state. Are most of the agencies small or large? How do your results compare with the information presented in this chapter?

REFERENCES

Doerner, W. G. *Introduction to Law Enforcement: An Insider's View.* Boston: Butterworth–Heinemann, 1998.
Hunter, R. D., and T. Barker. "BS and buzzwords: The new police operational style." *American Journal of Police* 12, no. 3 (1993), pp. 157–168.

Maguire, E. R., J. B. Snipes, C. D. Uchida, and M. Townsend. "Counting cops: Estimating the number of police departments and police officers in the USA." *Policing: An International Journal of Police Strategies and Management* 20, no. 1 (1998), pp. 97–120.

Reaves, B. A., and A. L. Goldberg. *Census of State and Local Law Enforcement Agencies, 1996*. Washington, DC: Bureau of Justice Statistics, 1998.

Swanson, C. R., L. Territo, and R. W. Taylor. *Police Administration: Structures, Processes, and Behavior*, 4th ed. Upper Saddle River, NJ: Prentice Hall, 1998.

Chapter 2

The Police Executive

M. L. Dantzker, University of Texas—Pan American

> Partly the task of leading and managing today's police organizations is a formidable challenge because even though the current executives are better prepared and educated than their predecessors, many have failed to recognize the full effects of the fundamental changes in their work force. (Stephens, 1992, p. 307)

The quote that opens this chapter comes from an individual who has spent more than 20 years in policing, many of them as a police chief. Who would know better than a police chief about the difficulties of the office, a position touted as being extremely important? Yet, despite the importance of the police chief, this position has not received proper attention. In all honesty, we know very little about the police department's top executive. Most scholarly discussion centers on whether the appropriate role ought to be one of leadership or management. Very little effort goes into trying to learn more about the person who fills that niche.

This chapter attempts to change that by addressing several issues associated with the role of police executive. It begins with a discussion of the issue of leadership versus management and then takes a peek at the qualifications for this position, selection procedures used to fill the position, the changing of the role of the police executive, and future developments.

LEADERSHIP OR MANAGEMENT?

Some people would argue that the police executive must be a manager and that providing leadership is one of a manager's tasks (Wilson and McLaren, 1977). My stance is that the police executive must be a leader who has strong managerial skills but who also knows how to delegate managerial duties. Taking this position, the concept of leadership, especially when we talk about strong and strategic leadership (Moore and Stephens, 1991), becomes a key consideration for the future of policing. Therefore, before we examine the police executive as a leader, it is prudent to explore the concept of leadership.

Leadership

Leadership plays an important role in any organization, an idea that is well-documented in the literature (Hunt and Magenau, 1993; Robinette, 1991; Stamper, 1992). Leadership affects how agency members conduct themselves. It also guides the organization toward fulfilling its mission, objectives, and goals. The foremost expectations for the person who occupies a leadership role is to be a stellar model of organizational values, norms, and beliefs. The capability of communicating and demonstrating these to other organizational members is of paramount importance. This holds true for police agencies, which are no different from any other people-oriented organizations.

> All police departments need leadership that guides and excites people toward
> desired social ends, but this is especially true of those agencies whose personnel
> have no conception of their purpose except to arrest "assholes" and answer radio
> calls. (Stamper, 1992, p. 134)

The reality of policing for the future is that leadership is a vital aspect that should not be lost or merged with the concept of management. This outlook has lead to the development of a model that advocates creating two distinct positions: the executive leader and the executive manager (Stamper, 1992).

This model relies on an appreciation of the distinction between management and leadership. *Management* can be defined as that element which leads, directs, or engineers the organization toward its goals. *Leadership*, on the other hand, is defined as that entity which influences and motivates others to fulfill their roles enthusiastically (Dantzker, 1999). One easily could conclude that leadership is a "motivator to action" while management provides the plan of action or direction. Therefore, a police leader must be one who can motivate subordinates to complete the necessary actions that make the organization effective and efficient. Professor Heidingsfield, a former police chief, will explore this theme in greater detail in Chapter 3. For the time being, suffice it to say that this quality makes the police leader a very necessary individual. Given this background, we are ready to ask, Who are police leaders?

The Police Leader

One of the most criticized elements in the history of policing has been the quality of its leaders and managers. The quality of police leadership has been called into question ever since the 1920s, when studies lamented how mediocre the upper police echelon was in this country. Unfortunately, it is an issue that scholars have not pursued to any great extent (see Cox, 1990; Goldstein, 1977; Lynch, 1975; Witham, 1985). The reality is that very little is known about police chiefs because the quantitative or qualitative information describing the police chief role or the person who becomes a police chief is extremely limited. For example, while researching this chapter, I discovered that neither of the two major associations in this country that deal with police leaders, the International Association of Chiefs of Police (IACP) and the Police Executive Research Forum (PERF), has a database that includes enough descriptive information to form a picture of just who are the police chiefs in this country. This is an extremely disturbing phenomenon when one considers the importance of the position of police chief. "Police executives are the most critical group related to improving law enforcement. Police organizations are unlikely to be better than their leaders" (Witham, 1986, p. 45). Furthermore, Witham (1987, p. 6) contends that

> It is widely recognized that the most critical ingredient in the success of an organi-
> zation is the quality of its leadership. Although police leaders cannot single-hand-
> edly upgrade law enforcement, there is no single group as important to the process.

What little information that does exist tends to support Witham's position (see Chandler, 1982; Enter, 1986a; Goldstein, 1977; Maniha, 1973; Masini and Playfair, 1978; Witham, 1985). Still, research on policing has paid very little attention to who or how qualified this person is. However, this situation is starting to change (Dantzker, 1994a, 1994b, 1996, 1997). Most recently, PERF attempted to survey "518 U.S. city and county police chiefs and other non-elected law enforcement agency directors policing jurisdictions with populations of 50,000 or more" (Police Executive Research Foundation, 1998, p. 1). However, it received only 358 valid responses. The picture formed by these participants is that police chiefs are primarily men, Caucasian, between 46 and 55 years of age, and hold a bachelors degree. Despite the small sample when compared against the almost 18,000 police agencies in this country, the PERF snapshot very well may be a good representation of police chiefs in this country. This leads us to the next question. From where do these police chiefs hail?

Historically, many police chiefs work their way up through the ranks (Chandler, 1982; Crank, 1987; Enter, 1986b). The PERF study (1998, p. 2) found that over half the respondents had been promoted from inside the agency. Unfortunately, in many instances progression through the ranks provides very limited training and prepa-ration for the position of police chief. We see more on this point in Chapter 3. Therefore, despite the advantage of being an insider, these rising chiefs are not adequately prepared for a leadership role (see Lynch, 1975; Witham, 1985, 1986, 1987).

> The quality of leadership in police organizations has varied tremendously. Some
> police organizations currently carefully select entry personnel, carefully evaluate
> their potential for promotion, promote based on merit, and prepare those who are
> promoted by sending them to appropriate training and/or educational programs.
> Others do none of these things. (Cox, 1990, p. 175)

The fact remains that there is much discrepancy as to who becomes a police chief. Regardless of who gets elevated and whether that person is promoted from within or hired from outside the agency, one would think that the requirements for being a police chief would be relatively consistent from one department to the next and that they should include criteria that best suit the job (see Cox, 1990; Goldstein, 1977; Hunt and Magenau, 1993; Maniha, 1973; Witham, 1986). Unfortunately, here is another associated problem. There is no standard in the criteria for the position of police chief or the skills a candidate should possess. Granted, police administration textbooks may offer flowery, theoretically based answers. However, the application of these theories often receives little support in the practical arena, and there is little corroborating research (Dantzker, 1994a). Perhaps, a question we should think about here is whether the police chief's qualifications are all that important? The answer is a resounding "yes."

QUALIFICATIONS AND SKILLS

As previously noted, very little research examines the qualifications or skills needed to become a police chief. However, a content analysis of 300 advertisements for police executive vacancies that appeared in *The Police Chief*, a prominent industry source of information, sheds some light on prevailing practices (Dantzker, 1994a, 1994b). The results indicate that three common criteria were mentioned in the advertisements: education, experience as a sworn officer, and police management experience. Despite an initial appearance of uniformity, the actual job descriptions really were quite diverse. For example, the level of education being sought ranged from the high school diploma to possessing a master's degree. The amount of police experience desired was overwhelmingly in the range of 6 to 10 years; 3 to 5 years was the more popular range for requisite police management experience. Other than these three areas, little commonality existed among the positions advertised.

This research supports the contention that there is no standard or core of qualifications for the position of police chief. The stance is an interesting anomaly. Despite no consistent background requirements, police executives must possess or accomplish a standard set of essential skills or tasks if they are to be successful. These skills or tasks are linked to qualifications.

Requirements, Skills, and Tasks

Discussions, debates, and research about the employment requirements for entry-level police recruits have continued over the years (Doerner, 1997). Oddly enough, the same is not true for police chiefs. Because the head of the organization holds an extremely critical position, it makes sense to expect there would be an abundant interest in what it takes to become a police chief. Yet, to date, the majority of the research regarding requirements for a police chief has focused primarily on education (Dantzker, 1994a; Enter, 1986a).

Ever since the 1931 Wickersham Commission, recommendations for raising the level of education expected of police officer candidates have not gone unnoticed. In fact, many current observers would agree that education is an important entry requirement. While an overwhelming majority of police agencies have not rushed to accept or implement higher education requirements, the level of education among active police officers continues to rise (Carter, Sapp, and Stephens, 1989; Shernock and Dantzker, 1997). Therefore, with improving educational levels among members of the bottom rung of the agency, one might expect the same would be true for police chiefs. Unfortunately, while educational requirements for line officers has been in the spotlight over the past century, the concept of educated police chiefs did not really garner any attention until the 1960s.

The first national recommendations regarding educational levels for police chiefs came from the 1967 President's Commission on Law Enforcement and the Administration of Justice. It recommended that all police chiefs should have a baccalaureate degree. By 1985, one study found that 75% of the chiefs surveyed held a diploma from a four-year college (Enter, 1986b).

No one will argue that education is not an important consideration. However, should level of formal education be the *only* requirement for a police chief? My own research (Dantzker, 1994a, 1994b, 1996) indicates many other vital requirements for the position of police chief: police management experience, extensive education and training, a record of continuous training, knowledge of police science, sensitivity to multiethnic concerns, experience with media, attendance at the FBI executive training academy or other professionally recognized institutes, and exposure to college management classes. When asked to rank a list of job requirements from high to low, police chiefs valued police management experience, extensive professional education and training, and knowledge of police science more highly than possession of a college degree (Dantzker, 1996). Despite the insights gained from this study, supportive research is sorely lacking. Despite the limited knowledge on what and how much is required to be a police chief, these job qualifiers must be linked explicitly to the tasks and skills of the position.

Many sources list the skills or tasks police chiefs need. I favor the selection that O. W. Wilson, a prominent expert on police administration, offers. According to Wilson (Wilson and McLaren, 1977), 11 areas or skills are essential for a police manager: organizing, leading, planning, communicating, controlling (placing of responsibility), decision making, budgeting, productivity, labor relations, disciplining, and job enrichment. In addition, three other skills appear to be critical ingredients: politics, managing, and empowering (Dantzker, 1994b, 1996; Dewitt, 1992; Lurigio and Rosenbaum, 1997; McElroy, Cosgrove, and Sadd, 1993; Trojanowicz and Bucqueroux, 1990; Tunnell and Gaines, 1996). My own research confirms that sitting police chiefs also hold these skills in high esteem (Dantzker, 1996).

Other loopholes remain. For instance, it would be interesting to see if the underlying philosophy of a department (traditional versus community policing) carries any implications for executive career preparation. Consider, for a moment, how drastically law enforcement has changed in recent years. Should the next generation of police chiefs concentrate on amassing the same set of credentials as their predecessors? Or, are the requirements and skills unfolding in a different direction? To better understand what the future might hold, a brief exploration of the police role with respect to community policing is prudent.

The Community Policing Role

Developing the community policing role requires a complete overhaul of the police culture (Kelling, Wasserman, and Williams, 1988; Lurigio and Rosenbaum, 1997; Sparrow, 1988; Trojanowicz and Bucqueroux, 1990). The traditional police culture portrays the job as tough crime fighting with little or no concern for targeting the underlying causes of crime. Police officers usually deal only with immediate problems for which their service has been requested.

Community policing, in contrast, requires that the police address the underlying causes and sources of problems in the community that lead to calls for service. This strategy may involve notifying the Street Department of a missing stop sign before an accident happens as well as dealing with any accident that does occur or contacting building inspectors or code enforcement officers to help vacate, and perhaps eventually tear down, an abandoned building that has become a haven for drug dealers or gang members. As you can see, this approach demands a new way of thinking for police officers. The role of the community police officer must be developed and the police culture must be changed to admit values and orientations consistent with this new role. As Deputy Chief Hauptman from the Omaha Police Department explains in Chapter 4, setting the tone for change is a primary executive concern. At the same time, if the officer's role must change, is it not reasonable to assume that the police chief's role must change as well?

The development of the community police role requires a multitude of organizational changes. For example, the infrastructure of the department must be modified to support a decentralized organization (Friedmann, 1992; "Community policing in the 1990s," 1992; Kennedy, 1993). This is necessary so that individual officers have greater use of discretion and problem-solving skills, which often go untapped. Community policing also requires systematic incorporation of community problem solving, mobilization, interpersonal relations, cultural awareness, and advocacy skill development in police training curricula (see McElroy et al., 1993; Trojanowicz and Bucqueroux, 1994). While the implementation and acceptance of community policing require cooperation from both the citizenry and police officers, its adoption and acceptance by police chiefs are mandatory. This is why it has become increasingly important to look at the qualifications and skills of individuals seeking to become police chiefs, particularly those who will be involved in community policing.

The preliminary success attributed to community policing is prompting many police departments to implement similar strategies. However, initiating a community policing effort, whether as a project, strategy, ethical mandate, or philosophy, is no easy task (see Bayley, 1994; Kennedy, 1993; Murphy, 1988; Riechers and Roberg, 1990; Sparrow, 1988). Several issues must be confronted to implement community policing successfully: (1) acknowledgment of the tenets of community policing, (2) development of the community policing role, (3) cultivation of supportive administrative leadership, (4) promotion of citizen participation, and (5) adaptation of community policing strategies to the community context (see Bayley, 1994; Brown, 1989; Dewitt, 1992; Riechers and Roberg, 1990; Sparrow, 1988; Trojanowicz and Bucqueroux, 1990).

As you can see, it takes a lot to make community policing a successful venture. Evidently, it also takes a very special type of a person to lead the effort. Who that person will be and what qualifications, requirements, and skills he or she should bring to the job are yet to be determined. One thing, though, is certain: The selected person must be an exceptional leader. This concern raises the issue of executive selection.

Originally, I planned on offering a discussion on selection of police chiefs. However, the reality is that, like qualifications and requirements, there is no standard and the criteria used vary from one government entity to the next. Still there are some common elements, such as using an outside firm to screen applicants, in-depth background checks, assessment centers, and oral board reviews. Ultimately, the individual is selected by the lead government official and perhaps approved by a governing body (e.g., city manager and city council). This decided lack of standardization, though, has led me to focus more on the hows and whys of being a police executive rather than actually getting to that position.

Regardless of how the police executive is selected, how a person operates as a leader will have a direct bearing on how well the organization functions. The question then is, What are the characteristics of a successful leader?

CHARACTERISTICS OF SUCCESSFUL LEADERSHIP

The answer to the question of what characteristics are needed by a successful police leader has a few good possibilities. However, I tend to support the response that offers a list of particular traits for successful leadership. Some fundamental traits would include intelligence, interests and aptitude, communication, mental and emotional stability, drive and motivation, cooperation, and administrative skills (Goode, 1951).

Intelligence

For policing, *intelligence* might best be defined as the ability to confront new or unforeseen situations and incidents rapidly and effectively adjusting behavior to recognize and readily understand the significant factors associated with the problem or situation no matter the complexity. Education long has been said to be a supportive element of intelligence.

A growing number of those entering law enforcement are college educated. Indeed, many agencies have adopted the corresponding expectation that police executives ought to be college educated as well (Dantzker, 1994a, 1994b). Even though a college education does not bestow "greater intelligence," it allows for the possibility more than just a high school diploma. Ultimately, the police leader will need to demonstrate intelligence beyond that of most subordinates because of the diversified roles the chief is expected to fulfill.

Interests and Aptitudes

A successful leader cannot be unidimensional, an all too common characteristic among older police leaders, who have been inundated with their careers and have little room left for anything else. A good police leader must have broader interests and aptitudes, particularly if he or she expects to communicate successfully with newer, younger, and sometimes better-educated officers, who may resist limitations in their own thinking or interests. For example, a police leader might strongly suggest or even limit off-duty employment to nonpolice activities (e.g., sales, construction) or create a program that allows officers to take a leave of absence to partake in another area of interest (e.g., going to graduate school). Dealing with labor interests, as Professors Hunter and Merritt explain in Chapter 9, may require nontraditional thinking. Regardless of how or what, a successful police leader must demonstrate a multidimensional persona and not be hemmed in by traditional expectations.

Communication

A police leader cannot spend all day behind closed doors at a desk. He or she must interact with a variety of people. As a result, the ability to communicate is an extremely important trait. In fact, this trait is so essential that a whole chapter (Chapter 5), written by Professor Southerland, is devoted to just this topic.

A good portion of what a police leader does is communicate with various internal and external groups, either verbally or in writing, to provide direction. The inability to be a good communicator will all but seal any attempts at good leadership. Why? Because an inferior command of language skills opens the door for a lack of respect from officers and the citizenry.

Mental and Emotional Stability

Any endeavor that requires a calm and rational demeanor must be accompanied by mental and emotional stability. Of course, this is true of the line officer as much as the leader. However, an unstable line officer probably would not be as detrimental to the organization as an unfit leader. The successful police leader must demonstrate a strong constitution, control of emotions, and a mental alertness that officers can count on and even emulate when situations become difficult. A leader who is weak in this area will not be successful.

Drive and Motivation

The leader guides and motivates members toward fulfilling goals. Therefore, he or she must display the drive and motivation that equals or surpasses what is expected from subordinates. More will be said about this in Chapter 6, where Professor Golden talks about evaluating employee performance. A leader who lacks the determination or will power to succeed affects subordinates by creating doubt as to the necessity to be productive and attain organizational goals. A "do-nothing" leader eventually will perpetuate "do-nothing" followers.

Cooperation

To be a successful leader, individuals must understand and accept the idea of cooperative efforts and support participatory activities. For example, if the police leader unilaterally makes decisions that affect the entire organization and its members with no input from others or refuses assistance during a crucial investigation, why would subordinates seek assistance or cooperate with others? Despite popular belief, policing does not occur in a vacuum. It requires input from many sources in the community. An uncooperative leader will not succeed in any arena.

Administrative Skills

The successful police leader must rely more on administrative skills than the technical skills used in nonleadership roles. In other words, he or she must possess the ability to understand and integrate information. For example, a good leader does not have to be a superior marksman. Instead, a good leader must be a competent disseminator of information.

Incumbents who adapt all the preceding skills are destined to be good leaders. However, a good leader must not be content to rest on his or her laurels. A key consideration is that leadership must be willing to accept change when the circumstances warrant.

CHANGING POLICE LEADERSHIP

Considering the ever-changing diversity, nature, and demands of society, police organizations need leaders who can best meet these changes. This is especially true if community policing continues and becomes the norm rather than the exception.

> Community policing represents a significant shift in organizational power and control from administration to operations. This power shift requires a new and flexible leadership style to emerge in organizations that have traditionally engaged in centralized command and control management. (Walsh, 1998, p. 20)

Historically, police leadership is best described as authoritarian and reactive. At times, this type of leadership has been somewhat successful, especially in a quasi-military organization. But future police leaders will need to adopt a different type of leadership. The question is, What type of leadership will be required?

To begin with, police leaders will need to accept and even embrace change (Enter, 1996). This will require leaders who are not reactive but rather are proactive, anticipatory, and adaptive (Gaines and Ricks, 1978).

By being proactive, the police leader is not afraid (1) to make decisions based on information that suggests that a problem can be headed off before it worsens and (2) of being creative or innovative. The proactive police leader will be a strong advocate of community policing, which, by its very nature, is strongly proactive.

Being anticipatory supports the concept of being proactive. The anticipatory or preemptive element allows the leader to anticipate what might occur and plan for it. As Professor Wright explains in Chapter 12, allowances must be made if we are to understand multicultural concerns. This forward-looking approach differs from the proactive element by foreseeing possible problems and addressing them before they can arise. For example, having witnessed how people react when an area team wins a sports championship, the anticipatory leader would have a plan in hand should a similar occasion occur in his or her jurisdiction.

Finally, an adaptive leader can react to conditions, situations, problems, and circumstances in a manner that is best suited to the time. Adaptation includes a continuum that "extends from dictatorial to democratic" (Gaines and Ricks, 1978, p. 259). Flexibility, as opposed to blind adherence to canons, is the hallmark of adaptive leadership.

Although all four elements (reactive, proactive, anticipatory, and adaptive) can be viewed as individual leadership styles (Dantzker, 1999), realistically a good police leader must incorporate all of them into his or her leadership style. The police leader who can blend the appropriate leadership elements in the right amounts will be the most successful. Sadly, traditional leadership (reactive, classical, authoritative) still is very much the norm, even though it does appears to be losing its grip on policing.

Obviously, it is not easy to be a good leader. Nor do good leaders become successful naturally. While many of the suggested characteristics can be innate, most leadership qualities need to be developed. This has been a major shortcoming in policing for years. Fortunately, this, too, may be changing.

DEVELOPING LEADERSHIP

While some may argue that leadership is an innate quality, others feel that "Leadership skills *can* be learned, developed, and improved upon, provided the proper medium exists to pass this knowledge onto the next generation of leaders" (excerpted from personal communication about a 1994 IACP proposal for a Police Leadership Institute, p. 11, sent to me by an IACP representative in 1995). Historically, there have been few avenues for developing leadership except through on-the-job training, which was minimal at best. Today's prospective police leaders can take advantage of several different learning environments, such as the FBI's National Executive Institute, the Southern Police Institute, the Southwestern Law Enforcement Institute, the Jepson School of Leadership at the University of Virginia, and California's Law Enforcement Command College. Other possibilities include courses offered by the International Association of Chiefs of Police, Police Executive Research Forum, the Institute of Police Technology and Management at the University of North Florida, the Bill Blackwood Law Enforcement Institute of Texas at Sam Houston State University, and other facilities located on university and college campuses. In any event, the point is clear: There is a distinct need to groom prospective police leaders.

In fact, there no longer is a shortage of means for developing good, strong police leaders. The problem still is the shortage of desire or opportunity for police leaders to take advantage of the means. In Chapter 3, Chief Heidingsfield talks about mentoring and entering the mainstream as necessary ingredients in the development of the next generation of police leaders. This area needs to be addressed as policing continues to balance the challenges posed by a changing society.

THE FUTURE OF POLICE LEADERSHIP

While current police chiefs are much better prepared when they assume their positions than their predecessors, the reality is that they and future police executives have an already difficult job that continues to become more complex (Stephens, 1992). The need to establish and support strong police leadership in the future is obvious.

> Police chiefs in America are presiding over structures whose features function as formidable barriers to organizational effectiveness, communication, and morale, as well as a mutually satisfying relationship with the community. (Stamper, 1992, p. 4)

Eliminating barriers will require police chiefs to become better leaders and managers. Perhaps a key to taming this dilemma could very well be the separation of management and leadership functions (Stamper, 1992; Dantzker, 1999). Additionally, because the future may become even more difficult than what we have already faced, policing requires visionary leaders who can provide a clear and consistent organizational vision.

> An organizational vision presents a clear picture of what direction the organization plans to take in the future. It should represent an achievable, challenging, and a worthwhile long-range target toward which personnel can direct their energies. (Garner, 1993, p. 2)

The future police leader must establish this vision and the framework from which the organization will succeed, communicate a clear outlook of what the organization's future may entail, and then steer the organization in the most appropriate direction. This includes forging a clear mission statement as to where the organization is going, imprinting a meaningful values statement, and empowering the members to achieve these goals (Garner, 1993). Future leaders must be willing to accept challenges (Mendofik, 1994). They also should be able to recognize and adapt to economic, technological, legal, and demographic changes and trends (Enter, 1996). Furthermore, successful leaders need to fulfill certain responsibilities, which include matching structure to objective, not falling into an activities trap (that is, paying attention to outcomes and not just process, such as how officers go about writing tickets as opposed to the number of tickets written), enriching the traditional roles, mixing creativity with accountability, being stable amid change, and creating community alliances (Stephens, 1992).

Police executives, today and tomorrow, have their work cut out for them. The traditional style of leadership (reactive, authoritarian) will not be successful. New leaders must be open, articulate, responsive, and willing to meet whatever challenges they confront.

DISCUSSION QUESTIONS

1. Considering that in many smaller agencies, the police executive must be both the top leader and manager, how would you suggest this person approach his or her roles? Even in the smaller agencies, can the top executive position possibly be divided into distinct leader and manager roles? Why or why not?
2. The police chief has been a staple of policing since its beginnings. Why do you think less attention has been paid to police chiefs than to line officers? Should the national and international organizations have more information available?
3. What qualifications should a person who wants to become a police executive possess? How important is it that the qualifications meet the tasks this person is expected to perform?
4. Police chief selection, in most cases, can be a very political process. How should a police chief be selected? Should the individual chosen come from within the agency or be an outsider?
5. How much effect do you think community policing should have on the selection of a police chief? Does it require a "new" type of chief? Why or why not?
6. Can successful leaders be created or is it simply a matter of innate ability? If they can be created, what types of courses or training would you recommend?

REFERENCES

Bayley, D. H. *Police for the Future*. New York: Oxford University Press, 1994.
Brown, L. P. "Community policing: A practical guide for police officials." *NIJ Perspectives on Policing*, no. 12 (September 1989).
Carter, D. L., A. D. Sapp, and D. W. Stephens. *The State of Police Education: Policy Direction for the 21st Century*. Washington, DC: Police Executive Research Forum, 1989.

Chandler, K. I. "A study of education of police chiefs in Illinois." Unpublished master's thesis, Western Illinois University, Macomb, 1982.

"Community policing in the 1990s." *NIJ Journal*, no. 225 (August 1992), pp. 1–8.

Cox, S. M. "Policing into the 21st century." *Police Studies* 13, no. 4 (1990), pp. 168–177.

Crank, J. P. "Professionalism among police chiefs." Doctoral dissertation, University of Colorado, 1987.

Dantzker, M. L. "Identifying employment criteria and requisite skills for the position of the police chief: Preliminary findings." *Police Forum* 4, no. 3 (1994a), pp. 9–12.

_____. "Requirements for the position of municipal police chief: A content analysis." *Police Studies* 17, no. 3 (1994b), pp. 33-42.

_____. "The position of municipal police chief: An examination of selection criteria and requisite skills." *Police Studies* 19, no. 1 (1996), pp. 1–17.

_____ (ed.). *Contemporary Policing: Personnel, Issues, and Trends.* Boston: Butterworth–Heinemann, 1997.

_____. *Police Organization and Management: Yesterday, Today, and Tomorrow.* Boston: Butterworth–Heinemann, 1999.

Dewitt, C. B. "Community policing in Seattle: A model partnership between citizens and police." *NIJ Research in Brief* (August 1992).

Doerner, W. G. "Recruitment and retention." In M. L. Dantzker (ed.), *Contemporary Policing: Personnel, Issues, and Trends*, pp. 53–73. Boston: Butterworth–Heinemann, 1997.

Enter, J. E. "The role of higher education in the career of the American police chief." *Police Studies* 9, no. 2 (1986a), pp. 110–119.

_____. "The rise to the top: An analysis of police chief career patterns." *Journal of Police Science and Administration* 14, no. 4 (1986b), pp. 334–346.

_____. "Police administration in the future: Demographic influences as they relate to management of the internal and external environment." In G. W. Cordner and D. J. Kenney (eds.), *Managing Police Organizations*, pp. 175–188. Cincinnati: Anderson Publishing Company, 1996.

Friedmann, R. R. *Community Policing: Comparative Perspectives and Prospects.* New York: St. Martin's Press, 1992.

Gaines, L. K., and T. A. Ricks. *Managing the Police Organization.* St. Paul, MN: West Publishing Co., 1978.

Garner, R. "Leadership in the nineties." *FBI Law Enforcement Bulletin* 62, no. 9 (1993), pp. 1–4.

Goldstein, H. *Policing a Free Society.* Cambridge, MA: Ballinger Publishing Co., 1977.

Goode, C. E. "Significant research on leadership." *Personnel*, 25, no. 5 (1951), p. 349.

Hunt, R. G., and J. M. Magenau. *Power and the Police Chief.* Newbury Park, CA: Sage Publications, 1993.

Kelling, G. L., R. Wasserman, and H. Williams. "Police accountability and community policing." *NIJ Perspectives on Policing*, no. 7 (November 1988).

Kennedy, D. M. (1993). "The strategic management of police resources." *NIJ Perspectives on Policing*, no. 14 (January 1993).

Lurigio, A. J., and D. P. Rosenbaum. "Community policing: Major issues and unanswered questions." In M. L. Dantzker (ed.), *Contemporary Policing: Personnel, Issues and Trends*, pp. 195–216. Boston: Butterworth–Heinemann, 1997.

Lynch, R. G. *The Police Manager.* Boston: Holbrook Press, 1975.

Maniha, J. K. "Structural supports for the development of professionalism among police administrators." *Pacific Sociological Review* 16, no. 3 (1973), pp. 315–343.

Masini, H. J., and M. B. Playfair. "The nature of the police executive's role." *Police Studies* 1, no. 2 (1978), pp. 39–44.

McElroy, J. E., C. A. Cosgrove, and S. Sadd. *Community Policing: The CPOP in New York.* Newbury Park, CA: Sage Publications, 1993.

Mendofik, P. J. "Reflections on leadership." *FBI Law Enforcement Bulletin* 63, no. 8 (1994), pp. 24–27.

Moore, M. H., and D. W. Stephens. *Beyond Command and Control: The Strategic Management of Police Departments.* Washington, DC: Police Executive Research Forum, 1991.

Murphy, C. "Community problems, problem communities, and community policing in Toronto." *Journal of Research in Crime and Delinquency* 25, no. 4 (1988), pp. 392–410.

Police Executive Research Forum. *Police Executive Survey.* Police Executive Research Forum web site at http://www.policeforum.org /home/ExecSurv.html, 1998.

Riechers, L. M., and R. R. Roberg. "Community policing: A critical review of underlying assumptions." *Journal of Police Science and Administration* 17, no. 2 (1990), pp. 105–114.

Robinette, H. M. "Police ethics: Leadership and ethics training for police administrators." *The Police Chief* 58, no. 1 (1991), pp. 42–47.

Shernock, S., and G. D. Dantzker. "Education and training: No longer just a badge and a gun." In M. L. Dantzker (ed.), *Contemporary Policing: Personnel, Issues and Trends*, pp. 75–97. Boston: Butterworth–Heinemann, 1997.

Sparrow, M. K. "Implementing community policing." *NIJ Perspectives on Policing*, no. 9 (November 1988).

Stamper, N. H. *Removing Managerial Barriers to Effective Police Leadership.* Washington, DC: Police Executive Research Forum, 1992.

Stephens, D. W. "Executive responsibility." In L. T. Hoover (ed.), *Police Management: Issues and Perspectives*, pp. 305–322. Washington, DC: Police Executive Research Forum, 1992.

Trojanowicz, R., and B. Bucqueroux. *Community Policing: A Contemporary Perspective.* Cincinnati: Anderson Publishing Company, 1990.

———. *Community Policing: How to Get Started.* Cincinnati: Anderson Publishing Company, 1994.

Tunnell, K. D., and L. K. Gaines. "Political pressures and influences on police executives: A descriptive analysis." In G. W. Cordner and D. J. Kenney (eds.), *Managing Police Organizations*, pp. 5–17. Cincinnati: Anderson Publishing Company, 1996.

Walsh, W. F. "Policing at the crossroads: Changing directions for the new millenium." *International Journal of Police Science and Management* 1, no. 1 (1998), pp. 17–25.

Wilson, O. W., and R. C. McLaren. *Police Administration*, 4th ed. New York: McGraw-Hill, 1977.

Witham, D. C. *The American Law Enforcement Chief Executive: A Management Profile.* Washington, DC: Police Executive Research Forum, 1985.

———. "Management reform and police executives." *The Bureaucrat* (1986), pp. 45–50.

———. "Transformational police leadership." *FBI Law Enforcement Bulletin* 56, no. 12 (1987), pp. 2–6.

Chapter 3

Bumps in the Road to Advancement: A Chief's Perspective

Michael J. Heidingsfield, Rio Salado College

Every formal organization, whether located in the private sector or public sector, must replenish itself periodically with new personnel if it is to continue to exist. Vacancies can arise through retirement, termination of employment, voluntary and involuntary separation, and expansion. These slots, if left unfilled, would spell the eventual demise of the organization.

One also must realize that personnel turnover sometimes creates multiple opportunities for internal movement or upward mobility within the organization. Agency leaders are left with unique opportunities whenever promotional opportunities occur because of the domino effect that quickly materializes. A chain reaction is set off any time an upper-level vacancy is filled with an internal candidate from a lower rank. For example, if a person is promoted from the lieutenant level to a captain, an opening is created for a new lieutenant. If a sergeant moves up to the vacant lieutenant spot, the vacuum creates yet another promotional opportunity. Should a corporal be tapped to step up to this sergeant position, this movement will stimulate a search for a new corporal. Thus, a single vacancy can generate a rejuvenating impact.

The domino effect can produce profound ramifications for the organization. The elevation of minority-group members, women, or persons with differing viewpoints into the supervisory ranks can alter the complexion of the agency. Such promotions might send a message as to the philosophy that a new executive brings into the department or signal an administrative change in the direction an agency is headed. In any event, internal mobility can serve as a vehicle for change or indicate that the leadership has set a new agenda in place.

As a police executive, I have had the opportunity many times throughout my career to use the promotional process to set the tone within my agency. Not unlike corporate America, decisions to identify those people best prepared to assume a leadership role ideally should be based on merit and ability. The challenge in any organization is the path that the agency follows to reach that ideal and the requirements candidates must meet to gain serious consideration. We travel that path in this chapter and talk about the selection process, the candidate's preparation, the change in perspective that accompanies upward mobility, and the keys to success in the new role. In this chapter, you get the view of a police chief who's been there.

No discussion of promotion can be undertaken without an exploration of the dynamics arrayed behind that incredibly critical decision by the aspiring police officer to seek advancement. Likewise, no inquiry as to the best possible path to follow to ensure success as a supervisor would be complete should the subtle nuances of the decision to pursue promotion not be reviewed and fully understood.

THE SUPERVISOR SELECTION PROCESS

One of the points in Chapter 1 deals with the typical structure of police organizations. After looking at organizational charts and becoming familiar with things like chain of command, we also encounter the term *span of control*. Basically, the hierarchical structure of an agency involves a series of relationships based on the authority of the incumbent. First-line supervisors, usually sergeants, are in charge of a squad of officers. Sergeants, in turn, answer to lieutenants, and so on up the line.

Getting knighted as a supervisor can occur through either an appointive or a competitive process. Despite a multitude of variations on each procedure, some basic themes characterize each approach. The following material investigates these two systems for making rank.

The Appointment Process

Agencies that rely on the appointive process operate under the premise that all the power and authority in that organization is vested undeniably within the senior leadership. The notion of appointive authority suggests the senior leadership is empowered to make critical decisions. There is no requirement that the decision maker consult with or seek the counsel of others. The ultimate choice as to who will become the organization's next supervisor rests with a decision rendered and based on the individual preference of the decision maker.

The appointive process may or may not enjoy the support of the agency members. Furthermore, promotion decisions may not be associated with the traditional values of fairness, equity, and parity. In some instances, rank-and-file officers may express genuine support for such a process. More often than not, this visible blessing suggests that three organizational dynamics are at work. First, a strong patriarchal system with a strongly embedded historical foundation supports such a practice. Second, a nonparticipative and autocratic organizational environment is in place. Third, the agency size or mission makes a competitive process moot because there is no legitimate or demonstrable need to proceed competitively.

One very predictable consequence of the appointive system is the perception that genuine decision making reflecting the traditional values suggested earlier is not at work. Instead, an unspoken politicization of the decision-making process has occurred. Such impressions, whether real or imagined, create conclusions that favoritism, cronyism, or disparate treatment may be at work.

On the other hand, the practice of appointing supervisors produces expeditious decision making. Swift and unencumbered executive action eliminates any prolonged organizational agonizing over what might appear to be the interminable decision making of distant leaders and agency heads. For agencies where trust is exceptionally high between the workforce and the leadership, this can be a highly favored catalyst for action and change within the organization. An organization's reliance on such a system calls for extraordinary cohesion within the agency and a long-term commitment to a mission and purpose that energizes and coalesces every member of that agency. For the appointive process to not only survive but prosper, the agency must have created an overwhelmingly powerful sense of service over self and selfless visionary leadership. Unfortunately, the highly political environments within which most law enforcement agencies operate make a strong appointive process a near impossibility. As Professors Hunter and Merritt explain in Chapter 9, the influence of unions and the deeply held mistrust between labor and management are important factors to consider. In addition, the history of racial and gender discrimination within American policing and the evolution of scientific assessment processes have combined to relegate the appointive process to a much-diminished role in police promotional systems.

The Competitive Process

Competitive practices as the tool by which promotional decisions are made are not new to law enforcement. They are based in the generations-old civil service systems found in many of the oldest and largest police agencies in the United States. During the post–World War II era, law enforcement experienced sweeping changes. The political cronyism and patronage of the day was pushed aside in the interest of uniformity, standardization, and consistency. One good example of this reform effort is the movement away from the subjective promotional decisions of police chiefs, who were susceptible to political influence. Competitive promotional practices amount to an initiative aimed at ensuring fair treatment and accurate prediction of future behavior.

While the methodology of competitive practices may vary widely, one can identify eight fundamental themes:

- Consistency in the process.
- Equal opportunity for success.
- Testing processes that have achievable outcomes.
- Outcomes that have been validated.
- Results that permit comparison between candidates.
- Processes that reveal depth of knowledge.
- Processes that simulate, illustrate, or replicate the circumstances that will be encountered by a supervisor.

- Processes that accurately predict the candidate's behavior as a prospective supervisor.

Competitive processes may range from the very straightforward objective examination consisting of preselected questions to the very sophisticated assessment center techniques developed in the 1980s. Regardless, "every police department needs a system for determining which officers should be promoted to higher ranks and responsibilities" (Nowicki, Sykes, and Eisenberg, 1991, p. 284). Large, traditional, and often rule-bound agencies, as a matter of necessity or practicality, tend to rely on the administration of *standardized examinations*. These tests often consist of objective questions that, when scored, yield a ranked list of candidates from which to make a selection for promotion. The appeal of such testing procedures is their ease of administration, scoring, and their ability to depict relative differences between candidates. Such a format permits consistency from one year to the next, strong defensibility for the individual questions on the examination, and a low potential for criticism of inequity, unfairness, or manipulation of results.

Competitive tests are not immune from criticism. Written examinations aimed at discerning the knowledge, experience, or aptitude of a prospective supervisor often are criticized for encouraging memorization and assessing "test-taking" capabilities as opposed to the capacity to manage and lead. Critics argue that these types of examinations reflect only the retention of studied material. They do little in the way of forecasting future success. Nevertheless, objective examinations prevail today in many police departments as the procedure of choice.

The successor to the traditional objective examination is the *assessment center*. This process creates an environment designed to mimic the tasks real supervisors face. Candidates are given a series of exercises that simulate the job they are seeking. An assessment center may test candidates in areas that focus on experience and training, job-related knowledge, judgment, managerial and leadership skills, as well as written and verbal communication. Candidates may be asked to respond to questions that cover various areas or to participate in role-playing scenarios. For example, in the area of experience and training, a candidate might be asked to advise how he or she keeps current with professional developments and would try to stay current. For job-related knowledge, the candidate may be handed a budget and told to reduce it with cost effectiveness as a goal. In terms of judgment, the candidate might be asked to field questions at an impromptu news conference, where one person continually interrupts him or her. As for management and leadership skills, the candidate might be told to develop a management team to respond to an equipment issue. Communications skills might be evaluated through either writing a memo or role playing a telephone conversation with a city official.

Trained assessors grade candidate performance on these exercises using a predetermined list of dimensions. For example, assessors might resort to a three-point scale with 1 being extremely satisfactory, 2 denoting a satisfactory showing, and 3 being reserved for unsatisfactory. The scores on all the test components are totaled and a recommendation is made. Suppose, for the moment, a total of ten tasks or items are being assessed with this scoring system. A grade of 10 would be a perfect score and a top promotional candidate. Persons with scores above 25 would not have a very good chance for the position. Ultimately, the match between a candidate's behavior (or score) and the agency's expectations is thought to ensure an accurate prediction of future compatibility.

MANAGING ONE'S POLICE CAREER

The transformation from civilian to sworn officer status is marked by several distinct changes. According to Van Maanen (1973), the police career consists of the preentry, admittance, change, and continuance stages. The *preentry* stage involves all the activities that go into making the decision to become a police officer; *admittance* centers on the academy experience and the introduction to the police world. The *change* stage takes place when the novice first hits the streets and has to absorb the harsh lessons of reality. *Continuance* references the ongoing adjustments that take place throughout the course of one's police career.

One also might suggest that the decision to position oneself for a move up the ladder also involves serious career planning and several distinct strategies. When Van Maanen (1984) looks at the career trajectory of officers trying to advance to the rank of sergeant, he notices several things that separate the failures from the successful officers. My own personal experience of climbing through the ranks, as well as grooming officers for upward mobility, provide the framework for the following discussion.

The Anticipatory Stage

Career progression into a supervisory position requires the aspirant to choose one of two different paths. The first strategy calls for a prolonged assignment in uniformed patrol. The goal here is to establish credibility and accumulate a suitable experience base for future supervisory decision making. The second avenue is to amass as many specialized assignments as possible. The idea here is to corral a diverse work experience and a breadth of knowledge about all facets of the organization. As Box 3–1 demonstrates, some agencies have instituted formal mechanisms to help employees establish and pursue career goals.

The choice of which path to pursue is overlaid with time lines of widely varying duration. Every agency has officers who eagerly seek advancement at the earliest possible opportunity. They may be motivated by personal ambition, a compulsion to succeed, perceived pressure from their peers, a natural competitive drive, or a strong passion for leadership. Those who choose an *accelerated opportunity path* inevitably face both positive and negative consequences. Some of the positive outcomes I have observed over the years include

- Quickly becoming part of the next generation of leadership for the organization and, thus, ensuring management succession.

Box 3–1   An Example of Agency Policy Regarding a Career
Development Program for Officers

I.   Purpose. It is the policy of the Tallahassee Police Department to
provide an opportunity for individual growth and development at all
levels, both personally and professionally. In keeping with this goal,
a Career Development Program has been established with the
following objectives:
   A.   To provide employees with an opportunity to continue their
formal education to achieve a minimum of a Bachelor's Degree
from an accredited college or university.
   B.   To provide employees with an annual review of the training,
transfer, and promotional opportunities available at their level.
   C.   To provide supervisors with the training, staff support and
resource materials needed to fulfill their counseling and evaluation responsibilities.

II.   Shift Preference. Personnel may request, via the chain of command,
temporary assignment to a shift in order to attend classes at local
schools or institutions. Efforts shall be made to assist personnel
who desire to further their education in accordance with their
Career Development goals.

III.   Enrollment in the Career Development Program.
   A.   The Career Development Program is a voluntary program.
Personnel wishing to participate shall fill out a Career Development Request and return it to the Training Section.
   B.   Career Development positions are "Temporary Duty Assignments." Personnel will be evaluated continuously throughout
their tenure in the assignment.
   C.   When the allotted time period for a "career track" assignment
ends, officers will be rotated to the Patrol Division. The officer
would not be eligible for another career development assignment
for at least one year.

IV.   Career Counseling Responsibilities. Career counseling will assist in
developing an employee's personal and professional career. It will
enable an employee to make informed decisions regarding the
attainment of personal goals. The employee's supervisor will serve
as the Career Counselor. Each employee and the supervisor/
counselor shall conduct a joint review of the employee's program to
ensure continued applicability to his or her goals. The supervisor's
specific responsibilities are as follows:
   A.   Explaining the Career Development Program to subordinates.

B. Explaining the Salary Incentive Program to subordinates.
C. Providing guidance to the employee in the selection of career goals.
D. Providing guidance in setting realistic priorities.
E. Making the employee aware of strong and weak points in skills, knowledge, and abilities.
F. Reviewing the employee's training record.
G. Identifying training programs offered by the State of Florida Career Development Program which will meet the employee's goals.
H. Providing the employee with lists of appropriate schools and/or training programs for his or her career goals.
I. Reviewing the requirements and procedures for lateral transfer.
J. Reviewing the requirements and procedures for promotion within the Department.
K. Providing a review of current Equal Employment Opportunity Commission objectives established by the Department and City Government.
L. Documenting career counseling by attaching a completed Career Development Checklist to each employee's performance evaluation.

Source: Tallahassee [Florida] Police Department, *Manual of Written Directives*.

- Serving as a visible incentive for advancement for others and a point of inspiration to those who otherwise might not compete.
- Providing a role model for those who follow and who seek someone successful to emulate.
- Ensuring that the organization is continuously injected with the fresh thought and new perspective of the next generation of leadership.
- Symbolizing the value that the organization attaches to those willing to pursue promotion promptly, thus countering the notion often found in police departments that time and seniority are the only real litmus test for success as a promotional candidate.

Candidates who pursue the accelerated opportunity path may face a number of challenges that materialize time and time again and include

- Provoking criticism from more senior officers who perceive the candidate as unprepared and insufficiently skilled to be a supervisor.

- Limiting future opportunities because a commitment to becoming a supervisor means that special career-broadening and experience-building assignments no longer will be available.
- Sowing the seeds for regret when the successful aspirant realizes that a premature immersion into a supervisory role is irreversible and much more narrow than the decision to experience the depth and breadth of the department before seeking promotion.
- Contributing to the perception that the experience base of an agency's first-line supervision is either shrinking, too limited, or both, which can affect the new or young supervisor's credibility.
- Thrusting the new supervisor into a role and responsibilities for which he or she is inadequately prepared.

There are a parallel set of advantages and disadvantages for officers who select the second track. The *extended experience path* is the more traditional route, whereby one seeks to accumulate a broad base of assignments. This choice brings the following advantages:

- A greater degree of comfort due to the extensive experience base on which the new supervisor can draw.
- Fulfillment of the traditional need for patrol officers to see the traits of experience, maturity, and seniority in their new supervisors.
- Ensuring that the department's management ranks are not overrun by young and minimally experienced new supervisors.
- A greater understanding of the philosophy, strategy, and vision of the organization.
- A reduction in the likelihood that the newly chosen supervisor, once well into his or her management career, will be influenced by the disappointment or latent resentment that stems from advancement that outstrips the need to experience a variety of line-level opportunities.
- Organizational recognition of the value of maturity and life experience in its supervisory ranks.
- Slow growth and seasoning of those who fill the critical role of supervisors.

Similar to the accelerated opportunity model, a parallel set of concerns arise with the choice of the extended experience path. Some of these would include

- The notion that talented and prepared promotional candidates are forced to languish and lose their edge because of an organizational predilection for supervisors with extended seniority.
- Greater employee turnover because good prospective supervisors may seek opportunities elsewhere, where there are immediate chances to manage and lead.
- A dulling or blunting of the enthusiasm and interest by the brightest candidates, whose tolerance for organizational obstacles, real or imagined, is particularly short.

- An internal struggle for the candidate who has chosen the extended experience path but suffers frustration and competing emotions as he or she watches peers forge ahead as they forsake experience for opportunity.
- Sending an organizational message that may communicate a lack of interest on the part of the senior leadership in cultivating management succession.

The Self-Assessment Stage

The decision about which promotional strategy to pursue should trigger a self-assessment of what career, professional, or personal preparation is needed (see Box 3–2). One particular initiative emerges as the single most important step one can take to ensure professional growth: the pursuit of higher education. The educational entrance requirement at some agencies may make the college diploma a moot issue. Even though some agencies may harbor mixed feelings about the value of a college degree and its relevance to professional success, one should not underestimate the value of higher education. As Shernock and Dantzker (1997, p. 85) suggest, "the fact is that policing requires a better educated individual than when it began its modernization [and is] . . . part of the answer to creating more efficient police personnel."

Box 3–2   Announcement of the Selection Process for Police Sergeant

The Tallahassee Police Department will conduct a promotional process for the position of Police Sergeant in accordance with the terms and conditions of this announcement.

Minimum Eligibility Requirements

In order to be eligible to compete in the promotional process, a candidate must meet the following criteria on or before September 8, 1998, which is the beginning of the announcement period:

A.   Graduation from an accredited community college with an A.A. or A.S. degree and have three (3) years of experience as a sworn police officer, or

B.   Successful completion of ninety (90) quarter hours or sixty (60) semester hours at an accredited college or university and three (3) years of experience as a sworn police officer.

NOTE: Education cannot be substituted for the required years of experience.

All candidates meeting the minimum eligibility requirements are encouraged to participate in the promotional process. The department will make every effort to ensure that schedules are adjusted appropriately so that all candidates employed by the department desiring to participate in the process have that opportunity.

Application Process

Each candidate who wishes to participate in the promotional process must submit a City of Tallahassee Application for Employment to the City of Tallahassee Human Resources Department, First Floor, City Hall, no later than 5:00 P.M., Friday, September 25, 1998.

Candidates shall attach a resume to their application.

Selection Process

The promotional process for the position of Police Sergeant will consist solely of an oral board. An interview panel, selected by the Chief of Police, will conduct the oral board. The oral board will be comprised of two components, as follows:

Part One: Each candidate will be give the first fifteen (15) minutes of the oral board to present himself/herself to the interview panel. Candidates may use this opportunity to provide information about themselves to the interview panel which they feel will enhance their standing as the most viable candidate.

Part Two: The remaining thirty (30) minutes of the oral board will be reserved for interviewing the candidate. Each candidate will be asked to respond to a predetermined list of questions prepared in advance by the interview panel.

Material for the questions will be taken from the following sources:
1. Tallahassee Police Department Written Directives Manual.
2. Tallahassee Police Department issued Florida Criminal and Traffic Laws booklet, 1998 edition.
3. Provisions of the Collective Bargaining Agreement for the Police Officer Unit between the City of Tallahassee and the Big Bend Police Benevolent Association, Inc., in effect on September 8, 1998.

A copy of the materials will be available in the Department's Employee Resources Office.

All candidates will be scored on a pass/fail basis.

Establishment of the Promotional Eligibility List

At the conclusion of their evaluation, those candidates who have scored a "pass" will be placed on the promotional eligibility list in alphabetical order. The effective dates of the promotional eligibility list shall be displayed on the list and the list shall remain in effect for one year following the establishment of the list.

Promotional Appointments

The Chief of Police shall, at his sole discretion, select any candidate for promotion whose name appears on the promotional list.

Source: Tallahassee [Florida] Police Department.

During my tenure as a police officer and a member of the "brass," I recognized at least six predictable outcomes associated with the performance and success of college-educated police officers and supervisors (Heidingsfield, 1995). First, the ability to conceptualize, embrace, and fulfill the often intangible processes of community policing seems greatly enhanced when officers have a college education. Second, the majority of adults in many communities are college educated. There is an unspoken but prevailing presumption that the officers who serve these citizens should have equivalent education. Third, while there always will be a debate about the relative merit of life experience, formal education, and human maturation, only the baccalaureate educational process synthesizes all three dynamics into one. Fourth, college-educated officers have reflected on their life's goals and made decisions by undertaking an arduous educational process to choose a career. This spells commitment and a competitive quest for pursuing leadership opportunities. Fifth, the institutionalization of college education helps law enforcement close the circle in the pursuit of professional recognition and stature. Finally, the ever-growing crisis of public confidence in American policing demands a substantive response. Seeking higher education for officers legitimizes our response and is restorative by its very nature.

The "Guardian Angel"

The next most important consideration when pursuing a management opportunity is seeking out a mentor or a "guardian angel," a role that can be filled equally well by a wide array of people. The actual position the mentor occupies within the organization is not as important as the grooming that takes place. Most police agencies do not formally encourage mentorship and have no such program in place. Nevertheless, the search for a mentor by a prospective supervisor can be a valuable pursuit.

The candidate should look for a mentor who exhibits several characteristics. The mentor should be someone worthy of emulation. This person should embody and embrace the organization's core values. He or she should have the wisdom and experience that provide a foundation of knowledge to be passed on to an underling. The mentor should be a person who approaches the law enforcement profession with thoughtfulness and reflection. He or she should have a steady record of making the right decisions and understand that the police service is a higher calling and requires a continuous attention. Above all, the mentor should appreciate the responsibility and obligation to nurture and shape the organization's future leadership.

Getting into the Mainstream

Rounding out the top three most important considerations when preparing to compete for the supervisory ranks is the need for the candidate to ensure that he or she is in the mainstream within the organization. The decision to pursue a supervisory position, particularly for those who have chosen the extended experience model, may be made while an incumbent is in a highly specialized assignment. That special assignment may bring with it a sense of prestige, greater value to the organization, and even elitism. These three intangible benefits may compete strongly with a decision to pursue promotion.

Understandably, with the passage of time in a particularly desirable special assignment (homicide investigation, undercover operations, special weapons and tactics, task force assignments, etc.), an individual's skills become more developed and, perhaps, even highly prized. At the same time, another dynamic is at work quietly undermining that officer's likelihood of success. That is, the individual grows more isolated from the mainstream of the organization.

Typically, the competitive process used to select new supervisors is based in knowledge of the patrol function and the ability to confront and manage patrol situations as they are encountered every day on the street. Even more important is the acknowledgment that virtually every new sergeant or supervisor selected will be assigned immediately to patrol management responsibilities. This tour of duty can create a severe disadvantage for the highly successful, but highly specialized, officer whose assignment substantially removes him or her from the critical work of patrol. His or her body of collective knowledge about patrol operations often is limited, dated, or simply obsolete. This slack erects two barriers to success. First, the hitherto upwardly mobile officer is unable to compete in the promotional process because of the lack of grounding in patrol operations. Second, the new supervisor must bridge an enormous gap if the most recent experience has been an extended special assignment.

The remedy for this concern is directly reflected in the rationale that the candidate must have already considered for his or her decision to seek promotion— prepare as fully as possible, including surrendering the prestige of the special assignment, for a return to patrol to work on a revival of the perishable skill sets needed on the streets and a reorientation to the delivery of patrol services. This is a painful decision for many people and often is made only reluctantly after a failed promotional experience has revealed that there is no substitute for being part of the mainstream of the organization and what it does.

THE METAMORPHOSIS OF PERSPECTIVE

The decision to become a supervisor implies a fundamental commitment to a change in the candidate's organizational perspective. There must be an honest and frank realization that relationships and associations inevitably must change. Former peers will become subordinates. Former supervisors are transformed into peers. Senior executives who were distant will now share a greater sense of focus. For some fledgling supervisors, this transition can be a painful and arduous journey that is never successfully concluded. As Bennett and Hess (1996, p. 553) put it, "sergeants find themselves in a position fraught with potential role conflict."

New supervisors who are ill-equipped to undertake this metamorphosis will resist the need to evolve professionally. They will deny the necessity of doing so or simply never understand that this transformation is a crucial element in their professional transition. The decision to become part of the organization's leadership, indeed, is just that. It requires a new perspective about the day-to-day operations and demands that the new supervisor start seeing the world through a new window.

Expectations will change dramatically in all directions and quarters. The required adjustments can be bewildering for the new supervisor. According to Goldstein (1990, p. 157), "Most officers do not see their sergeant as sources of guidance and direction, but rather as authority figures to be satisfied."

This view creates an immediate challenge for the rookie supervisor. At the same time, the new supervisor must contend with administrative expectations that he or she may not have ever contemplated. These can include expectations that the new supervisor

- As the element of management closest to the daily operations of police service, act as the conscience of the organization as a whole.
- Embody the core values of the organization without reservation and these values "are the beliefs, purpose, mission and goals that define what is essential to the organization" (Southerland, 1992, p. 287).
- Not be reluctant or hesitant to step up to the toughest situations and make equally difficult decisions.
- Appreciate that his or her actions often will purposely or inadvertently reflect the position of the agency's chief executive.
- Be held to higher expectations as to performance and conduct than ever before, yet function in an environment that is much more subjective with far fewer specific benchmarks for success to follow.
- Realize that, short of voluntary demotion or conscious misconduct, this decision to become a supervisor essentially is irrevocable.

- Clearly understand that advocacy, loyalty, a larger perspective, the ability to anticipate issues, the skill to craft solutions, and the talent to make others successful
largely will replace the traditional earmarks of a patrol officer's success.

Realistically, these expectations are not easily realized in many organizations
and settings. The traditional paramilitary structure is diminishing in many law
enforcement agencies. The ranks are swelling with college-educated, ambitious, and
sophisticated new officers, who often style their professional perspectives after
corporate America. Traditional notions of loyalty and personal accountability often
are difficult to sustain. Military service and its accompanying influence are much less
likely to have been part of the officer's past. The extraordinary power of police labor
unions in some areas contributes to this seeming reluctance regarding personal
responsibility as well. Finally, the new generation of police officers is immersed in
the quest for material success that characterizes the American way of life. All these
trends contribute to the danger that every organization must recognize as new leaders
are chosen. That is, sophistication, education, and ambition cannot replace
commitment, dedication, and a willingness to be held accountable.

Similarly, the expectations of line officers who were former peers will be
altered as well. Some of those expectations will be appropriate. However, the newly
promoted officer will encounter expectations that are entirely inappropriate. Here,
the new supervisor will confront the greatest struggle and the most difficult of
dilemmas as friendships, collegiality, and shared past experiences become the
ammunition of former peers unprepared or unwilling to adjust to the new super-
visor-subordinate relationship. This can manifest itself in inappropriate expectations of preferential treatment, protection from inquiry or discipline from the
department, inflated evaluations, blind loyalty, and reduced expectations in terms of
daily performance.

At the same time, the organization as an institution should have at least one very
dramatic expectation of the new supervisor that may be less apparent to those who
are line officers without formal leadership responsibilities. It is not enough to have
said that the new supervisor must embody the core values of the organization. The
institutional expectation is that the new sergeant or supervisor will reflect the
principle of "service over self." This principle suggests that, while contemporary
policing styles value the autonomy, empowerment, and wide-ranging discretion of
the individual officer and supervisor, in its extreme this philosophy can produce an
organizational selfishness that can be very damaging.

On the eve of the 21st century, American law enforcement enjoys unprecedented
opportunity within its ranks in terms of the sheer number of officers that now police
our country's communities and the availability of federal funding associated with the
institutionalization of community policing, both of which are buoyed by an
outspoken national consensus to reduce crime. At the same time, law enforcement
salaries are competitive with other entry-level job opportunities in the private sector.
One consequence of this convergence, which is exacerbated by the attitudinal change
seen in many of today's officers, is the emergence of a personal philosophy that
individual success and reward are of greater importance than the organizational good

and the agency's mission on behalf of the community it serves. This approach to individual achievement may imply short-lived personal success for the new supervisor. However, it is very problematic for the organization over the long term. Instead, the organization has a right to expect that its new leaders shall make a conscious effort to place the institutional good over personal accomplishments so as to ensure that the community is receiving the most focused, enlightened, and impactful police service available. Implicit in that individual commitment to subordinate one's self to the organization is the understanding that police agencies working as one collective body ultimately will be the most successful and with organizational success will come personal success and advancement.

This metamorphosis of perspective fundamentally suggests that the prospective supervisor must have a clear rationale in mind when he or she embarks on the path to leadership. In the interest of honesty to one's self and the organization, the candidate must engage in some introspection that reveals to his or her satisfaction the reasons for the choice to become a supervisor. That decision must be conscious, thoughtful, and reflective.

EMBARKING ON THE NEW ASSIGNMENT

Once the decision making is past and the promotional process has been successfully undertaken, the role change has begun. Acquiring the skills necessary for the job becomes of paramount importance to the new sergeant. Time is of the essence if the new supervisor is to be successful and prepared for what lies ahead.

Training the Rookie Supervisor

The first consideration at this point should be how to train the new supervisor. Modern policing, as a whole, does not enjoy a particularly good reputation in terms of its ability to train prospective sergeants. Most agencies employ training regimens that can be best characterized as ad hoc, informal, and most often, tied to traditional experience-it-as-it-goes (or on-the-job) training.

An interesting contradiction is at work here. For better than a generation now, American law enforcement has employed a sophisticated, well-developed field training program for new recruits. Unfortunately, this obligation to ready the next generation of police officers has not carried over to a commitment to prepare its newest leaders. The even greater irony is that, even though many agencies acknowledge this omission, the impetus to create a remedy simply is not there. The resolution to this dilemma is in an organizational commitment that "manager training should be initiated only after determining both individual and organizational training goals" (Bennett and Hess, 1996, p. 391).

The new sergeant can expect to encounter a model of training that falls somewhere within the spectrum of no formal training to an in-depth management school (see Box 3–3). The training program often is dictated by financial constraints, the need to assign the new sergeant quickly to field duty because of critical gaps in supervision, or the mistaken presumption that those who have fared well in the promotional process have demonstrated the innate ability to lead and require no further growth or development. Obviously, nothing could be further from the truth. The cold, hard reality of vicarious liability and civil litigation that Professor Camp visits in Chapter 7 reveals a myriad of ways for this negligence to haunt an agency. Just as the academy graduate must be prepared and tempered through an extended learning experience, such as the field training program, so must the new supervisor be educated and shaped.

Too often the senior leadership is satisfied with a modest training program that merely communicates the day-to-day skills required of the patrol sergeant. Unless within the rare agency that employs an extended and sophisticated supervisory training program, the new supervisor may want to keep an eye out for external training opportunities. It also becomes abundantly clear that the necessity of having a mentor, as discussed previously, becomes even more crucial.

Box 3–3   Levels of Supervisor Training

Level 1: No Training. A complete absence of formal training accompanied by only incidental or coincidental on-the-job training.

Level 2: Informal on-the-Job Training. An informal transfer of knowledge in which the new supervisor is partnered with an experienced sergeant for an unspecified period of time.

Level 3: Generic Training. Assignment to a generic employer-sponsored New Supervisors' Training module that does not recognize the uniqueness of the police sergeant.

Level 4: Formal on-the-Job Training. A formal on-the-job training program in which the new supervisor is partnered with one or a series of trained senior sergeants, who serve as assigned trainers. Such a program is similar to the rookie Field Training Officer Program and should include formal assessment of the trainee's progress, a satisfactory demonstration of the core competencies, and a pass/fail evaluation.

Level 5: Formal Specialized Training. Assignment to an extended training program within the police agency that reflects all relevant elements of the police manager's experience. An acceptable equivalent would be an assignment to recognized regional or national policing training body for an extended period of time that is considered a complete and self-sufficient training experience.

The First Supervisory Assignment

Once the training requirement has been met in whatever fashion organizational requirements or personal ambition dictate, the next step in the evolution is the new sergeant's first assignment. More often than not, the dominance of patrol, seniority, and the traditional desirability of some schedules over others combine to eliminate any real choice of assignment by the new sergeant. Quite often, the initial assignment will be in patrol operations serving as a first-line supervisor for a group of patrol officers. The new sergeant will encounter officers who were once peers and now are convinced the new sergeant is entirely incompetent.

The ability of the sergeant to persevere in this first assignment is paramount. It is not an overstatement to say that success in the first assignment is almost a prerequisite for career success as an organizational leader. Many eyes will be watching to determine whether the new sergeant can measure up in such ways as

- Quickly establishing himself or herself with the patrol squad being supervised.
- Not allowing ego to inject itself into the style of supervision chosen.
- Communicating credibility, a willingness to learn, and a grasp of the role.
- Not permitting the undesirability of the work hours or specific assignment to become an issue.
- Committing to the personal and professional development necessary to grow into the new role.
- Demonstrating the ability to accept constructive criticism and adapt accordingly.

Supervisory Responsibilities

The new sergeant can expect to encounter at least four categories of responsibilities. They include the traditional chores of first-line supervision, serving as a subject matter expert, being the lead worker, and managing a program. We now look more closely at each of these duties.

In a typical patrol setting, the sergeant functions as the immediate supervisor of a squad of officers who provide basic police services within a particular community or geographic section of a city. The sergeant must ensure that staffing is adequate to meet the workload, officers are properly equipped, operational resources can be shifted and realigned as calls for service or events dictate, and sound decisions are being made in the field. This last item is a daunting task. The new sergeant must oversee and manage the "in-the-trenches" operationalization of police service delivery. Sometimes, dramatic and extraordinary events will require the field supervisor to assume command of a situation. These critical incidents require split-second decision making, tactical thinking, and strategic use of available resources. At the same time, the new sergeant must handle tasks related to building a team and the leadership and development skills imperative for the smooth operation of a professional patrol unit.

Much different from the responsibility of first-line supervisor is the concept of the sergeant as a subject matter expert. Here, little or no emphasis is placed on either the supervision of people or the management of resources. Instead, this role recognizes that the sergeant is strategically placed within the organizational structure. By default, he or she possesses a deeper knowledge about different dimensions of the department's operations.

Perhaps the best illustration of the sergeant as a subject matter expert occurs when a sergeant serves as an agency's accreditation manager. In Chapter 10, Professor McCabe explains what accreditation is and what the process of self-study entails. One member in an agency seeking accreditation will be appointed to serve as the "accreditation manager." This person will become the most knowledgeable member when it comes to accreditation standards and what the agency has done to gain compliance. Obviously, the person will serve as the voice of authority within the agency on those matters. The sergeant in this position often will enjoy a special relationship with the command staff. Because the subject matter expert wields authority and influence, organizational interaction dynamics change.

The third responsibility for the new sergeant is that of lead worker. Here, the sergeant is responsible for executing certain tasks or assignments traditionally considered line-level work. However, because of the significance of that particular duty, the organizational culture or policy requires that the position be filled by a manager or supervisor. The best example here would be a sergeant's assignment to the internal affairs function. In that setting, the sergeant routinely conducts investigations of alleged employee misconduct. Any standard supervisory responsibilities are either limited or absent. But the nature of the work, the importance of how the assignment is executed, and the credibility of the position all suggest that a sergeant should serve as the lead worker.

Finally, as a program manager, a sergeant will be the supervisor responsible for the oversight and direction of a particular function of the agency. These duties could range from specialized investigative functions to crime analysis to the canine program. In these instances, the sergeant not only ensures the operational capacity of that activity but must meet certain specialized performance measures, prepare a functional budget, and conduct workload or deployment analyses as well.

Supervisory Roles

While supervisory responsibilities tend to be well defined and formalized within an organization, supervisory roles are not as clear and often overlap with one another. Understanding these roles is essential to understanding the process of management, which Bennett and Hess (1996, p. 39) characterize as "a complex relationship between employees of different levels, ranks, authority and responsibility." Nevertheless, a baker's dozen roles have become fairly well institutionalized in most law enforcement organizations. Every new supervisor should be familiar with the range and depth of the expectations that these roles imply.

Source of Agency Authority.   In many instances, dictated either by the time of day or operational necessity, the sergeant can expect to speak on behalf of the organization as a whole. These opportunities can range from daily decisions about departmental policy to exchanges where the sergeant talks as the official voice of the agency.

On-Scene Supervisor.   Calls for service, emergency situations, and the complexity of the human behavior encountered by officers on the street periodically demand the intercession of the supervisor. The aim is to ensure that agency members respond to circumstances as professionally and properly as possible. These opportunities can run the gamut from the management of police pursuits, supervision of a barricaded suspect situation, responding to an officer's use of deadly force, and much more mundane tasks at crime scenes.

Role Model.   Embedded throughout the narrative in this chapter is the clear consensus that a supervisor must serve as a role model to those for whom he or she is responsible. This emulation should extend to organizational values, credibility, trustworthiness, leadership capacity, and integrity.

Mentor.   Sergeants must be prepared and willing to not only supervise those for whom they are responsible but provide stewardship as well. The ability to shape another's professional development, encourage growth, and fashion sound career choices is an absolute must. Block (1993, p. 3) goes so far as to suggest that stewardship can replace leadership. According to other commentators (Bennett and Hess, 1996, pp. 321–322), mentors are "wise, trusted teacher[s] or counselor[s] . . . working in close emotional quarters."

Coach.   The parallel here to athletic teams is unmistakable. The sergeant must be prepared to motivate, train, support, and shape a team of professional police officers. This role implies a commitment to development of skills, the ability to deliver criticism constructively, and the capacity to encourage and produce high morale and dedication. At the same time, the astute supervisor also must allow his or her officers to pursue and reach the highest levels of self-actualization.

Disciplinarian.   The least liked of the supervisory roles, dealing with disciplinary issues, is essential to managerial success. This function calls for the appropriate level of knowledge about agency policy and requirements, the courage to confront and deal with misconduct, and the overriding responsibility to be fair and equitable in subsequent decision making. Bennett and Hess (1996, p. 470) maintain that "first-line supervisors are the key to law enforcement agencies' discipline."

Leader.   The notion of leadership receives extensive coverage from many quarters and no attempt will be made here to replicate that dialogue. Leadership in a paramilitary setting necessitates that the incumbent possess some basic traits. These include the ability to inspire others, the capacity for creating followers, the broadest possible perspective of the police industry and culture, the capability to lift service delivery to the next higher level, personal integrity beyond reproach, and the strongest possible reputation for credibility and professional knowledge.

Manager.   Although one might be tempted to use this term interchangeably with the word *leader*, the two are not synonymous. As discussed earlier, this term may imply a particular function within an agency. In a broader context, *managing* suggests the operational or administrative deployment of resources and activities to support the organizational mission. *Leadership* connotes strong humanistic values, while *management* tends to rely on technical, logistic, or administrative decision making. The sergeant, of course, should be capable of both.

Representative of Senior Leadership.   In a number of different circumstances, the first-line supervisor will speak on behalf of the department's senior leadership. This can occur in a setting as routine as a shift change briefing, where a policy decision is explained and interpreted. Often during nonbusiness hours, the senior patrol supervisor on duty may formally or informally represent the chief of police, a responsibility that may be delegated through the agency's operational orders or simply understood to be the case.

Communicator.   No supervisor can be successful without the skill to share and receive information. It is generally acknowledged that kinesics (body language) represent the predominant way in which a sender effectively sends a message. Bennett and Hess (1996, p. 108) suggest that "of all the skills needed to be an effective manager . . . skill in communicating is the most vital."

Effective Listener.   Linked directly to the ability to be an effective communicator is the obligation to do more listening than speaking, to be reflective and perceptive as a listener, and to be attuned to the subtle nuances of communication. As Bennett and Hess (1996, p. 118) explain, "the weakest link in the communication process is listening."

Performance Overseer.   This aspect is included simply as a reminder that there is no shying away from the obligation to oversee performance and intervene when necessary to either reinforce the decisions made or correct improper behavior.

Evaluator.   A logical extension of the role of performance overseer is the responsibility to assess the performance of those for whom a supervisor is responsible in the interest of individual and organizational success and effectiveness.

SUPERVISORY TRAPS AND PITFALLS

No discussion of the successful path to promotion and the ability to stay on that path would be complete without an honest and candid appraisal of things that can go awry. Several unintended dynamics can emerge and trip up the otherwise successful supervisor. They include role convolution, sergeants as union stewards, the tendency to creep back into being a crime fighter, and the collegiality syndrome.

Role Convolution

Although role convolution can occur at a number of junctures, it always includes a single characteristic misstep. There is a tendency, especially for new sergeants, to drift away from the expectations of the position. Usually, the new sergeant experiences some confusion over his or her proper role and reshapes the job to exclude certain inherent responsibilities. For the sergeant who dislikes dealing with disciplinary issues, this may be marked by an unspoken indifference to misconduct. For the supervisor who feels that evaluations are a waste of time, there will be a corresponding lack of formal performance appraisals for subordinates. For the sergeant who has become fearful of dealing with field incidents that are part of the daily regimen of law enforcement, this loss of confidence may drive him or her to ignore operational responsibilities and retreat entirely into an administrative role that is inappropriate. As you can see, withdrawal from one or more functions renders the supervisor less than complete.

The Union Steward Mentality

A second trouble spot arises when a sergeant behaves as a union steward or representative. Regardless of whether a supervisor works in a unionized environment or not, sergeants are part of the management side of the organization. Many sergeants will have to confront the tendency to overly protect subordinates. The inclination is to be an advocate to the exclusion of all else and to deny responsibility for misconduct when it is clearly evident. This mismatch can be a fatal barrier for those who cannot overcome the hurdle.

Crime Fighting

This dilemma arises when a supervisor cannot moderate the urge to become directly involved in street law enforcement or the investigation of incidents to which patrol officers can respond. While the tactical edge and the sixth sense of police intuition should never be denied or compromised, the value a sergeant brings to the job is his or her ability to lead and manage, not respond to calls. This hazard stems from two sources. The first is the need to understand and appreciate the expectations and roles discussed thus far. The second is to ensure a balance in daily activities and understanding the organizational priorities that are in place.

The Collegiality Syndrome

Perhaps the most deadly supervisory sin is the "collegiality syndrome." Sergeants must strike a delicate balance between their supervisory responsibilities and the human need to surround oneself with a personal support system of friends, confidants, and companions. The challenge comes when this collegiality intrudes on decision making and creates the potential for conflict. Inappropriate fraternization or excessive demands from friends who are fellow officers compromise the sergeant's integrity and are precursors to bad decision making. As McGrath (1997, p. 157) explains, among police officers the "level of interdependence creates a sort of camaraderie that can simultaneously support and undermine the . . . behavior of fellow officers."

ROLE SATISFACTION AND CAREER SUCCESS

Just as there are a myriad of barriers to overcome and mistakes to be avoided, a number of things, if done right, are key ingredients to long-term success as a police supervisor. A new supervisor who is interested in front loading for success should make a conscious effort to develop a persona that is described by others as a "can do/go to" attitude. What does that expression mean? Simply put, the successful "can do" sergeant is the supervisor who is prepared to solve problems on behalf of the organization, anticipate issues on behalf of leadership, and willing to accept virtually any challenge in order to move the agency forward. Others can count on this sergeant to seize the opportunity and not bemoan the burden.

Likewise, the "go to" sergeant is regarded as a resource of exceptional value. This esteem is reflected in the willingness to turn to that supervisor in a crisis, when urgency is essential, or when circumstances demand a particularly difficult resolution. Agency leaders are confident that the end product is virtually assured. The downside for the "go to" sergeant, though, is the reaffirmation of the classic hypothesis that suggests that those who work the hardest, work the most often, and are willing to step up whenever asked will work more than anyone else because it is such an easy option for an administrator to choose. Nevertheless, in its totality, the "can do" or the "go to" approach to management breeds success, mutual confidence between the department and the incumbent, and the promise of future advancement.

CONCLUSION

Successful career paths rarely happen by accident. Instead, the aspiring officer must take a deliberate and reflective approach to charting out a sound career path. Career path decisions may require the incumbent to integrate what, at first, might appear to be conflicting desires. That is, emerging leaders within an organization often are faced with the dilemma of choosing between that which is interesting, prestigious, or exciting and that which is tough, not particularly glamorous, but critical to the organization. No doubt, there are plenty of lackluster assignments within an agency. A transfer to internal affairs, research and planning, or accreditation management may not be as glamorous as other, front-line posts. However, these positions will provide upcoming supervisors with very substantial and crucial organizational skills. But more important than choosing any particular career path is to have a plan that is well thought out and then to follow it. After all, there always is the promotion to the next rank to consider.

DISCUSSION QUESTIONS

1. Distinguish between the appointive and competitive processes for promotion selection. What are the advantages and disadvantages to each?
2. Contrast and compare the "accelerated opportunity path" with the "extended experience path." If you were a police officer, which route would you choose to follow and why?
3. From a chief's perspective, what are the six outcomes associated with the behavior and performance of college-educated police officers?
4. Explain what the "metamorphosis of perspective" entails.
5. Discuss the concept of "service over self" as the basic premise of successful police supervision.
6. Examine the supervisory traps and pitfalls. Are they peculiar to just policing or are they applicable to other occupations?

REFERENCES

Bennett, W. W., and K. M. Hess. *Management and Supervision in Law Enforcement.* St. Paul, MN: West Publishing Company, 1996.

Block, P. *Stewardship: Choosing Service over Self-Interest.* San Francisco: Berrett-Koehler Publishers, 1993.

Goldstein, H. *Problem-Oriented Policing.* New York: McGraw-Hill, 1990.

Heidingsfield, M. "Six reasons to require college education for police officers." *Subject to Debate* 9, no. 12 (1995), pp. 5, 7.

McGrath, E. "Professional ethics and policing." In M. L. Dantzker (ed.), *Contemporary Policing: Personnel, Issues, and Trends*, pp. 145–166. Boston: Butterworth–Heinemann, 1997.

Nowicki, D. E., G. W. Sykes, and T. Eisenberg. "Human resource management." In W. A. Geller (ed.), *Local Government Police Management*, 3rd ed., pp. 272–306. Washington, DC: International City Management Association, 1991.

Shernock, S., and G. D. Dantzker. "Education and training: No longer just a badge and a gun." In M. L. Dantzker (ed.), *Contemporary Policing: Personnel, Issues, and Trends*, pp. 75–97. Boston: Butterworth–Heinemann, 1997.

Southerland, M. D. "Organizational communication." In L. T. Hoover (ed.), *Police Management: Issues and Perspectives*, pp. 281–303. Washington, DC: Police Executive Research Forum, 1992.

Van Maanen, J. "Observations on the making of policemen." *Human Organization* 32, no. 4 (1973), pp. 407–418.

————. "Making rank: Becoming an American police sergeant." *Urban Life* 13, no. 2–3 (1984), pp. 155–176.

Chapter 4

Ethical Leadership

Barbara J. Hauptman, Omaha, Nebraska, Police Department

As we head toward the new millennium, headlines continue to bombard us about police organizations around the nation dealing with corrupt, brutal police practices. "Three Officers Charged in Beating of Motorist," "Vice Squad Detective Faces Robbery Charges," "Undercover Officer Kills Fellow Officers," "Police Officers Indicted in Drunken, Off-Duty Melee," "Officers Arrested for Robbery and Extortion," and "Federal Official Held in Kidnap-Death Plot" are just a sampling of such news stories. When these instances do occur, the main spotlight is on the unsavory officers. At the same time, some people also point fingers at police leaders, especially the police chief. Former Los Angeles police chief Daryl Gates really stirred the pot when he claimed that he was not responsible for his officers' actions in the beating of Rodney King. Yet, some observers suggest that the officers' behavior was indicative of the atmosphere Chief Gates created. Do leaders exert an influence on their subordinates? Many would answer with an emphatic "yes." They also would add that this is exactly why police leaders must be ethical.

Leaders are responsible for the practices within their organizations. The upper layer sets the tone for how the organization is managed. Therefore, if an organization and its members are to be effective, the leadership must be effective, too. One major issue revolves around the question of just what is effective leadership? In addition, a major corollary of effectiveness is ethical behavior by the leadership. What do we mean by *ethical leadership*? These two fundamental questions form the basis for this chapter.

LEADERSHIP

One of the more interesting debates in policing is the division between managing and leading. Reality requires that the two not be recognized as synonymous, as seems to be the rule rather than the exception among police chiefs (Dantzker, 1999). A simplistic way to distinguish the two is that managers create the policies and procedures. Leaders encourage and influence members to follow policies and procedures. While both managers and leaders are important to any police organization, it seems that leadership often takes a backseat to management. For the agency to be effective, leadership must be developed and encouraged. That, of course, leads us to the next question: What is leadership?

Defining *leadership* is a rather simple task; accepting a standard definition is not so simple. Because a number of definitions are available, "it is important to understand that there is no single 'correct' definition of leadership" (Hughes, Ginnett, and Curphy, 1995, p. 42). The following are merely examples of what other writers think:

> *Leadership* is "the reciprocal process of mobilizing, by persons with certain motives and values, various economic, political, and other resources, in a context of competition and conflict, in order to realize goals independently or mutually held by both leaders and followers." (Burns, 1978, p. 425)
>
> *Leadership* is "the process of influencing an organized group toward accomplishing its goals." (Hughes et al., 1995, p. 43)
>
> *Leaders* are "persons who, by word and/or personal example, markedly influence the behaviors, thoughts, and/or feelings of a significant number of their fellow human beings." (Gardner, 1995, pp. 8–9).

Other commentators talk about leaders as being motivated by a concern for others or from a keen sense of duty (Kanungo and Mendonca, 1996; Cavaliere and Spradley, 1995). Simply put, leaders are people who can affect and influence the behavior of others. One of the most effective ways for the leader to influence others is through his or her behavior. In other words, talking about being a good leader is not enough. He or she must act like a good leader.

Walking the Talk

For starters, we must realize that "Leadership has a major impact on people" (Oakley and Krug, 1991, p. 230). If a leader's behavior is not congruent with what he or she says, all trust in the leader is lost. Setting an example is extremely important for effective leaders (Blanchard and Peale, 1988; Gardner, 1995; Morris, 1997). Leaders who do not practice what they preach are known as hypocrites, diminishing any effectiveness they may have as a leader. Effective leaders demonstrate integrity by being consistent in both action and word (House, 1995).

Suppose, for example, a police lieutenant continually stresses the evils of sexual harassment. He says something about this wrongful act at every roll call. This person encourages all the officers under his command to avoid any behavior that might even remotely be construed as sexual harassment. However, each evening the lieutenant is observed riding with a rookie female officer. One evening he is spotted in a city park engaging in amorous activities with this subordinate while on duty. All the talk about avoiding sexual harassment and doing the right thing suddenly is worthless.

Effective leaders share a gift for defining a vision and for moving people toward a direction for the future (Goodwin, 1998, p. 29). Effective leaders "walk the talk" or practice what they preach. They do not break trust. They accept responsibility for their actions and move on. However, part of walking the talk requires a leader to have certain skills and abilities.

Skills and Abilities

According to Bennis and Mische (1995, p. 9), an effective and visible leader of an organization should possess creativity, visionary influence, solid knowledge of the business, credibility achieved through a track record of successful experiences, exceptional people skills, an impeccable character, and excellent judgment. Senge (1998, pp. 17–18) believes that

> an effective leader has a mission, where the mission provides an orientation . . . a direction, not a destination. Without a sense of mission, there is no foundation for establishing why some intended results are more important than others. Leaders who lack vision fail to define what they hope to accomplish in terms that can ultimately be assessed.

A vision is critical if a leader is to guide followers toward the intended goals of the organization. An effective leader clearly communicates this vision at every available opportunity. Professor Southerland devotes much more attention to this topic in Chapter 5.

Goodwin (1998) suggests that today's leaders should adhere to ten simple lessons if they are to be successful (see Box 4–1). It is believed that effective leaders follow these lessons when communicating the organization's vision. Furthermore, by following these lessons, one increases the chances of demonstrating one of the most important traits, ethics, which can influence a leader's viewpoint.

Box 4–1   Goodwin's Ten Leadership Lessons

1. Timing is (almost) everything.
2. Share the glory.
3. Trust, once broken, is seldom restored.
4. Leadership is about building connections.
5. Leaders learn from their mistakes.
6. Confidence counts.
7. Effective partnerships require attention to partners.
8. Personal renewal is important.
9. Leaders must be talent brokers.
10. Language is one's most powerful tool.

Source: D. K. Goodwin. "Lessons of presidential leadership." *Leader to Leader* 9 (Summer 1998), p. 27.

Morris (1997) provides a convenient backdrop for defining ethical and nonethical persons. A *nonethical person* has a viewpoint that is narrow, shortsighted, and maintains an exclusive allegiance to self. The *ethical person*, on the other hand, takes a long-term point of view and has a very broad, more inclusive concern for others. The ethical person truly uses the "golden rule" and treats others the same way he or she would want to be treated. When properly applied, this guide will establish and sustain morally strong relationships. The ethical leader constantly communicates his or her concern for others to anyone who is watching. It is apparent that many skills may be required to be a good leader. However, none is as important as ethics.

Ethics

If leadership sets the tone within an organization, then ethical leadership should ensure an extremely healthy and honest relationship between the organization and the community it serves. But, what exactly are ethics?

Ethics, in reality, are not the behaviors we expect from individuals. Instead, they are a form of a philosophy that focuses on what is considered *right* and *wrong*. What we really are referring to when we speak of ethical leadership is *moral* leadership. That is, we are identifying someone who practices acceptable standards of behavior and readily differentiates between what is right and wrong. Therefore, a person who abides by an established code of conduct is perceived as behaving in an ethical and forthright manner. Any departure from that code leaves us with a person who is behaving in an unethical fashion. Unfortunately, many of us, including our leaders, often are accused of practicing "situational ethics." Instead of steadfastly adhering to a set of expectations, duplicitous behavior or a "double standard" emerges (i.e., the lieutenant in the earlier example). Leaders must embrace a certain set of core values if they are to be morally correct or behave ethically.

Core Values

Ethical leaders embrace "higher" values and principles and challenge their followers to embrace these universal principles, too. Burns (1978), Kouzes and Posner (1992), and Milton-Smith (1995) also recognize that leadership is connected to followers' desires, emphasizing the process that revolves around shared visions and goals. What are these higher values?

According to O'Toole (1995, p. 108),

> successful leaders share certain core values that allow them to overcome ever-present resistance: all employees have inalienable rights, particularly that all are entitled to be treated with respect and to be treated as ends, not means.

He continues with talk about universal truths or core values that should serve as the foundation for making ethical decisions:

There is no circumstance where it is permissible for a leader to treat followers with disrespect; there is never a valid reason for leaders to abuse followers. There are universal truths and principles—trustworthiness, respect, promise-keeping, service, and faithfulness.

Actions define leadership and decisions are precursors to action (Nair, 1994). Decisions should be evaluated against the absolute values of truth and nonviolence and the universal code of conduct: to treat others as we would like them to treat ourselves. Senge (1998, p. 18) reminds us that "to be values-guided is to hold up lofty standards against which every person's behavior can be judged." Using these "lofty" standards as the basis for weighing available alternatives and consequences of one's actions places a person well on the path to leading in an ethical way. These values are especially important because leaders often carry the mandate to shepherd in organizational change.

LEADERS AS CHANGE AGENTS

Ethical leaders also are agents of change. According to Souryal (1992, p. 186), they "are driven by principle, seek moral solutions, mix values with technology, and adjust their strategies to ill-defined environments." Souryal acknowledges that the

power of ethical management is the power of knowledge, vision, decency, and good faith. When ethical management is pursued, all aspects of illegality, falsity, unfairness, exploitation, and corruption are unjustified. (1992, p. 186)

Because leaders are interested in making things better, change becomes a top priority on the agenda. They grow and change with the times. According to Katzenbach (1995, p. 13), leaders tend to share certain traits. Some common characteristics of change agents include

- Commitment to a better way.
- Courage to challenge existing power bases and norms.
- Personal initiative to go beyond defined boundaries.
- Motivation of themselves and others.
- Caring about how people are treated and enabled to perform.
- Keeping a low profile, not grandstanding.
- Having a sense of humor about themselves and their situations.

Real change leaders think and act differently than traditional leaders. Real change leaders look to upgrade the skills and behaviors of the people in their organizations. Their motto is "continuous improvement." At the same time, though, they are fair and truly care about people.

Melendez probably sums it up best. Ethical leaders are

people of vision, effective communicators, effective decision makers, and intelligent; they respect and value individuals and their dignity; they are committed to service; they have total honesty and integrity; they are kind; and they often see themselves as teachers. (1996, p. 293)

Whether as teachers or change agents, leaders can vastly influence and shape an organization's culture.

Shaping the Organization's Culture

According to Ciulla (1995, p. 494), "organizations need to be places where ordinary life is not a daily moral struggle." It is also important that "ethical responsibilities are, or should be inseparable from business policies and practices and that morality in the workplace should not be drastically different from morality in the culture outside of it" (p. 499). In other words, leaders should practice the same behavior inside the organization as they do outside of it. By behaving ethically, leaders influence how others act and, thus, shape the culture of the organization. If a leader is corrupt, brutal, or discriminatory, chances are very good that the followers will be that way, too. The argument about the L.A.P.D. and its officers' behavior under Chief Daryl Gates is a good example of how leadership could shape an organization's culture. Leaders must create a work environment conducive to ethical behavior.

The Work Environment

First and foremost, the leader of an organization must have a vision. Most visions are translated into working plans through a process known as *strategic planning*. Strategic planning involves gathering input from all those affected, both inside and outside the organization. Goals are carved out, along with specific objectives and plans for achieving these ends. Assigning time lines, responsibilities, and accountability for follow-up are important steps in the strategic planning process. The strategic planning process establishes the framework for determining priorities and should be a continuous process.

Next, leaders can shape the organization's culture by promoting an ethical work environment. How can they accomplish this? Leaders can promote an ethical work environment by

making a formal commitment to advance ethical behavior throughout the organization; developing and communicating an ethical vision for the organization; demonstrating ethical behaviors or "walking the talk"; establishing appropriate ethical performance criteria and conducting training, and rewarding ethical achievements and responding to misconduct in a timely, thorough manner. (Larimer, 1997, pp. 5–6)

Once the leadership establishes goals and sets examples of prized behaviors based on absolute values and a universal code of conduct, moral progress is made (Nair, 1994, pp. 118–119) and an ethical work environment exists. Shaping the work environment involves monitoring the decision-making and policy-making practices.

Decision Making

Nothing can tarnish an organization's reputation quicker than the absence of solid value-based decision making (Ramsey, 1996, p. 15). Basing decisions on firm moral principles allows audiences to grasp the larger picture that the leader wishes to convey. Nair (1994, p. 140) seizes on this point:

> When those in leadership positions act on principles, they set an example for all who follow. One person can make a difference. Your life is your message. Leadership by example is not only the most pervasive but also the most enduring form of leadership.

The effects of decisions made by leaders reverberate throughout the organization and the community. The decisions made by leaders send a clear message to all about what will be tolerated, accepted, or unacceptable. In a police organization, decisions made are likely to end up on the evening news.

Nair (1994, p. 99) identifies four steps as essential to infusing a moral dimension into a leader's role in society and for providing a path for organizational members to follow:

- Establish principles of governance.
- Create integrity in the decision process.
- Change the criteria for decision making.
- Implement decisions within moral constraints.

Ethics revolve around what we do, not what we say we should do. According to Kidder (1995, p. 32), "ethics defines the way we participate in the community around us." It is not always easy to take a stand. However, Nair (1994, p. 136) explains that leaders "have an obligation to call attention to discrimination, unethical behavior, and intimidation. We have to do it not for personal gain, but to improve the system."

An organization's policies should reflect the values of the organization. Policies are the foundation for making decisions and influencing behaviors in the organization. The organization's leader is accountable for the effects the organization's policies have on the organization, the employees, and the community.

Leaders with integrity can question the status quo and influence decision making within their organizations (Gottlieb and Sanzgiri, 1996). Leaders with integrity can provide the framework for ethical decision making and are "responsible for the effectiveness of organizations" (Bennis, 1989, p. 15).

Leaders need accurate, current data when making policy decisions. They also should seek information from a variety of sources. Messick and Bazerman (1996) assert that unethical decision making often results from faulty or inaccurate assumptions leaders have about the world, other people, and themselves. As long as leaders understand how decisions based on faulty assumptions can lead to unethical outcomes, they will strive to enact better, more ethical decisions.

A commitment to the truth also provides the best defense against two of the most common errors in strategic decision making: rush to judgment and group think. *Rush to judgment* refers to the ill-advised notion that taking some type of immediate action is the best prescription. *Group think* is defined as the "unwillingness of top management to consider critical information which might disturb their own view of reality" (Danley et al., 1996, p. 278). What is the best defense against these mistakes? A commitment to the truth (Nair, 1994, p. 126). Unfortunately, because police leaders often must exist in a political environment, being ethical and moral can be very lofty goals.

The Role of Politics

Zajac (1997) posits that ethical failures in organizations (such as corruption and other forms of wrongdoing) are equally as powerful as shortcomings of efficiency and effectiveness. Ethical failures can have a corrosive effect on public faith, especially for a law enforcement agency. The damage to public faith can be far more significant over the long term and be extremely difficult from which to recoup.

John W. Gardner emphasizes the role leaders play in society today:

> Leaders have a significant role in creating the state of mind that is the society. They can serve as symbols of the moral unity of the society. They can express the values that hold society together. Most important, they can conceive and articulate goals that lift people out of their petty preoccupations, carry them above the conflicts that tear a society apart, and unite them in pursuit of objectives worthy of their best efforts. (quoted in Bennis, 1989, p. 13)

When an organization experiences an "ethical lapse," the public trust is shattered. Leaders must understand the heavy burden they carry to maintain the public's trust in their organizations. Leaders of police organizations, especially, need to understand the difficulty of rebuilding trust after it is lost. All future actions, no matter how honorable, are considered suspect.

According to Cropanzano and his colleagues (1997), politics in an organization causes stress and uncertainty. They define a political environment as "characterized by groups and individuals who competitively pursue their own ends" (p. 160). In this environment, building power bases is perceived as the road to success. Instead, it leads to less predictability, more uncertainty in the workplace, and being blinded to the concerns of others. The ethical leader understands "politics" exist in any organization but does not cross the line. Astute leaders do not justify illegal behaviors. They do not treat people unfairly nor do they exploit others for personal gain. Ethical leaders are guided by the universal values mentioned earlier.

Cropanzano et al. also found that

> job involvement, job satisfaction, and organizational commitment positively correlated with perceived organizational support and negatively correlated with perceived organizational politics. (1997, p. 169)

An employee who perceives the work environment to be politically charged will experience greater levels of anxiety and tension and lower levels of general health. Ethical leaders can ensure a healthy work environment by establishing ethical practices through the organization's policies and processes.

People expect more of police organizations today than ever before. The community looks to be included in decision-making and policy-setting processes. As societal issues become more complex, police leaders must be prepared to face competing interests and tightened budgets. Regardless of the societal challenges, the ultimate challenge for police leaders is to adopt an ethical system appropriate for the organization. Probably the best model one can employ is the "justice ethics" system (Lynch, 1998), which advocates equal opportunities, team leadership, and power through groups (coalitions, associations, or employees). However, because policing is a strongly bureaucratic entity, this type of system is difficult to implement. Regardless, police leaders must do their best to adhere to a strong, ethical leadership or accept the negative effects an unethical organization will bring.

CONCLUSION

Leadership sets the tone for the entire organization. Ethical leaders can ensure a healthy relationship between the organization and the community it serves. Leaders must have a vision or mission and be able to effectively communicate it to the organization's members and the community it serves.

Successful leaders must possess certain core values and let those values guide them in making decisions, values such as trustworthiness, honesty, respect, promise keeping, service, and faithfulness. Leaders must "walk the talk" and practice what they preach. Any inconsistencies will be remembered and will reduce a leader's effectiveness.

A leader can shape the organization's culture by shaping its policies. The ethical leader's viewpoint understands the long-term, inclusive concern for others. Finally, the ethical leader commits to "doing the right thing" when it may not be the most popular thing to do.

DISCUSSION QUESTIONS

1. What can law enforcement leaders do to ensure an ethical work environment exists in police organizations?
2. Define ethics. Are ethical leaders more successful than nonethical leaders?
3. What skills and abilities should an effective, ethical leader possess?
4. What effect do "ethical lapses" or "ethical failures" in a police department have on the public?
5. How can police leaders shape the organization's culture? How important is having a mission or vision to a leader?

REFERENCES

Bennis, W. G. *On Becoming a Leader.* New York: Addison-Wesley Publishing Company, 1989.

_____ and M. Mische. *The 21st Century Organization: Reinventing through Reengineering.* San Francisco: Jossey-Bass Publishers, 1995.

Blanchard, K., and N. V. Peale. *The Power of Ethical Management.* New York: Ballantine Books, 1988.

Burns, J. M. *Leadership.* New York: Harper & Row, 1978.

Cavaliere, F. J., and L. W. Spradley. "Is teaching 'the social responsibility of business' a responsible activity?" *Education* 116, no. 1 (1995), pp. 86–92.

Ciulla, J. B. "Messages from the environment: The influence of policies and practices on employee responsibility." In J. T. Wren (ed.), *The Leader's Companion: Insights on Leadership through the Ages*, pp. 492–499. New York: The Free Press, 1995.

Cropanzano, R., J. C. Howes, A. A. Grandey, and P. Toth. "The relationship of organizational politics and support to work behaviors, attitudes, and stress." *Journal of Organizational Behavior* 18, no. 2 (1997), pp. 159–180.

Danley, J., E. Harrick, D. Schaefer, D. Strickland, and G. Sullivan. "HR's view of ethics in the work place: Are the barbarians at the gate?" *Journal of Business Ethics* 15, no. 3 (1996), pp. 273–280.

Dantzker, M. L. *Police Organization and Management: Yesterday, Today, and Tomorrow.* Boston: Butterworth–Heinemann, 1999.

Gardner, H. *Leading Minds: An Anatomy of Leadership.* New York: HarperCollins Publishers, 1995.

Goodwin, D. K. "Lessons of presidential leadership." *Leader to Leader* 9 (Summer 1998), pp. 23–30.

Gottlieb, J. Z., and J. Sanzgiri. "Towards an ethical dimension of decision making in organizations." *Journal of Business Ethics* 15, no. 12 (1996), pp. 1275–1285.

House, R. J. "Leadership in the twenty-first century: A speculative inquiry." In A. Howard (ed.), *The Changing Nature of Work*, pp. 411–450. San Francisco: Jossey-Bass Publishers, 1995.

Hughes, R. L., R. C. Ginnett, and G. R. Curphy. "What is leadership?" In J. T. Wren (ed.), *The Leader's Companion: Insights on Leadership through the Ages*, pp. 39–43. New York: The Free Press, 1995.

Kanungo, R. N., and M. Mendonca. *Ethical Dimensions of Leadership.* Thousand Oaks, CA: Sage Publications, 1996.

Katzenbach, J. R. *Real Change Leaders: How You Can Create Growth and High Performance at Your Company.* New York: Times Books, 1995.

Kidder, R. M. "Tough choices: Why it's getting harder to be ethical." *The Futurist* 29, no. 5 (1995), pp. 29–32.

Kouzes, J. M., and B. Z. Posner. "Ethical leaders: An essay about being in love." *Journal of Business Ethics* 11, nos. 5–6 (1992), pp. 479–485.

Larimer, L. V. "Reflections on ethics and integrity." *HR Focus* 74, no. 4 (1997), pp. 5–6.

Lynch, R. G. *The Police Manager*, 5th ed. Cincinnati: Anderson Publishing Company, 1998.

Melendez, S. E. "An 'outsider's' view of leadership." In F. Hesselbein, M. Goldsmith, and R. Beckhard (eds.), *The Leader of the Future: New Visions, Strategies, and Practices for the Next Era*, pp. 293–302. San Francisco: Jossey-Bass Publishers, 1996.

Messick, D. M., and M. H. Bazerman. "Ethical leadership and the psychology of decision making." *Sloan Management Review* 37 (Winter 1996), pp. 9–22.

Milton-Smith, J. "Ethics as excellence: A strategic management perspective." *Journal of Business Ethics*, 14, no. 8 (1995), pp. 683–688.

Morris, T. *If Aristotle Ran General Motors: The New Soul of Business.* New York: Henry Holt and Company, 1997.

Nair, K. *A Higher Standard of Leadership: Lessons from the Life of Gandhi.* San Francisco: Berrett-Koehler Publishers, 1994.

Oakley, E., and D. Krug. *Enlightened Leadership: Getting to the Heart of Change.* New York: Simon and Schuster, 1991.

O'Toole, J. *Leading Change: Overcoming the Ideology of Comfort and the Tyranny of Custom.* San Francisco: Jossey-Bass Publishers, 1995.

Ramsey, R. D. "Are ethics obsolete in the 90's?" *Supervision* 57 (February 1996), pp. 14–17.

Senge, P. M. "The practice of innovation." *Leader to Leader* 9 (Summer 1998), pp. 16–22.

Souryal, S. S. *Ethics in Criminal Justice: In Search of Truth.* Cincinnati: Anderson Publishing Company, 1992.

Zajac, G. "Reinventing government and reaffirming ethics: Implications for organizational development in the public service." *Public Administration Quarterly* 20, no. 3 (1997), pp. 385–392.

Chapter 5

Communication: An Agency Imperative

Mittie D. Southerland, Murray State University

When passing the new general order to the deputy chiefs, the chief believed that it was understood and would be implemented throughout the organization with very little trouble. Unfortunately, by the time the new order reached the patrol officers, it had taken on an entirely different context than originally intended. The chief failed to consider that communications, regardless of the format, can be misunderstood or misinterpreted. A common problem among many organizations is a shortcoming in the concept of communication.

Communication is one of the most essential functions undertaken within a police agency. Through communication the organization's philosophy, vision, values, and expectations (hereafter referred to as *organizational direction*) are clarified to its members and the community at large. To be successful, police executives must identify an appropriate organizational direction and convey it to the appropriate audiences in a manner that the groups can understand.

Police leaders do not discover the organizational direction on their own. It is ascertained through consultation with and input from organizational and community members. The manner in which this direction is determined communicates volumes about the executive's belief system. If leadership determines the direction on its own and dictates it to the members and the community, the top executive is saying, "You are unimportant, you have no worthwhile ideas, and you have nothing to contribute. I am neither interested in developing your abilities nor in using your ideas." However, when the top tier involves organization and community members in mapping the direction and the direction results from that consultation, the message is, "I value your input, you have important ideas to contribute and you are necessary to the success of this organization." It is not hard to understand why community and organization members are more motivated and committed when they are involved directly in charting the organizational direction.

It is important that this organizational direction be appropriate for the community, its problems, and the skills and abilities of organization members. It also should be assumed that the organizational direction will change as these factors change. The organizational direction is more likely to fit the community and organization needs when their members play a critical role in its development. The executive's responsibility is to find the best ways to communicate the organizational direction and convert it into action. When the leaders effectively communicate an appropriate organizational direction, police officers, supervisors, and mid-level managers will be motivated and committed to putting its objectives into action. Thus, effective communication results in effective organizations.

Executive communication is embedded in every action and statement proffered by an executive. It includes oral, written, and nonverbal communication, such as voice inflection, body language, and facial expression. It also includes the congruence or conflict between what we say and do, the goals we set, and the policies that constrain those goals. Executives who *say* they are committed to community policing but whose *actions* fail to involve the community members or street-level police officers in decision making are communicating an incongruent message. The underlying message is simple. Lip service is important, but action is not expected; we will talk community policing, but we are not really serious about doing it. Or, as Deputy Chief Hauptman puts it in Chapter 4, credibility demands that leadership "walk the talk."

This chapter dissects the issues in communication that are imperative to the success of the police organization. The topic of interpersonal communication typically delves into the styles, forms, modes, and processes of communication. It examines the various forms of oral and written verbal communication, nonverbal kinesic communication, active listening, barriers to communication, and negotiation strategies. These are addressed only indirectly in the chapter. Interpersonal communication has important implications for organizational communication but has been covered well in a number of police administration texts. This chapter focuses on a smaller number of communication issues. We look at how to develop vision and values, accountability for the right type of values, hidden messages, communicating organizational expectations, policy development and implementation, and organizational communication style and message. A theme that emerges is that the proper approach to these issues is critically important in effectively communicating the organizational direction to community and organization members. Also, this chapter favors a community policing model and assumes that traditional styles of communication are unproductive in encouraging community-oriented policing (COP). It assumes the executive is responsible for setting the tone of communication both within the police organization and between the members of the organization and the community. The executive must lead by example through every form of communication in both public and private life.

NATURE OF EXECUTIVE COMMUNICATION

Executive communication involves both organizational and interpersonal communication. As mentioned in the previous section, this communication must be consistent; otherwise, confusion will reign. Relatively little literature has reported on police organizational communication compared with other policing topics. Nevertheless, the general research on the topic is easily applied to police organizations.

Communication is vitally important in determining the productivity and quality of policing. Police executives must be innovative and willing to develop partnerships with supervisors, officers, the community, businesses, and other government agencies to effect high-quality policing. Values are central to high-quality policing. As I previously explained,

> The right sorts of values must be clearly adopted throughout the organization and the police executive must take an active role in assuring that the organization is value driven toward quality policing. (Southerland, 1992, p. 297)

Organizations and their members must be capable of adaptation and transformation (Mink, Owen, and Mink, 1993). They must be continuous learners. Successful organizations will cultivate an organizational climate that accepts constructive criticism and permits members to express their feelings regarding job experiences. These open channels will promote consensus and collaboration, self-motivation, roles and procedures as evolutionary, high quality as a way of life, and ways to improve processes.

Organizational flexibility and *community responsiveness* must become the key watchwords. Peters (1994) challenges organizations to abandon everything and go beyond the latest fashionable clichés, such as the once in-vogue notions of decentralization, empowerment, reengineering, and total quality management. This dare to abandon everything and move to perpetual revolution may be a bit drastic for the traditional, conservative field of policing. However, it does allow us to take advantage of the intellect and imagination of police officers. The mind set and actions Peters (1994) promotes may be necessary if we are to capitalize on the wealth of talent lying at the "bottom" of our police organizations.

The fact that we still consider police officers as the "bottom" of the food chain in the organization is problematic. The word *bottom* transmits a message of less importance, left over, stale, not as good as, broken, and subpar. All too often, good ideas are discarded because they did not originate with the brass of an agency. What a completely different mind set there would be if we talked about police officers as the "heart" or "foundation" of the organization. Their ideas implicitly would gain value. As you an see, executives must assure that their words and actions, the organizational structure and symbols, and the rewards and punishment send a consistent message to organization and community members.

Much of what Peters (1994) advocates seems too radical for police organizations. Nevertheless, agencies can become ensnared in many of the same traps that destroy profit-oriented businesses. Take the absurdity of focusing the vast majority of our managerial attention on the tangibles of the job, which make up only a small percentage of the resource expenditures. The intangibles deserve far more attention than they get. For example, the bulk of most police budgets is spent on personnel costs and very little is earmarked for new equipment. Yet, it is not unusual for leaders to devote half a dozen meetings to a major capital equipment proposal, such as new uniforms or vehicle purchases. At the same time, relatively little time is set aside to discuss training issues. Furthermore, very little, if any, time goes to a consideration of how to capitalize on the imagination and intellect of the members of the organization.

Another prime example is the annual report. What does it communicate? How is it presented? More than likely, it focuses on crime, traffic data, and a handful of high-profile crime-fighting angles. In all fairness, the annual report usually includes a presentation of the program activities engaged in by officers who are specifically assigned to community-oriented policing programs to soften the law enforcement image. However, the annual report fails to report on the less tangible, and unaccounted for, community service activities of the typical officer. This omission ignores real community policing efforts while focusing attention on limited program-matic activity.

Policing may find that small, independent, self-contained units of 25 or fewer members can be more focused and effective at meeting community needs than that in place today. Why do little businesses work? They have to. During a recent field study of small police departments, several chiefs and officers said they had to be community oriented and adapt their policing strategies to their communities because the community would put up with nothing less than a responsive police department. Similarly, Peters (1994, p. 252) reports that "most companies don't get close enough to customers to hear them." One company broke itself into "itty-bitty businesses . . . that would have no choice but to schmooze and become intently, intimately, and emotionally involved" with customers (Peters, 1994, pp. 253–254). Although size is no guarantee, smallness may create the possibility for more intense communication with the community. More important, the value system that the police organization embraces will be the ultimate determining factor of whether meaningful communication will ever occur.

Peters (1994, p. 69) also suggests that each member of an organization should be a businessperson who "will go anywhere, find anyone, and break any box to get the job done fast and well." By *breaking any box*, Peters means workers will go beyond the artificial confines of the organizational chart and do what is necessary to accomplish the task. The key ingredient here is trust. "Without trust we cannot expect the human imagination to pursue value-added" approaches (Peters, 1994, p. 80). Each employee, whether a sworn officer or not, should have identifiable customers and a broad range of "whole tasks" to perform. This communicates trust and the importance of the individual to the police organization. To accomplish this also requires a willingness to allow and accept mistakes within the organization. As we experiment with new techniques and methods, officers must be free to take risks with the knowledge that errors made in "good faith" will go unpunished. Intentional mistakes or errors that violate the value system must be subject to the fullest extent of the disciplinary system. The nature of the value system is critically important under these conditions and receives attention in the rest of the chapter.

While the act of communicating is important, what stands behind the communication has even greater importance. Organizational values and visions can have a tremendous impact on communications. Therefore, it is important to address these issues. Furthermore, accountability is a mainstay of both vision and values.

ACCOUNTABILITY FOR THE VISION AND VALUES

Accountability is an absolute necessity for any organization that hopes to be successful. Holding each department, each division, each unit, and each employee accountable sets the foundation for achieving the organizational direction. However, accountability is not enough. First, we must disseminate a clear and proper vision for the entire organization. Then, we must hone in on measuring the right values.

In addition to stating the vision and values in very clear tones, the police executive must exhibit these standards in his or her behavior. The way he or she spends time, reacts to critical incidents, and champions the way sends a distinct signal to every employee. It also is important to break down tasks into manageable chunks. This way, the changes required to achieve the vision do not seem overwhelming or impossible.

The way executives communicate the vision and values is critical. Leaders are responsible for making values and beliefs tangible. This necessitates stepping out and showing what they want by their own actions. A sense of conviction is necessary. Executives must be extremely clear in everything they communicate about their vision, their values, their principles, and the criteria by which they judge themselves and others. This requires personal insight. The following questions must be answered: What do you stand for? What do you believe in? Where do you spend your time? Time probably is the clearest indicator to other people about what you believe is important (Kouzes and Posner, 1988, 1995a, 1995b). The successful police executive whose vision includes community policing will spend a significant amount of time with community members. The executive's reaction to every circumstance and every critical incident should reinforce the values.

The following parable illustrates the importance of matching actions to values and having consistent implicit and explicit communication. A police officer had worked under three police chiefs. The values these chiefs espoused explicitly were very much alike; their implicit communication was where they differed. They all told their officers that what they expected from them was to look sharp, keep in shape, treat everyone with respect and dignity, and solve the community's problems.

The first chief was a womanizer who went to conferences so he could spend time with his latest girlfriend without his wife learning about it. He spent very little time with community members, and when he did, he usually imbibed just a little bit too much. This chief lost all credibility with the officers and the city council pretty quickly. Within two years he was looking for a new job. Morale in the department suffered and some of the officers began to model the chief's behavior.

The second chief lasted a little longer. It took him three years to be removed from office. This chief started out pretty well. Everything was going fine until the department had a significant number of officers retire. The chief was now responsible for hiring replacements. Up to this point, the department had contained predominately white men. This chief had been telling the officers and the community that he was interested in making the agency more representative of the community and would do so as openings became available. The recruitment effort went fine. Lots of capable young people were in the applicant pool, including a record number of women and minority-group members. The selection process was working well and produced a list of diverse individuals from which the chief was responsible for selecting the newest members of the department. The chief's choices were all white men. His credibility was lost. An ensuing civil suit threw the organization into turmoil. The investigation into the chief's action that resulted from the litigation uncovered prior sex and race discrimination. The chief was removed from office and the department was left with a tarnished reputation. Officers who were closet chauvinists and racists felt free to express their views and to act on them.

The third chief knew the history of his two predecessors and was determined to do things differently. He knew that his actions would be under a microscope. In his first departmental meeting, he announced that he wanted everybody to do things consistently with the way he acted. "You can do anything that I do." He worked out at the gym, ate right, was family oriented, treated employees with respect and dignity, and spent a significant amount of time in the community learning about problems and supporting officers' efforts to solve them. He encouraged the members of the department and led by example. He was consistent in his actions, his words, and the pictures he put on his office walls and on his desk. Everything he did and every decision he made seemed to have been chosen with his vision and values in mind. This chief hired some highly competent women and minority-group members and started a leadership development program. He wanted every officer to be a leader within the community. He identified all the communities within the jurisdiction, created small "departments" with responsibility for those areas, and held them accountable for making their "communities" safe places to live and work. In doing this, the chief shrank the hierarchy of the department without cutting out any of the current rank. His intention was that the rank structure would change through attrition. He knew that most agencies that had reduced the rank structure faced serious opposition and recalcitrance from mid-level management. He was determined to utilize the skills and experience of the mid-level managers to support and make the needed organizational changes.

This last chief was successful. Everyone worked harder for this chief and the organization was transformed. This chief maintained credibility and was revered by the community and members of the police organization. All were part of a team working toward the same organizational direction.

DEVELOPING THE VISION

How is a vision developed? It begins as a quest for change. Kouzes and Posner (1988, 1995a, 1995b) identify two guidelines for developing vision. First, it is important to search out challenging opportunities so as to change, grow, innovate, and improve. The leader must think of the organization as being on an adventure. There must be new challenges regularly and opportunities to improve. Second, the leader must involve the organization in experimenting, taking risks, and learning from the mistakes that are made. It is important to institutionalize organizational processes for collecting creative ideas. Leaders should put "idea gathering" on their own agenda by spending time with beat officers, investigators, staff, and civilian personnel and asking what could be done better. Simply put, stagnation will strangle an organization.

The single most important thing the executive can do is to model risk taking. The questions that can help the executive to clarify the vision are these: How would you like to change the world for yourself and your organization? What is your dream about your work? What work do you find absorbing and enthralling? Once these questions are addressed the executive is ready to write a short, 25 words or less, vision statement.

The *vision statement* should describe the ideal, unique image the executive has formulated for the organization and what it means to be successful. Then, it is important to draw a picture of the vision or find a symbol that represents it. Pictures are a much more vivid form of communication than words.

Once the vision statement is developed, the executive's role is to breathe life into it. He or she needs to communicate it to others so they understand the vision and incorporate it into their own activities. One way to accomplish this step is to appeal to values, interests, hopes, and dreams. The executive can demonstrate important values by fostering collaboration and promoting goals that build trust. Trust is built by knowing the audience with whom one is communicating and the common ground. It is important to recognize what will be understood by the employees. The message sender must chose language carefully so that the audience immediately receives the full meaning of the message. Positive language is motivating. Words, such as *will*, *are*, and *can* convey strong conviction. The words *we*, *our*, and *together* promote collaboration and trust. Enthusiasm is contagious.

ORGANIZATIONAL VALUES

Values are enduring beliefs that certain, specific modes of conduct are preferable (Rokeach, 1973). *Organizational values* define the essential beliefs of the organization. They identify the things that are cherished. The value system serves as a guide and lets people recognize the range and limitations to organizational behavior. Organizational values include beliefs about which strategies and techniques work well in the organizational setting (Ouchi, 1981). Organizational values and beliefs must be expressed in concrete ways so that new members entering the organization can understand and embrace them (Southerland and Reuss-Ianni, 1992). A major problem with police values is that the implicit values often conflict with the explicit values; "This breeds confusion, distrust, and cynicism rather than clarity, commitment, and high morale" (Wasserman and Moore, 1988, p. 1).

Peters and Waterman (1982) found that every exceptional company they studied had articulated a clear set of values and was serious about the process of shaping those values. They (1982, p. 285) questioned whether it could be possible to be an excellent organization without having the following set of seven values:

• A belief in being the "best."

- A belief in the importance of the details of execution, the nuts and bolts of doing the job well.
- A belief in the importance of people as individuals.
- A belief in superior quality and service.
- A belief that most members of the organization should be innovators and, its corollary, the willingness to support failure.
- A belief in the importance of informality to enhance communication.
- An explicit belief in and recognition of the importance of economic growth and profits.

To translate these values directly to policing, we must modify the seventh one to read, "An explicit belief and recognition of the importance of upholding the Constitution and producing those outcomes that make our community safe and orderly." The police executive's role is critical to transmitting values to members of the organization so that they become "bone-deep beliefs." To that end, executives should follow this advice:

> Be confident in your beliefs. Live them with integrity. Remember that the "small stuff" is all there is. It's a pretty tough message. If your convictions about people aren't all that clear and strong, then it's tough to be confident and consistent. Maybe that's the secret, for good or ill, after all. (Peters and Austin, 1985, p. 212)

THE RIGHT TYPE OF VALUES

Why is the right type of values such a focal point for policing? This is the heart of the problem many police departments face. Many administrators do not know what they are trying to achieve. Sometimes, they unwittingly embrace values that are counterproductive to their mission. We see this happening in police agencies where there is little community support. The police are not trusted and the community fears police brutality. Think, for a moment, about the values that are reflected in the following approaches to policing: "We are always in charge." "We have the answers." "It is us against them and we must win." "We will strictly enforce the law for that is our mission." These statements lead to the macho police stance and the gung-ho mentality. They invite excessive use of force, inattention to community needs, insensitivity to the needs of crime victims, an unresponsive attitude toward community members, an insular attitude, and an unwarranted distrust or fear of anyone who is not a member of the police community.

How can such a counterproductive approach be changed? It will take the infusion of a fundamentally different value system. The alternate value system carries a host of distinct expectations. It says things like these: "All life is precious." "We are responsible for carrying out the guarantees of the Constitution and the Bill of Rights." "We serve our community." "We listen to our constituents." "We engage community members to join with us in making the community a safe place to live." "We take charge of situations where police action is necessary." "We protect life and property."

This value system promotes police behavior that deserves and wins respect, engenders trust and community support, and creates a view of police as authority figures. The ultimate goal is have the police seen as trusted authority figures, not as authoritarians to be feared.

The problem confronting many police agencies is that they adhere to some parts of each of the aforementioned sets of values. This incomplete alliance creates an inherent value conflict and causes officers to be confused as to what is truly desired and expected. The contradiction is evident only when the organizational communication (words and actions) are examined at both the implicit and explicit levels. A discussion of this issue is presented next.

HIDDEN MESSAGES

Unanticipated consequences can result when police executives fail to examine the implicit communication that occurs in the organization. Quite often, police officers and citizens act on the basis of *implicit communication* (what they believe will happen based on their interpretation of the oral or written message), while ignoring the *explicit communication* (what they are told to do through the oral or written message). This mix-up happens most frequently when there is conflict between the implicit and explicit communication. Box 5–1 contains a scenario that shows conflicting communications.

In Box 5–1, the supervisor is implying that the community's views are not important and that problem solving is not valued. Explicitly, this supervisor is advising the officer to ignore such information in the future. The supervisor does not come right out and prohibit the officer from taking action to resolve the problem. However, the officer is keenly aware that this supervisor evaluates her and is in control of potential rewards and punishments. Therefore, the officer chooses to do nothing more about this specific incident. Based on the supervisor's implicit communication, the officer disregards the official, explicit communication from the chief to "do more problem solving and be more community oriented out there."

A scenario such as this occurs more frequently than we would like. It also is a reminder of the age-old adage "actions speak louder than words." Police agencies communicate much more loudly by what they value implicitly than by what is valued explicitly. It is crucial that implicit and explicit communication are consistent.

If this supervisor were interested in supporting the new organizational values, then he or she would have taken this opportunity to reinforce the problem-solving training. The supervisor could have responded, "You've done a nice job of problem solving. You've looked at the problem and enlisted community input about it. The solution sounds very workable. I know you'll be able to use your persuasive skills to get the public works department to do what's needed. What are your follow-up plans?" After the officer's ideas are discussed, the supervisor could close with, "Keep solving problems and remember—positive interaction. You're sure on the right track."

Box 5–1   A Scenario Illustrating the Conflict Between Explicit and Implicit Communication

The chief recently announced that the department will become a community-oriented police department. Part of the COP approach is an emphasis on problem solving. To prepare officers for this new role, the department sent every agency member to a training program on problem solving. One officer who attended the training notices that several traffic accidents have occurred at a particular intersection on her beat. She decides to try out the new problem-solving skills. She goes to the intersection and begins to scan the area for problems. She talks with people who live in the area to get their input. Her analysis leads her to conclude that tree limbs partially covering the stop signs and overgrown bushes that obstruct visibility contribute to the accident problem. Neighbors tell her that they have tried, without success, to get the public works department to cut the limbs and trim back the bushes. The officer decides to go to the public works department and meet the supervisor to see if she can get the trees and bushes cut back.

The officer reports her findings and her plan to her supervisor, "You know the intersection where we've had all those wrecks? I looked at it and talked with some of the residents in that neighborhood. We think the problem stems from reduced visibility due to overgrown trees and shrubs. I plan to get the limbs and shrubs trimmed. That should resolve the problem." The supervisor responds, "Why are you bothering with all this nonsense? You shouldn't waste your time on trees and shrubs. They aren't a police problem. Just write some tickets. That will satisfy city hall. Besides, we have more important things to do."

As you can tell, there is a lack of accountability within this organization. The chief is responsible for modeling such positive interaction and assuring that everything done in the organization on an implicit level supports the explicit messages. The upper echelon also must assure that the explicit messages support the vision and values established for the organization.

Police executives and leaders at all levels should examine every written document and action to uncover or decode any hidden messages that may create confusion or compromise the organization's thrust. Organizational negativity can result from conflicts between what is said and what is done in organizations.

The first major cause of organizational negativity is ineffective communication and ineffective management of change (Topchik, 1998). All too often, change creates confusion, anxiety, frustration, and false starts. Effective change can happen when people adopt VISAR: vision, incentives, skills, action plan, and resources. Employees are more positive when they understand the *vision*, the reason for the change. They have an *incentive* to be positive about change when they believe it will benefit them or the organization. Employees are more positive when they are tooled with the appropriate *skills* to meet the challenge of the change and know about the *action plan*, the specific steps that will be involved in the change. Given the time, tools, money, and other *resources,* people will have a more positive attitude toward implementing change. One estimate is that negativity costs U.S. companies $3 billion each year in low productivity, damaged customer relationships, and other performance problems (Topchik, 1998). Similar effects on American policing are not as easily estimated. Yet, the consequences may be more significant for the communities served. The customers of private corporations have other options for obtaining the desired product. Often, there are no other options for police services.

The second major cause of organizational negativity stems from a mismatch between trust and enablement of employees. *Trust* involves "allowing people to make decisions that affect their work and providing them with opportunities for growth and development" (Topchik, 1998, p. 63). *Enablement* is giving employees "the skills, knowledge, resources and motivation to do their jobs" (Topchik, 1998, p. 63). Peak performance comes from high trust and high enablement. Any other combination is problematic and results in negativity. When people are highly enabled but given little trust, they have wings but are caged and, therefore, cannot fly. The result is a frustrated employee. People who are trusted but not enabled are loose cannons. They have been turned loose without the appropriate skills and are doomed for failure. When organizations do not enable or trust their employees, they entrench their workers. Members quickly perceive that they cannot do much or are expected to do little. These employees just hide. Failure to trust and enable typically is a hidden form of communication that must be brought to the surface, made explicit, and subjected to planned change if negativity is to be overcome.

The third form of organizational negativity results from a hidden communication in the form of inappropriate norms. *Norms* are the accepted and expected behavior of individuals in the organization. Organizations develop norms regarding every behavior and action within the organization. Negativity results when the norms are inappropriate for accomplishing the organization's mission. Four steps are necessary for turning a negative norm into a positive norm. First, the norm that needs to be changed must be identified and its negative effect must be understood. Second, a specific replacement norm needs to be identified. Third, specific behaviors, actions, and procedures must be implemented for the new norm to become established. Fourth, once these changes are installed, there must be an appropriate follow-up to reward those who change and to hold people who have not changed accountable for their failure to change (Topchik, 1998). Periodic follow-up will be necessary to assure that the *desired* norm becomes a *true* norm.

HANDLING CONFLICT IN ORGANIZATIONS: DISAGREEMENTS VERSUS MISUNDERSTANDINGS

Misunderstandings result from poor communication, while *disagreements* come from differences of opinion, goals, or values. Organizations that fail to understand and acknowledge the differences between these two terms are likely to misdiagnose disagreements and classify them as misunderstandings. Efforts to avoid the conflict inherent in disagreements can create an unhealthy environment. Thus, supervisors tend to rely on the belief that any differences between employees result solely from misunderstandings due to improper communication (Pascarella, 1997).

The emphasis on having a common purpose and practicing teamwork in organizations causes many executives and managers to ignore disagreements, subvert them, or assume they are nonexistent. This approach is counterproductive. The key in any conflict situation is to determine whether it involves a disagreement or if it simply is a misunderstanding. If the conflict involves disagreement, then any attempt to resolve it may exacerbate the problem by exposing the disagreement and causing entrenchment. When handled properly, though, differences of ideas and values can be healthy for an organization. As police organizations interact more with citizens, especially in what Professor Wright calls a "multicultural environment" in Chapter 12, and as employees become more involved in making decisions, one should expect more disagreements and disputes to materialize.

Proper handling of disagreements and conflict within an organization will mean developing the capacity to bridge disagreements, overcoming them or learning to live with them. Sometimes, a compromise solution will be appropriate. Other situations may call for a hard stand to be taken. The critical thing when taking a stand is to do it in an appropriate way. As Stiebel (1997a, p. 32) cautions, "If you habitually walk into the room and announce, 'Here's my position, take it or leave it,' you risk making things worse."

As Box 5–2 explains, four fundamental elements must be considered when developing a strategy to resolve a communication problem. There are other valuable

---

Box 5–2   Four Strategic Steps for Handling Conflict

Strategic Step 1. Determine What the Problem Is
Determining whether the conflict stems from a misunderstanding or is a true disagreement aids in avoiding the trap of putting energy into solving the wrong problem. A *misunderstanding* is "a failure to understand each other accurately," while a *disagreement* is "a failure to agree that would persist despite the most accurate understanding" (Stiebel, 1997b, p. 31). The solution to each of these problems is different. If the problem is a

misunderstanding, it can be solved by getting the individuals to understand each other correctly. If the problem is a true disagreement, it can be solved only by getting one party to modify or change his or her position. Resolving disagreements and reaching a compromise is much more complicated and difficult than resolving misunderstandings.

Strategic Step 2. Know What the Goal Is

This step involves asking yourself, "What do I want the other person to do?" Answering this question will determine the goal of your strategic response. The most useful approach is to focus on determining what the other individual is willing and able to do for you right now. This may lead to an incremental accomplishment of your goal. Quite often, we are able to get the final result incrementally but not all at once. The purpose of this step is to create the other person's next move by deciding what we want and are most likely to get the other person to do.

Strategic Step 3. Look at the Issue from the Other Side's Perspective

In developing a method for leading the other party to see and accept a different point of view, one must begin by looking at the issue through that person's eyes. Stiebel (1997b, p. 32) warns that "People find their own perceptions the most convincing." Resolving a conflict is not a matter of convincing the other side. Instead, lead the other party to reach the same conclusion you did. People are not persuaded by efforts that try to explain why they are wrong. Attitudes and beliefs are very difficult to topple. Instead, the search should concentrate on locating a method that will work. Usually, that means starting from the other side's perspective and leading that side to a different position.

Strategic Step 4. Work Toward a Resolution

One can avoid major mistakes by being careful not to focus on what one wants the other person to do. Instead, predict how he or she is likely to respond. Avoid the emotional snares of arguments; they are often foreseeable. Instead, ask some basic questions. Given the approach being taken, what is the best response the other party can make? What is the worst response? Which response can the other side reasonably be expected to make? The answers to these questions will provide an assessment as to whether the planned approach is worth the risk.

Source: Based on D. Stiebel. "How to persuade others to cooperate with you." *Management Review* 86, no. 7 (1997), pp. 30–32.

approaches an astute leader will not ignore. For instance, experiential-based, or challenge, education involves participants in an active and interactive learning process. This type of group exercise can reduce conflict and open communication lines that may have shut down or never been open before (Goergen, 1996). Team-building exercises can be used at all levels of the organization and can assist in the development of trust, cooperation, communication, problem solving, critical thinking, and risk taking, all of which are important attributes of winning teams.

COMMUNICATING ORGANIZATIONAL EXPECTATIONS

Effective organizations require the clear communication of their expectations. What do we expect police officers and civilians to do? How do we expect them to act? Organizational expectations have implications for employee selection, training, and the discipline and reward systems.

Employee selection may be one of the most important ways for an organization to relay its desire to change. The organization's future expectations regarding the knowledge, skills, and abilities, as well as the character and attitude, of employees are communicated through hiring decisions. Current employees will scrutinize new recruits and "get the message," whether or not it was sent intentionally. If the organization takes great care in its hiring process to recruit and select highly qualified applicants, current members will take pride in the process and the recruits. However, the response most likely will be negative if the organization is careless and its new recruits are less qualified than current employees.

Some departments that have embraced community policing have found it necessary to modify their recruitment and selection processes, incorporate citizen input, and seek different types of attitudes and values in their police recruits. Such action not only is helpful in rerouting the organization by introducing new officers who have desirable organizational values but also proclaims that the organization is serious about making some deep-seated changes. The incorporation of the vision and values in the implicit and explicit messages of the hiring process sends a clear message to any recalcitrant members that the organization is moving in this direction and joining the team would be in their best interests.

In an examination of how to improve productivity through human performance modeling and engineering, Furman (1997) touches on a key issue relevant to the communication of expectations through training. Representing skills in language form is difficult because the actions that make up the skill often are unconscious. He uses the example of trying to tell someone how to tie a shoe or a necktie. The result often is frustration because, in our attempt to transfer the skill through language, we usually teach others what we *think* we do and not what we *actually* do (Furman, 1997, p. 19).

In the police world, executives often use language to describe skills they want officers to incorporate in their performance. Unfortunately, these words do not translate easily without specific scenarios and examples of the skill in action. For instance, leaders say they want officers to engage in community policing. However, the upper echelon often fails to describe what this means and gives no specific examples of officers in action.

Police organizations should develop policies that clearly outline workplace conduct, including clear expectations for communication based on respect for all people. Policy should encourage employees to avoid communication that could be offensive. This embargo includes telling jokes, making remarks, posting or distributing cartoons, using profanity, and involvement in gossip that is based on race, color, gender, religion, and the like. Training that is situational and includes opportunities to practice handling such issues through role playing is important. Officers need more training on defending themselves against verbal abuse because it is encountered much more frequently in organizations than any form of physical abuse (Padgett, 1997).

Discipline and reward systems are the factors in organizational communication that have the greatest potential to influence long-term change in officer behavior. The frequency and magnitude of reinforcement and the delay between behavior and reinforcement are factors "which can be used to predict what choices a person will make when given two or more attractive situations" (Furman, 1997, p. 21). We should increase the frequency and magnitude of positive reinforcement and reduce the delay between behavior and reinforcement. The timing and the type of reinforcement communicates the value of the behavior to the organization. Lack of response to behavior communicates its lack of importance. Therefore, failure to respond to minor ethical breaches by a police officer may send a stronger message than firing an officer for a serious ethical violation. The same theory applies as with "broken windows" (Wilson and Kelling, 1982). Overlooking minor indiscretions communicates the willingness to overlook major indiscretions. Eventually, the culture will have moved to one in which minor indiscretions are commonplace and major ones occur frequently. The executive must communicate by his or her vigilant and active involvement that minor problems will be fixed quickly. Repair of the broken window in an expeditious manner sends the message that we care about behavior here and ethical values will be enforced. Those who aspire to excessive use of force and corruption will go elsewhere to apply for a police position.

POLICY DEVELOPMENT AND IMPLEMENTATION

Policy is one of those areas about which many people are ambivalent. Some departments have no written policies while others attempt to put everything they do in a written format. As Professor McCabe explains in Chapter 10, the accreditation movement is responsible for the emphasis on policy development.

One reason why criminal justice agencies engage in policy making is to let members know just what the organizational expectations are. Another pressing reason, one to which Professor Camp devotes a great bit of attention in Chapter 7, is to avoid the financial repercussions of a tort action. The degree to which policy should be designed to control behavior and the type of accompanying implementation strategy depends on the frequency with which the activity occurs and the degree of risk the activity entails. One should consider this risk from the perspective of not only potential litigation but also its impact on the department's relationship with the community.

Alpert and Smith (1994) present a continuum that distinguishes among the various needs for organizational intervention to control behavior. The most restrictive point on this continuum is *strict control*. Here the agency not only establishes clear policy and procedures that allow no deviation but also commits substantial training resources and careful enforcement to prohibit deviation from the policy. Use of force would be one such example.

Structured or *values-driven guidelines* are more appropriate where protection of life and defense against injury are not directly involved and where the officer needs to be able to choose an appropriate response (Greene, Alpert, and Styles, 1992). Structured guidelines are appropriate for topics like the initial case contact and follow-up investigations of a criminal incident.

The third level of policy is the provision of *summary guidance*. Here the agency provides a statement of philosophy and general guidance in terms of the attitude and approach for officers to take. Courtesy standards for general police-citizen contacts would fall here.

The very process of policy development can communicate the organizational vision and values. For example, a department concerned about use of force incidents could identify that action as an expected low frequency event, thereby sending an implicit message that the department expects it to happen rarely. On the other hand, identifying security checks for businesses after closing hours as an expected high frequency activity will send the implicit message that it is expected to occur often.

Agency administrators must take great care when wording statements to ensure that the reality of frequency and the desirability of frequency are clear. There are a number of other fundamental considerations. First, policy statements must be developed with a clear purpose of facilitating the accomplishment of organizational values. If a directive has no relationship to the vision or values, it probably has no place in the policy manual. Policy should be designed to help organizational members do their jobs better.

Second, policy must be made with the input and involvement of all organizational members. Civilian police personnel often are left out of the loop in this process even when the organization has involved police officers at all levels. It is particularly important to include those members of the organization who, most likely, will have to carry out this policy. These members often have the most diverse experience with the issue and, therefore, the most information to bring to bear on the policy development process. It also is important to have citizens examine and review policies as they are being developed or revised. A citizen's advisory board can be helpful in this regard.

Third, policies should be workable in the real world of policing. Guidelines should be specific yet flexible. They should provide examples of behavior so that officers can evaluate their own performance, serve as the basis for performance evaluation on the most important activities of police employees, be developed to assist trainers in training police employees for excellent performance, and incorporate relevant laws or ordinances so as to be instructive without interfering with the overall understanding provided to the officer.

Finally, policy statements should follow a standard format. However, some policies may be shorter or longer depending on the frequency and risk factors discussed earlier and the degree to which they are designed to control or to instruct behavior. Box 5–3 displays a general outline of the headings that should be included in a model policy and the description of what each section should contain.

Box 5–3   Standard Format for a Model Policy Statement

I. Mission Statement

Each policy should begin with a restatement of the mission of the department. This practice will communicate that this guiding principle is worthy of repeating and should always be in the front of each member's mind when making decisions.

II. Value(s)

The policy should make a specific statement identifying the value(s) this policy is designed to facilitate.

III. Purpose

This section is an overall statement of the intent regarding the issue at hand. This statement should include how the officers should approach decision making and what factors should be considered most important.

IV. Policy

Here is the statement of philosophy regarding what is expected in terms of attitude and behavior, why it is expected, whose behavior the policy is designed to instruct, and how the topic of the policy is to be approached in general terms.

V. Definitions

These are the operational definitions of terms used in the policy and procedure sections. Only those definitions essential for understanding the implications of the policy should be placed here. A lengthy list of definitions contributes to officers skipping over this section. Putting in only the essential definitions allows for ease of reading and understanding. Specific legal definitions and other definitions that might be useful but not essential for understanding of the policy should be placed as an end note to the policy.

VI. Procedures

Here the parameters for action or inaction should be described in such a way as to instruct officers in specific actions to take and in what sequence.

VII. Policy Implementation

A. Training Requirements

Here the type, amount and frequency of training should be specified.

B. Reporting Requirements

This section should describe the form and content of reporting for evaluation of performance with respect to the policy. Typically, reporting requirements are in place only for actions that subject the department to potential risk, such as use of lethal force or vehicular pursuits, or for serious social problems, such as domestic violence. However, the organization has an opportunity in this section to set up a systematic method for measurement of officer choices that reduce the risk to the department. For example, the reporting requirement could be established for officer use of nonlethal force. This could capture the effectiveness of such action in circumstances that might otherwise justify the use of lethal force. Care must be taken to limit the degree to which reporting requirements become an unnecessary burden without providing useful information.

C. Administrative Review

This section should detail the procedure for reviewing the actions of members under the policy. It should specify the potential disciplinary action that might be appropriate for misaction or inaction under the policy.

VIII. Policy Review and Evaluation

This section specifies the method for reviewing and evaluating the effectiveness of the policy for guiding organizational behavior.

COMMUNICATION STYLE AND STRUCTURE

Why are the communication style and structure important? If examined and understood, they can help predict the accepted forms of officer behavior toward citizens. The styles and structures used by the formal organization and allowed by the informal network will set the standard by which officers will be evaluated. The styles and structures also have implicit messages, as discussed earlier, that transcend the training officers receive and what they are told.

Traditional police agencies use a *closed form of communication*. When a decision must be made, management considers only its own view in reaching that decision. Chapter 1 introduced this idea when it discussed the concept called *chain of command*. The knowledge and views of street officers, individual citizens, and the various communities within the department's jurisdiction are ignored. This form of communication is ineffective in contemporary policing. It assumes that the chief and a few top managers are the only ones who have any worthwhile ideas about the way policing will be done in this jurisdiction. This type of communication not only separates the administration from the officers, but it also reinforces the separation of officers from the community.

The *open model of organizational communication* functions differently. Some observers consider it the hope for high-quality policing (Couper and Lobitz, 1991; Sparrow, Moore, and Kennedy, 1990). Under the open form of communication, decisions are made not only in consideration of officer and citizen views but in consultation with them as full partners in the venture of policing. As the department encounters problems or issues, the potential sources of pertinent information or ideas regarding solutions are identified. The problems or issues then are faced at the lowest possible organizational level and resolution is sought with full input from those sources.

These open and closed models are polar extremes in decision-making and communication styles. They require completely different management approaches. The open model of organizational communication cannot function in the classical organizational structure with its top-down chain-of-command bureaucratic emphasis. The paramilitary symbols (i.e., rank and insignia) that remain in many police organizations pose obstacles or barriers for open forms of communication. If communication is not viewed from the open model, the community cannot be substantively involved in assisting the department to identify and solve community problems.

The most frequently proposed structure for communication is a network approach. One might picture this style as a fishnet or a bunch of wires piled on the floor. There is no apparent starting place, center, or end. The message behind this structure is that communication should serve the needs of the organization. However, organizational mechanisms must be put in place to assure that information is disseminated to the right people in a timely fashion. Many organizations face problems that result from poor internal and external communication. There must be a balance between allowing a free flow of communication and assessing the degree to which the structure requires proper occurrence of communication. There must be some design to the formal communication structure. Informal communication fills the gaps and with newer organizational structures, but it is not as much a necessity as it was when organizations were tall hierarchies with top-down communication. The current communication philosophy is to inform everyone who has a need or might have a need to know. More communication is considered better than less. The approach implies that information should not be considered power but should be shared. Individuals who withhold information to build their own power bases create substantial problems for this kind of an organization.

The most successful executives focus on three things. They set priorities, communicate them, and hold people accountable through action plans (Kouzes and Posner, 1988). The real key here is communication. A variety of communication tactics are used to accomplish these goals. Organizationwide meetings are held regularly. People are informed about how they are doing and what they are trying to do. Information, whether good, bad, or indifferent, is not held back. These executives recognize individuals and teams that make contributions and meet the short-term goals. They set up a newsletter, manage by wandering around the organization for up to five hours a day, and get to know everybody's name and face. Their philosophy is fix it, do it, try it. Try anything.

Another recent phenomenon at the heart of most new management and leadership philosophies is the concept of *empowerment*. Ettorre (1997) examined the status of empowerment in American businesses and found that it is a lot easier said than done. The problem is that empowerment has to be put into practice to be useful. Empowered employees are more effective, more efficient, more committed to their organizations, and not in need of supervision to stay on top of things.

The dialogue Ettorre (1997) uses to demonstrate the "reality" of executive views about empowerment in the business sector sounds much like what we might hear in a police organization about empowerment or about community-oriented policing. The following script converts some of this business jargon to fit policing:

Chief: I want to talk about empowerment. [Waits for groans to subside.] Look, I know it's touchy-feely, but I think we ought to do it. Other police departments say they are doing it, and it would look good in our vision statement.

Captain A: But you can't measure the damned thing, and it has nothing to do with crime control.

Chief: Yeah, but we only have to tell the officers that they're empowered. It'll make them feel good and make things a lot easier for the sergeants.

Captain B: Besides, we can always phase it out next year if we don't like it. This empowerment stuff—why can't they leave the Human Resources people out of it and let us run the police department?

The problem with the way many executives approach empowerment is that they shy away from going far enough. It is not enough to have a participatory culture or to stay the course when the going gets tough. Empowerment is not laissez-faire management. It must involve accountability and evaluation. "For empowerment to be vital and measurable . . . it must be directly aligned with strategic goals and individual accountability all the way to senior management, customers, and stockholders. It must be measured in a way that clearly shows its impact" (Ettorre, 1997, p. 12).

The critical difference is that police officers should be partners in the task of community problem solving. If organizations operate this way, empowerment should result in "higher retention rates, better productivity, attraction of good job candidates and more effective team interaction" (Ettorre, 1997, p. 13).

McCoy (1996) identifies three things that must be done by the organization for its employees if the organization is to be optimal in achieving its objectives. First, it must educate workers so they will know what to do. Second, it must enable them to know how to do it. Third, it must empower them to have the authority to do it.

The extent to which individuals within an organization have the authority to do a task or job can be assessed in a number of ways. The premiere way is to raise one simple question: Do members possess the ability to make a decision without prior approval from a superior?

A critically important way to engrain the vision and values in the organization is through making your expectations explicit. This can be accomplished by developing, writing down, and distributing your leadership credo. The best way to develop your leadership credo is to pretend that you will be going to be away from the organization for at least nine months. You want to leave behind a one-page sheet that tells your employees what they should focus their efforts on while you are gone (Kouzes and Posner, 1988). The following is a hypothetical example of a leadership credo that police chiefs might wish to develop:

- We will handle all personal interactions inside and outside the department in a positive manner.
- We will treat all people with respect and dignity.
- We will act with the highest professional ethics.
- We will be problem solvers.
- We will develop programs that we believe in, that will make our employees feel good about themselves, and that will contribute to the betterment of our community.
- We will set our organization apart as a positive and progressive place to work.
- We will help each other grow professionally and be the best that we can be individually and as a group.
- We will, in every instance, uphold the Constitution of the United States, the Bill of Rights, and the principles for which they stand.

On completion of your personal leadership credo, it is important that it be published and widely distributed. It also can provide the basis for work team discussions. The key is to obtain a commitment from all organizational members. Therefore, the credo could be presented as a discussion point. From here, the organization could develop and adopt its own credo. However, a credo is just one element of good communications. Another element is to have a plan.

The importance of a plan cannot be overstated. The plan will provide those milestones, measurable steps along the way and fundamental deadlines, we all need to accomplish our tasks. The plan encourages us to take things one step at a time. By having lots of milestones, we have more opportunities to celebrate reaching them. Communicate your appreciation by visibly demonstrating that each individual's contributions are recognized. Do this on a regular basis. Select an appropriate acknowledgment for each employee. Recognition is important. It can be as simple as a flower, a thank you, or a thank you note.

What do you measure? People do what gets rewarded. One of the ways that we know what gets rewarded is by paying attention to by what is measured. In what do you show an interest? When you return from a trip or vacation, what is the first question you ask? Make sure that the things that go first are the things that are the most important. Make sure that the people you reward are the people who are doing the right things and doing them right. This comes from clarity in your own mind in the first place about the kinds of actions and values that you consider to be paramount.

Ultimately, an effective leader will be a good communicator. Not only is the form and method of the communication important but so is what stands behind it, such as values. Through good values, clear vision, and a strong plan, there is no reason why police leaders cannot be good, effective communicators.

CONCLUSION

The vast majority of organizational communication occurs through the culture, climate, and management style of the organization; the organization's system of rewards and punishments; the symbols adopted for use in the organization; the adopted values, mission, and role the organization pursues; the mechanisms and standards for measuring police performance; the apparatus for government account-ability for police action; and the expected relationship between the police and the community. Each of these components shapes the range of possibilities for commu-nication and determines the forms and atmosphere of that communication. One by one, each of these elements sets up a range of expectations and assumptions about the behavior of others. That is, both the police and the public have a basis for antici-pating certain forms of response from each other. These expectations may be implicit or explicit and either correct or incorrect.

Sometimes, executives fall into the trap of communicating to employees that the organizational direction is all about the executive. It is not. It is about the organi-zation members. When they succeed, the organization flourishes. How do we make employees realize that it is all about what they do? We must coach, encourage, support, and occasionally push them (Doerr, 1997). Executives need to transform their leadership style into a coaching style. If we can develop long-term credibility in our employee teams, we can replicate them (Kouzes and Ponser, 1988). The key is to have the vision and values so ingrained that an organization can continue to achieve success without the presence of a person in its top leadership slot.

As with the orchestra conductor, the leader's job is to communicate in such a way that the members' efforts blend together in a harmonious and dynamic perfor-mance. The conductor never makes a sound during a performance, even though his or her job is to get the best music possible out of the musicians. The conductor commu-nicates via nonverbal instruction and body language. This person takes pains to ensure that every participant has the appropriate background and ability to perform. The maestro makes sure that every member of the orchestra knows what type of sound is desired and clarifies those expectations. On the day of performance, the conductor communicates in a manner consistent with what has been practiced. The best conductors have done their jobs so well that they really are not needed at performance time. They are there merely to put on the finishing touches for the audience.

This analogy is what organizational communication entails. A great leader transforms mechanics into artistry and makes great performance second nature. That is what policing is all about.

DISCUSSION QUESTIONS

1. Think of the police organization as a collection of "service packages." Make a list of all the service packages done by the police organization. Identify alternative sources for each.
2. What are some ways a new chief could use communication to solve the problems of a corrupt police department?
3. What values do you think need to be changed in police departments?
4. Assume that you are the new police chief on your campus. How will you convey your ideas of community to all the relevant audiences?
5. Suppose you are a member of the search committee to hire a new police chief or safety director for your campus. After reading this chapter, what three questions would you pose to the final slate of candidates?
6. Suppose you have been selected the new police chief or security director on your campus. What vision and values will you promote? How?

REFERENCES

Alpert, G. P., and W. C. Smith. "Developing police policy: An evaluation of the control principle." *American Journal of Police* 13, no. 2 (1994), pp. 1–20.

Couper, D. C., and S. H. Lobitz. *Quality Policing: The Madison Experience.* Washington, DC: Police Executive Research Forum, 1991.

Doerr, J. E. "Global leadership: It's not about you." *Management Review* 86, no. 7 (1997), p. 5.

Ettorre, B. "The empowerment gap: Hype vs. reality." *Management Review* 86, no. 7 (1997), pp. 10–14.

Furman, M. E. "Reverse the 80–20 rule." *Management Review* 86, no. 1 (1997), pp. 18–21.

Goergen, T. "'Challenge' education: Handling conflict in a supervised situation helps employees move forward." *Law and Order* 44, no. 2 (1996), pp. 96–99.

Greene, J., G. P. Alpert, and P. Styles. "Values and culture in two American police departments: Lessons from King Arthur." *Contemporary Criminal Justice* 8, no. 3 (1992), pp. 183–207.

Kouzes, J. M., and B. Z. Posner. *What Followers Expect from Leaders: How to Meet People's Expectations and Build Credibility.* San Francisco: Jossey-Bass Publishers, 1988.

_____. *The Leadership Challenge II: How to Get Extraordinary Things Done in Organizations.* San Francisco: Jossey-Bass Publishers, 1995a.

_____. *Credibility: How Leaders Gain and Lose It, Why People Demand It.* San Francisco: Jossey-Bass Publishers, 1995b.

McCoy, T. J. *Creating an "Open Book" Organization: Where Employees Think and Act Like Business Partners.* Saranac Lake, NY: AMACOM, 1996.

Mink, O. G., K. Q. Owen, and B. P. Mink. *Developing High-Performance People: The Art of Coaching.* Reading, MA: Addison-Wesley, 1993.

Ouchi, W. G. *Theory Z.* New York: Avon Books, 1981.

Padgett, R. "What can I say? Keys for positive communication in the workplace." *Law and Order* 45, no. 2 (1997), pp. 56–57.

Pascarella, P. When misunderstandings are really disagreements. *Management Review* 86, no. 7 (1997), pp. 30–32.

Peters, T. *The Tom Peters Seminar: Crazy Times Call for Crazy Organizations.* New York: Vintage Books, 1994.

_____ and N. Austin. *A Passion for Excellence: The Leadership Difference.* New York: Random House, 1985.

_____ and R. H. Waterman, Jr. *In Search of Excellence: Lessons from America's Best-Run Companies.* New York: Warner Books, 1982.

Rokeach, M. *The Nature of Human Values.* New York: Macmillan, 1973.

Southerland, M. D. "Organizational communication." In L. Hoover (ed.), *Police Management: Issues and Perspectives,* pp. 281–303. Washington, DC: Police Executive Research Foundation, 1992.

_____ and E. Reuss-Ianni. "Leadership and management." In G. W. Cordner and D. Hale (eds.), *What Works in Policing? Operations and Administration Examined,* pp. 157–177. Cincinnati: Anderson Publishing Company, 1992.

Sparrow, M. K., M. H. Moore, and D. M. Kennedy. *Beyond 911: A New Era for Policing.* New York: Basic Books, 1990.

Stiebel, D. *When Talking Makes Things Worse! Resolving Problems When Communication Fails.* Dallas: Whitehall and Nolton, 1997a.

_____. "How to persuade others to cooperate with you." *Management Review* 86, no. 7 (1997b), pp. 30–32.

Topchik, G. S. "Attacking the *negativity* virus." *Management Review* 87, no. 8 (1998), pp. 61–64.

Wasserman, R., and M. H. Moore. *Values in Policing: Perspectives on Policing.* Washington, DC: National Institute of Justice, 1988.

Wilson, J. Q., and G. L. Kelling. "Broken windows: Police and neighborhood safety." *Atlantic Monthly* 249, no. 3 (1982), pp. 29–38.

Chapter 6

Productivity and Performance Evaluation

James W. Golden, University of Arkansas at Little Rock

Although it has long been part of manufacturing- and production-related occupations, productivity and performance evaluations of employees is becoming more and more a part of social service-oriented occupations, especially policing. A major issue that today's police executives face is how to evaluate productivity and performance. Simply put, how does the police leader determine whether the agency is fulfilling its mission? Closely related to the issue of agency productivity and performance is the question of how well individual personnel are working. In essence, how does the police leader determine whether officers are carrying out the agency's mandates? One well-known means is examining how an agency is meeting its mission statement.

Most police agencies have no unified mission statement. Instead, they merely list the various functions performed by the agency (Hoover, 1992). A *mission statement*, like the one contained in Box 6–1, describes the top priorities of the agency. Immediately following the mission statement comes a series of statements that expand the beliefs that police leaders feel are beacons or guideposts for agency members. There may be declarations like "We value all human life," "We are committed to the protection of the community from violence and disorder," "We

---

Box 6–1   An Example of an Agency Mission Statement

The mission of the Tallahassee Police Department is to protect the rights of all people, ensure order, and provide for the public's safety through the effective delivery of law enforcement services while maintaining the highest level of professional standards.

Source: Tallahassee [Florida] Police Department, *Manual of Written Directives.*

---

recognize that crime is a community problem," and "We are committed to meeting the needs of all persons who look on us for service." As you can see, these statements are crucial because they set the tone within the department. With no clear mission statement that sets out the operating philosophy, administrators are unable to relay a vision of agency goals to its employees and community members.

Traditional mission statements often spoke of what the police were going to accomplish for the community (Wilson and McLaren, 1977). Employees generally were given a clear understanding of police agency goals, but community input was rare. Performance, productivity, and accountability were based on agency-driven measures. While the rise of police-community relations programs in the 1960s and 1970s (Carter and Radelet, 1999) changed the relationship between the police and the community to one of cooperation, the community was still not an equal partner with the police. Not until the advent of the community policing model did the police begin to share the responsibility of solving crime problems with the community in a collaborative or equal partnership effort. Mission statements then changed to reflect the new model of policing. Along with the changes in mission and goals, new methods of accountability were needed.

The adoption of a community policing orientation, which represents a huge departure from traditional police work, compounds the issue of accountability. Trojanowicz and his colleagues (1998, p. 24) point out that community policing "is a paradigm shift that emphasizes a combined police-citizen attack on community problems." Conceptually, community policing also requires a decentralization of management and authority, with community police officers assuming a much different role than the job description of a conventional patrol officer. Decentralization also means that police administrators must redesign individual and agency performance evaluation systems to match the new expectations that go along with the community policing paradigm.

This chapter examines productivity and performance evaluation for both individual officers and police agencies. It examines productivity and performance issues from the past but concentrates on the impact of community policing. First, it looks at performance evaluation for police personnel, followed by a discussion of performance evaluation at the agency level. Finally, the impact of community policing on performance and accountability is addressed.

A HISTORICAL BACKDROP

Organizational thinking at the turn of the century was dominated by concepts emerging from the new perspective of "scientific" management (Wren, 1987). The evolution of management into the study of organizations is germane to this discussion of police administration issues.

When Congress passed the Civil Service Act of 1883, more commonly known as the Pendleton Act, the result was a sweeping reform for public personnel practices. This act mandated that federal government workers be hired on the basis of grades achieved on competitive examinations. A probationary period was required before an employee gained job tenure. In addition, political contributions were removed as a fundamental job requirement. While the Pendleton Act affected only federal workers, local civil service ordinances eventually made similar protections available to municipal police officers (Bopp and Whisenhand, 1980).

The turn of the century also brought about the beginning of police professionalism. One of the major figures in this movement was August Vollmer, the chief of police in Berkeley, California. Among his many innovative programs were requiring officers to complete college courses, using bicycles to replace foot patrols, and incorporating scientific procedures to help solve crimes (Vollmer, 1936). The cornerstone of Vollmer's vision of a professional police officer would center on high-quality personnel. Although some of his ideas were unpopular with more traditional, conservative police administrators, others did not hesitate to copy his blueprints (MacNamara, 1989).

From an administrative standpoint, Vollmer perhaps is best known for his emphasis on efficiency in the delivery of police services. Vollmer (1936, p. 236) asked, "how can Americans expect police efficiency when, at every step in the apprehension and prosecution of criminals, political influence interferes, and soon a truly vicious circle is started[?]" He further noted that for police to be truly productive, society "must also require, and make provision for, a professionally trained police, personnel fit not only in body, but also in character, education, and ideals of service" (Vollmer, 1936, p. 237).

O. W. Wilson, a student of Vollmer, further advocated the cause of efficiency through the use of scientific techniques. Arguing that the public deserved better service, Wilson pioneered the use of one-officer patrol cars, finding them to be efficient and effective (Uchida, 1997). With the first edition of his book *Police Administration* (1950), Wilson quickly became the leading figure in police administration. Wilson asserted that professionalism was a direct result of organizational efficiency and crime fighting.

The central theme in Wilson's concept of police administration was managerial efficiency. He recommended the use of workload formulas, which reflected both crime and calls for service, to set beat boundaries. Efficiency, particularly in terms of response time, was of critical importance to police professionalism (Wilson and McLaren, 1977).

Other factors also were molding police professionalism during this period. The 1931 Wickersham Commission gave police reform a major boost. This blue-ribbon panel, formally known as the United States National Commission on Law Observance and Enforcement, conducted the first major nationwide study of the criminal justice system. Out of 14 reports that the commission produced, 2 were devoted to policing (1931a, 1931b). Bopp and Whisenhand (1980, p. 25) point out that the Wickersham Commission provided "a blueprint for progress." Unfortunately, a major tenet, the need to reduce the influence of politics, was all but ignored by municipalities.

The 1960s brought a number of forces to bear on the police. These included Supreme Court decisions on police procedures; the civil rights movement, which challenged discriminatory police practices; a series of riots in major American cities between 1964 and 1968; a dramatic rise in the crime rate; protests against the war in Vietnam; and the spread of drug use among college students, which also increased hostility among young people toward the police (Walker, 1992, p. 20). The result was a period marked by tension and rapid change for the law enforcement world.

President Johnson, in response to public concern, appointed the President's Commission on Law Enforcement and the Administration of Justice. Two years after its formation, the President's Commission issued its report *The Challenge of Crime in a Free Society* (1967a). Among other things, this document called for increased police professionalism through higher personnel standards, more training, increased supervision, and better management. Accompanying this report were nine task force studies, including one devoted specifically to the police (President's Commission, 1967b).

Following a series of urban riots in 1967, the National Advisory Commission on Civil Disorders was formed to sift through these disturbances. This group, known as the Kerner Commission, scrutinized the role of the police and the relationship to the community. It found ample evidence of hostility between the police and the policed. Ironically, the Kerner Commission (1968, p. 301) noted "many of the serious disturbances took place in cities whose police are among the best led, best organized, best trained, and most professional in the country."

Gaines, Kappeler, and Vaughn (1997, p. 55) point out that these commissions performed a valuable service as "blunt force instruments whereby citizens could not avoid seeing and comprehending the problems associated with their police." Although it might appear that the police were being hammered by boards and commissions intent on finding fault, several positive benefits materialized. The passage of the Omnibus Crime Control and Safe Streets Act of 1968 created the Law Enforcement Assistance Administration (LEAA). LEAA sponsored crime-related education programs for the general public. It also created the Law Enforcement Education Program (LEEP), which provided funds for law enforcement officers to attend college. Although critics were quick to point out that more funding was provided for police hardware than education, the act and its successors provided a major impetus for the refinement of police professionalism (McShane, 1989; S. Walker, 1992).

One such successor was the Police Foundation, established in 1970 with a $30 million dollar grant from the Ford Foundation. Since then, the Police Foundation has sponsored a number of major police research projects. Also during this period, the Ford Foundation helped form the Police Executive Research Forum (PERF). This organization is composed primarily of police executives, with additional membership categories for criminal justice practitioners, chiefs of smaller agencies, police practitioners, and academicians. PERF has undertaken a number of important research projects (Deakin, 1986). The creation of these practice-oriented research organizations set the stage for entertaining questions about police productivity and performance.

Another organization that had a major impact on policing is the International Association of Chiefs of Police (IACP). The IACP, formed in 1901 under the direction of Richard Sylvester, the superintendent of the District of Columbia Police, was to become the primary national organization for police professionalism. The association publishes a magazine, *The Police Chief*, which provides readers with short articles of legal orientation, summaries of police programs across the country, and short summaries of research articles. Between 1973 and 1991, the IACP published the *Journal of Police Science and Administration*, containing articles that were more academically oriented and more often based on systematic research (Walker, 1977).

The decades of the 1970s and 1980s brought about change as police agencies began to evaluate their own effectiveness and seek to change the organizational structure. One such concept was *team policing*, designed to balance the efficiency of the police with decentralization to meet community needs (Sherman, Milton, and Kelly, 1973). First used in Syracuse in 1968, the concept expanded to more than 60 police agencies (Schwartz and Clarren, 1977). By the late 1970s, many agencies realized that team policing was not producing the performance- and productivity-enhancing rewards to the organization expected by proponents.

Goldstein (1977, p. 236) suggested the use of *problem-oriented policing* to "develop a more systematic process for examining and addressing the problems that the public expects them to handle." The major focus is on solving the problems that often lead to repetitive calls for police service, rather than answering the same call time after time. This process has been compared with the public health model, which focuses on treating the problem, not the symptoms.

The two decades were filled with research on police effectiveness. Beginning with the landmark Kansas City Preventative Patrol Experiment (Kelling et al., 1974), researchers have examined rapid response to reported crimes (Pate et al., 1976), follow-up criminal investigations (Greenwood, Chaiken, and Petersilia, 1977), one-officer versus two-officer patrol cars (Boydstun, Sherry, and Moelter, 1977), directed patrol (Cordner, 1981), foot patrol (Trojanowicz, 1982), domestic disturbances (Sherman and Berk, 1984), and a host of other areas too numerous to mention. This condensed listing of research is not intended to be inclusive of all the performance evaluation research conducted over the last 25 years. However, it offers a flavor as to the hundreds of research projects which have influenced today's concept of police performance evaluation.

As presented in Chapter 10, one outgrowth of the research focus on police performance is the move toward accreditation, culminating in the creation of the Commission on Accreditation for Law Enforcement Agencies (CALEA), developed in 1979 as a joint venture of the International Association of Chiefs of Police, National Organization of Black Law Enforcement Executives (NOBLE), National Sheriffs' Association (NSA), and the Police Executive Research Forum. In 1983, the CALEA, a private, nonprofit organization, began accepting applications for accreditation from law enforcement agencies. The commission was formed to develop a set of law enforcement standards and, subsequently, to establish and administer a voluntary accreditation process.

Cordner and Williams note that

> the law enforcement agency accreditation program's standards should support and encourage "best practice"—the most effective programs and techniques known to the profession—without regard to ideology or temporary fad. (1995, p. 9)

Pertinent to our discussion of performance evaluation is Cordner and Williams's (1997) summary of the basis for the accreditation process. They note that the accreditation program stands "more for administrative efficiency than for anything else—and this is by conscious design." Cordner and Williams (1997) further suggest that those organizations which sponsor CALEA and the accreditation process would do well to focus on the concept that accreditation is about efficiency and effectiveness. Accreditation has many vocal proponents, as well as many vocal opponents. The process, however, offers opportunities for increasing police efficiency and effectiveness in the 21st century.

PRODUCTIVITY AND PERFORMANCE MEASURES

One by-product of the era of professionalism was the search for valid indicators of police productivity performance at both the agency and individual levels. Performance measures that reflected the application of scientific methods to determine how well the police were performing held a special allure.

As you might imagine, *productivity* can be defined in a variety of different ways. For our purposes, Crowe provides a good definition of *productivity*:

> Productivity may be defined simply as a measure of the results gained from a specific amount of effort. In its purest form, the word productivity implies the achievement of results. (1988, p. 12)

A major concern of police agencies is to be effective and efficient. This quest for enhanced productivity and better performance often translates into "getting more patrol units on the street, answering more calls for assistance, reducing police response time, or producing other valued service activities [including the reduction of crime]" (Whitaker, 1984, p. 1). As we shall see in a moment, this orientation has implications pertinent to our discussion.

Four measures of productivity and performance have been used to evaluate police performance: reported crime rates, arrests, clearance rates, and response times (Alpert and Moore, 1997, p. 265). Each of these performance and productivity measures receives attention in the following sections.

Reported Crime Rate

When police agencies use reported crime rate as a measure of productivity, they usually rely upon information taken from the *Uniform Crime Reports* (UCR). The UCR is a cooperative effort of approximately 16,000 law enforcement agencies that voluntarily submit reports to the Federal Bureau of Investigation about crime in their jurisdictions. The FBI has administered the program since 1930. The UCR standardizes crime reporting practices and allows a glimpse into crime seriousness, frequency, pervasiveness, and likelihood of notifying the police. It is designed to generate reliable statistics for use in law enforcement. Eight offenses constitute Part I of the UCR: murder and nonnegligent manslaughter, forcible rape, robbery, aggravated assault, burglary, larceny-theft, motor vehicle theft, and arson. Collectively, these crimes are known as the *crime index* (FBI, 1996).

These index crimes were chosen for several reasons (O'Brien, 1985, p. 18). First, they are most likely to be reported to the police. Second, police investigations can easily establish whether a crime has occurred. Third, these offenses occur in all geographical areas. Fourth, these crimes occur with sufficient frequency as to provide an adequate basis of comparison. Finally, they are serious by nature or volume.

From a productivity standpoint, reliance on the UCR has several benefits. Data are collected monthly by individual police organizations and aggregated at both the state and national levels. No other source of information on crime collects data on a monthly basis. Thus, trends can be easily established for given jurisdictions. Because the data are collected monthly, trends in arrest and clearance are stable and useful for forecasting. Even though the crimes reported to the police may substantially underrepresent the actual amount of criminal activity, comparisons with the National Crime Survey (NCS) (a way of counting crime victims) suggest that the trends are accurate and stable over time. Combining the UCR data with other readily available statistical information allows planners and policy analysts to make projections based on empirically observed crime trends (Inciardi 1978; Skogan 1974).

The UCR is not without its critics. The Wickersham Commission (U.S. Commission on Law Observance and Enforcement, 1931b) suggested that the collection method employed would produce inaccurate data and proposed that the Census Bureau would be better suited to ensure data integrity. Whitaker and his associates note that the Wickersham Commission was concerned that

> crimes reported to the police did not accurately indicate the true occurrence of crime; and that the causes of crime were difficult to determine and the fluctuation of the crime rate could not be attributed solely to police activities. (1989, p. 384)

Since outside forces in addition to police activity may affect crime data, the UCR loses value as the primary way to tap police productivity.

A number of other pressing problems are associated with reliance on UCR data. Hindelang (1974) points out that offenses, which vary from state to state, are lumped into broad general categories. Drug offenses, which have increased in importance as a measure of crime, are often committed in secret and not known to the police. Furthermore, a good deal of data is lost, as information about the nature of the offense is not collected by the UCR reporting program. Hindelang concludes that to

> complicate matters, most of the problems . . . are not invariant across time and geography, but rather are free to vary as a function of policy changes, increased sophistication in police detection and investigation, changes in reporting propensities of victims, penal code changes, changes in the local data needs and demands, etc. (1974, p. 2)

On top of this are even more criticisms that need to be taken into consideration (Whitaker et al., 1989, p. 385). For one thing, UCR reports require the cooperation of the local police departments and citizens who report crimes to the police. Crimes that citizens do not report or police do not record are omitted. Therefore, the data are more accurate in depicting police activity than patterns of crime.

Furthermore, the UCR is open to manipulation by agencies that want to appear to be doing better than they are. Agencies charged with reducing crime should not be responsible for collecting the data used to assess their own crime-control performance. Observers (Whitaker et al., 1989) have suggested that a separate enterprise obtain data independent of police agencies, since an external group would be less tempted to bias the data and would present information more widely usable to the public.

Black (1970), along with Maxfield, Lewis, and Szoc (1980), suggest that crime is a social fact. The argument here is that a crime rate is an empirical phenomenon and cannot be evaluated as inaccurate or unreliable. Crime rates are the result of the number of interactive factors between the police and the citizens whom they serve. Therefore, they should be considered methodologically as rates of detection and sanctioning of crimes by official agencies.

Despite a number of reasons for caution when using the UCR, there are some valid reasons for its use. Decker (1977) notes that comparisons with the NCS found the two data sources to be conceptually comparable. Although the NCS tended to yield significantly higher offense rates, both data sources yielded similar distributional patterns. This finding led Decker to conclude that the UCR provided an accurate indicator of the relative occurrence of crime.

Arrests

Citizens rely on the police to prevent crime and to catch criminals. When the crime rate goes up, the police are blamed for their failure to reduce crime. The public then demands more and better police protection. The police typically respond by suggesting that resources are stretched to their limits and more officers, whether through additional hiring or increased overtime, are needed to reduce crime. In effect, the argument here is that adding officers will make the agency more productive in its law enforcement role.

Britt and Tittle (1975) suggest a relationship between crime rates and police behavior. They analyzed arrest rates for serious and minor crimes to test the dragnet and the displacement hypotheses of police behavior. The *displacement hypothesis* holds that the relationship between arrests for serious and minor crimes is inverse. Police place minor crimes in a lower priority status during periods when serious crimes are more prevalent. On the other hand, the *dragnet hypothesis* posits that the relationship between serious and minor offenses is positive. The police make more arrests for minor offenses in the hope of obtaining information that will assist in solving major crimes.

According to Britt and Tittle, their data are "clearly incompatible with the displacement hypothesis" (1975, p. 447) and "increase the plausibility of the dragnet hypothesis" (1975, p. 448). The data show that "an increase of one unit in police is followed by an increase of .56 units in the rate of arrest for minor crimes" (1975, p. 445), but there is no corresponding increase for major crimes. The data reveal, however, that "arrests for minor crimes help clear serious crimes through arrests, and that this feeds back through the level of serious crime arrests to increase the number of minor crime arrests at a later point in time" (1975, p. 446). Britt and Tittle caution that reliance on a dragnet hypotheses to reduce crime would result in a stable relationship between crime trends and arrest rates after a period of initial effectiveness.

Sheley and Hanlon (1978) argue that societal and political public pressure on police with respect to certain types of crime changes the enforcement policy of the agency, which, in turn, affects the official crime rates, which are based on citizen reporting. They suggest that selective enforcement of certain criminal offenses, based on community pressure, may have unintended effects in terms of increased arrest rates for crimes that are not part of the enforcement effort. Implied, but never stated, is the idea that if the public perceives a crime problem in a particular locale, reporting to the police will raise the crime rate since it is based on offenses known to the police.

This concept underscores a fundamental problem when using arrests as a measure of police productivity. As police crack down on certain crimes, reporting rates for those crimes may increase. This certainly is an unintended consequence for agencies that hawk a reduction in crime as a positive agency performance.

Sheley and Hanlon (1978) examined the policy decision to strengthen the narcotics investigation unit in "Factoryville," an older city in the northeast with a population around 200,000 people. The city instituted an antiheroin campaign after a state official proclaimed the city was the distribution center for the region. An unintended side effect of the antiheroin campaign was a 228% increase in marijuana arrests "despite the absence of public and police sentiment against marijuana use" (Sheley and Hanlon, 1978, p. 273). The blitz produced a 25% increase in drug arrests based on a 100% increase in personnel in the narcotics unit, a 24% increase in overtime hours, and a 132% increase in investigation expenditures (1978, pp. 268, 270). However, the increase in marijuana arrests (228%) overshadowed any gain in heroin arrests (9%). As arrests for heroin possession became more difficult, arrests for marijuana rose. This situation was generated by enforcement against lower-level users, assisted by media publicity which "resulted in a greater number of 'tips' from the public regarding 'possible illegal drug activity'" (1978, p. 271).

Sheley and Hanlon (1978) surmise that arrest rates may not indicate an increased priority of enforcement by the police. In fact, an examination of the political and societal factors of the time is needed to separate those arrests that are latent or unintended effects from the primary thrust of a policy change. They caution that

> with the ability to define formal and informal police policy regarding a particular
> crime, one may not easily retrospectively determine the extent of systematic bias in
> statistics for that crime. Some statistics are simply not directly linked to public pol-
> icy. (1978, p. 274)

Simply put, arrest rates do not always reflect police emphasis on particular types of crime. As such, increases in arrest rates would be a poor performance indicator as the rise in the arrest rate may be a by-product of police emphasis on another crime.

J. Q. Wilson and Boland (1978) suggest that patrol strategies affect robbery rates. Aggressive policing reduces the robbery rate because "direct deterrence effects depend on the number and activity of patrol officers" (1978, p. 369). The rate of offending may be altered because criminals think that the chances of getting caught are greater. This perception may be driven by more officers on the street or more proactive patrol procedures, such as stakeouts.

They (1978) found robbery rates correlated negatively with the robbery arrest ratio. Repeated analysis with burglary and auto theft produced similar negative correlations. In other words, these crime rates were influenced by patrol deployment and workload. Wilson and Boland conclude that police practices

> do affect crime rates, directly or indirectly, and these practices are, as far as we can tell, the product of decisions made over the long term and not in response to short-term changes in crime rates or resource levels. (1978, p. 381)

Walsh (1985) takes a different view, focusing on the role of the individual officer. Police agencies generally do not prepare felony arrest strategies as they would robbery arrest strategies, as discussed previously by Wilson and Boland (1978). Walsh focuses on general felony arrests, rather than arrests for specifically targeted crimes, which are more similar to directed patrol strategies. Many agencies are reluctant to specify a required number of arrests, as such a policy would be interpreted by the community as a quota. Walsh (1985), in his examination of officer variation in felony arrests, deals with the issue of an "informal" quota that may masquerade as a measure of departmental performance. After looking at crime data, New York Police Department patrol supervisors determined that the average patrol officer should log nine arrests. A small number of officers was found to account for most of the felony arrests. Walsh identified four types of officers: Type 1, who made no arrests; Type 2, who made from 1 to 8 felony arrests; Type 3, who made from 9 to 20 felony arrests; and Type 4, who made from 25 to 69 felony arrests.

Police officers adapt to the role expectation of the job because the officer, governed by a policy that defines general procedures, responds to "the conflict created by the demands of both bureaucracy and community." In effect, service to the community is defined by patrol officers on the street, not the police bureaucracy. Thus, the goals and objectives of a police organization, "in this case community security and the enforcement of law, are mediated in terms of the beliefs, expectations, and self interests of the individuals required to achieve them" (Walsh, 1985, p. 288). Again, this calls into question the wisdom of using arrest rates as a measure of police productivity, given the effect of role adaptation by individual officers.

Kohfeld and Sprague (1990) find that demography plays a part in the interaction between police and criminals. In addition, there is a general communication phenomena between police and criminals, influenced by the number of police arrests in general. They conclude that

police communicate to burglars through arrests; arrests lead to generalized deterrence in the form of spatial and temporal displacement of burglary; fine time-scale
disaggregation allows identification of the theoretical parameters implicated in our
models of the general deterrence relationship; and finally, the interactions that
underlie this deterrence relationship are systematically conditioned by demography.
(1990, p. 131)

They suggested that their results speak only to the issue of effective police deterrence for burglary. The researchers further suggested that this deterrent effect may be
based on *displacement* or relocation, both spatially (across territory) and temporally
(across time), rather than causing a cessation of criminal behavior across the board.

The reality of any thought of the use of arrests or arrest rates as a form of police
performance measure is twofold. First, there are too many different crimes from
which to choose an appropriate performance measure and no clear consensus as to
which crimes should be picked. There would be too much variance among police
agencies, because each community would set its own standard, which may change
from year to year. Second, at the risk of sounding overly simplistic, it all comes down
to discretion on the part of the officer whether to make an arrest. J. Q. Wilson (1976,
p. 278) argues that the police officer "in the discharge of his most important duties,
exercises discretion necessarily, owing in part to his role in the management of
conflict in and in part to his role in the suppression of crime." As Manning (1997)
noted, police have a lack of clear guidelines to follow when exercising discretion. In
terms of evaluating agency performance, the selection of the appropriate departmental performance measure is weakened by the exercise of officer discretion. This
practice results in an inability to determine whether the reduction in crime is a true
decrease from stamping out crime or by causing crime to displace or relocate to
another location.

Clearance Rate

There are serious drawbacks to using clearance rate as a police performance
measure. According to the FBI, a crime is cleared when police

have identified the offender, have sufficient evidence to charge him, and actually
take him into custody, or in exceptional instances, when some element beyond
police control precludes taking the offender into custody. (1992, p. 206)

While some people might be tempted to adopt clearances as a productivity
measure, there are obstacles to this approach. First, clearance rates are based on
reported crimes. Since not all crimes are reported to the police, clearance rates must
be substantially lower than crime rates. Second, clearance rates are not stable since
they vary by crime. Third, the police can systematically unfound crimes or report
them in different categories. Fourth, investigators might promise a suspect in custody
immunity from prosecution if he or she admits to other crimes. Such practices could

inflate the clearance rate artificially. Finally, not all agencies use the same standards for reporting an arrest (Walker, 1992).

Cloninger and Sartorius (1979) examine crime rates, clearance rates, and enforcement patterns in Houston, Texas. They wanted to see if an increase in police expenditures would result in an increase in arrest and clearance rates for homicide and auto theft, thus reducing these future crime rates. Cloninger and Sartorius (1979, p. 395) found that "the previous year's auto theft rate was significantly and positively associated with the current year's law enforcement rate for each of the six enforcement input variables." In other words, clearance by arrest is affected more by the crime rate and size of the area patrolled than any other factor in their study. The researchers conclude that the risk of arrest does reduce the crime rate, but the factors causing this relationship remain unclear. As they explain, criminal activity is "progressively less sensitive to risk of arrest, risk of punishment, and severity of punishment, in that order" (Cloninger and Sartorius, 1979, p. 400).

Response Time

At one time, many agencies placed tremendous emphasis on response time as a measure of productivity. The belief was that a rapid response would increase the probability of an arrest and, thereby, increase public satisfaction with the police. The reality, however, is that response time has little effect on clearance rate and only a small impact on public satisfaction.

The landmark study on the effectiveness of patrol is the Kansas City Preventative Patrol Experiment (Kelling et al., 1974). One of three levels of patrol was assigned to an area: reactive, proactive, or control. *Reactive beats* received no preventative patrol and officers responded only to calls for service. *Proactive beats* were patrolled by two to three times the normal amount of cars with assistance from cars from reactive beats. *Control beats* were assigned the normal level of one patrol unit per beat.

The goal of this massive undertaking was to determine whether patrol deployment practices exerted any discernible impact. The outcome was that variations in patrol levels have no significant effect on criminal activity or citizen perception of safety. In particular, changes in level of routine patrol had no effect on response time. Furthermore, no consistent pattern of differences emerged among the three types of patrol districts in terms of citizen attitudes toward police services. Citizen fear of crime was not affected and the attitude of business proprietors toward crime and police services remained stable. Finally, patrol patterns did not appear to affect citizen satisfaction with the police.

As you might imagine, the findings from this study prompted lively discussion. Since the conventional wisdom that lower response time produces greater perceived police effectiveness was not upheld, critics pointed to design flaws in the study as intermediate explanations for the outcome. Two years later, researchers were back in Kansas City to revisit the effect of response time, particularly in the form of police dispatch and travel time, on arrests and citizen satisfaction. This subsequent study collected more detailed crime information and observers rode with police officers to gather travel-time data. Once again, the findings indicated no relationship between travel time and making an arrest. Furthermore, dispatch time and travel intervals were not strongly associated with citizen satisfaction (National Institute of Law Enforcement and Criminal Justice, 1978).

A Final Note

While research in the 1970s and 1980s focused more on styles of policing and crime-specific policing as performance indicators, the decade of the 1990s brought about a renewed emphasis on police productivity and crime rate. O'Brien (1996) examines the Uniform Crime Reports and the National Crime Victimization Surveys from 1972 through 1993 as they relate to the fluctuation in violent crime rate. Finding that they are related but not strongly, O'Brien (1996) concludes that changes in law enforcement agencies created the rise in violent crime rate, not changes in the incidence rates of violent crime. Dissatisfaction with these four ways of measuring productivity and performance (reported crime, arrests, clearance, and response time) prompted further thought. Hoover (1992) argues that peacekeeping or order maintenance governs the police response to societal problems. Since law enforcement is merely one facet of policing, police productivity measures should focus on more than just the crime fighting or crook catching role. However, one must be careful not to fall into the "activity trap."

Longmire (1992) cautions police executives against falling into the *activity trap*, which he defines as a focus on requirements that have no clear connection to departmental goals. The activity trap often occurs when police agencies evaluate effectiveness on the basis of crime rate, arrest rate, or other vague measures of police activity. Instead, the primary focus should be a call for a comprehensive evaluation of police services to determine whether community needs are being met.

Other observers expect that efforts to switch from traditional measures of police performance will meet with considerable resistance. They contend that long-standing reliance on these factors by the media, the public, and municipal management has contributed to their virtual institutionalization. In fact, Alpert and Moore warn that

> these measures reflect an increasingly outmoded model of police tasks and fail to capture many important contributions that police make to the quality of life. More important, these measures may misguide police managers and lead them and their organizations towards purposes and activities that are less valuable than others that can be achieved with limited and diminishing resources. (1997, p. 266)

INDIVIDUAL PERFORMANCE MEASURES AND APPRAISAL

Individual performance assessment is the next step in evaluating how well an agency is doing in its delivery of police services. These instruments provide two basic functions. First, they give a clear picture of how each individual officer is functioning. Second, when aggregated, they yield a clear picture of how well the agency is responding to citizen needs.

The reader should be aware that this section is not intended to be an encyclopedia of every single device available for measuring individual performance. However, it will discuss the basic concepts of individual performance evaluation, sources of error, and how the individual performance appraisal fits within the overall evaluation cycle. There are three basic elements in the performance evaluation cycle: objective assessment, appraisal interview, and remediation (More and Wegener, 1996). We finish with an examination of employee interviews and the remediation process.

Employee Performance Evaluations

Landy and Goodin remark that

> the process and concept of performance evaluation began as an example of the cart leading the horse; performance evaluation has therefore never quite attained the role it needs in order to be effective. (1974, p. 166)

Perhaps one reason for this failure is because it

> is often disliked and misunderstood by both the supervisors doing the evaluation and the officers being evaluated. This occurs many times because the purposes of performance evaluation are not understood. (Swanson, Territo, and Taylor, 1998, p. 280)

Employee performance evaluations serve five major purposes. They help gauge performance, assist in career development, relay supervisory interests, alert participants to promotional opportunities, and trigger salary decisions. Philosophically, Landy and Goodin view performance appraisals as an effort to

> (1) standardize the nature of the personnel decision-making process so that the rights of the job incumbent are fully represented, (2) assure the public that the agency representatives are fully qualified to carry out their assigned duties, and (3) give the job incumbent necessary behavior modification information to maintain behaviors which are appropriate from the organization's standpoint and eliminate those which are inappropriate. (1974, p. 167)

Performance appraisals can focus on traits, behavior, or accomplishments. *Trait-based systems* are relatively easy for supervisors to complete, which probably accounts for their popularity despite criticism about their subjectivity. Examples of traits that are often rated would include loyalty, friendliness, efficiency, and reliability. As you can see, trait categories range from performance qualities to personal qualities to job-related ability. *Behavior-based systems* generally involve documenting specific employee actions. The *critical incidents approach* requires listing only good and bad incidents that are considered extraordinary. This documentation eventually becomes part of the evaluation record. *Behaviorally anchored rating systems* (BARS), on the other hand, present a list of specific tasks for a job and employees are rated against these standards. *Results-based systems* focus on employee outcomes. One drawback of this system is that it is more complicated and time consuming. However, this type of appraisal system can be fashioned so that it relates directly to the agency mission and goals (Bennett and Hess, 1996; Holden, 1994).

Regardless of the method chosen, performance appraisals should exemplify some central features. For one thing, they should be job related and focus on performing specific tasks. They also should be stated clearly and simply. Evaluations should be based on observable, as well as objective, behavior. In addition, evaluations should target actual on-the-job performance. Finally, supervisors should use measures that reflect predetermined performance standards (More and Wegener, 1996, p. 168).

Sources of Error

The first thing we must realize is that no appraisal system is perfect. There always will be room for error, particularly when humans judge other humans. This phenomenon is more of a problem with the rater than with the rating system itself. The focus, then, should be on keeping these intrusions to a minimum. Iannone (1994) suggests that proper training can reduce rater errors and make the performance appraisal process more worthwhile.

What kind of errors tend to surface? Latham and Wexley (1981) identify five rating errors: leniency, strictness, halo error, central tendency error, and recency bias. *Leniency,* the most common error, is the tendency to give people the benefit of the doubt. Supervisors often are lenient with subordinates to be popular, avoid criticism, and protect less talented or more vulnerable workers. Others are lenient to ensure that their subordinates have a fair chance at promotional opportunities.

Strictness is the opposite of leniency. When raters are overly tough, subordinates are rated artificially low. This downgrading puts employees at a disadvantage when it comes time for promotion.

A *halo error* occurs when one outstanding incident adversely affects the rating. More and Wegener (1996) state that the error can be positive or negative, while Holden (1994) suggests that it is halo error only if the subordinate is evaluated higher based on a single characteristic. In any event, a halo error can skew an evaluation to the point that the process becomes meaningless.

A *central tendency error* occurs when every ratee is considered average. Average evaluations are often the safest and certainly the least controversial, particularly when the rater is compared with others who may be very lenient or very strict. If raters are unfamiliar with the person being rated or there is a lack of verifiable performance data, it often is easier for the supervisor to assign an average rating. Unfortunately, central tendency errors reward marginal employees while penalizing outstanding ones, stifle creativity and kill morale, and destroy the credibility of the appraisal process (More and Wegener, 1996).

Recency bias occurs when individual performance over the last few months is given more weight than performance during the first few months of the rating period. Bennett and Hess (1996, p. 712) refer to this phenomenon as "late inning results count most." Supervisors may rate an employee who has a good first six months of an annual rating period followed by a bad six months lower than the employee who has a bad six months followed by a good six months. In reality, both employees had a good six months and a bad six months. Recency bias rewards the employee who has a good last six months and penalizes the employee with the bad last six months in the rating period.

Evaluation Interview and Remediation

The purpose of conducting an evaluation interview with the employee is to discuss the strengths and weaknesses observed by the supervisor and chart a blueprint for improvement. Employee performance evaluations are worthless if they are not communicated to the employee along with recommendations for remediation or change. If the interview is handled appropriately and the employee is able to see that the criticism is deserved, constructive, and fair, then the interview is beneficial. If not, the process quickly degenerates into an exercise in futility that breeds distrust, resentment, and outright hostility.

Once the basic rewards and criticisms are discussed, the process turns to the collaborative goal of solving any identified problems. As More and Wegener explain, the "ultimate value of the interview will depend . . . on a police officer's ability to recognize the need for self-improvement and the sergeant's ability to stimulate that subordinate's desire to change" (1996, p. 189). This process is highly complex. It involves evaluating, teaching, coaching, and counseling skills. The interview process may become a meaningless exercise without proper talent, experience, leadership skills, and training in performance interviewing.

Remediation is the final step in the formal performance evaluation process. It is defined simply as using available and appropriate resources to correct a deficiency. First-level supervisors, usually sergeants as Chief Heidingsfield explains in Chapter 3, are responsible for resolving performance problems. Since squad sergeants prepare the employee appraisal and conduct performance interviews, they are in the best position rectify any deficiencies.

Many agencies embrace a system of *progressive discipline*. That means lower levels of discipline are exhausted before escalating to more severe actions. Box 6–2 contains an example of policy guidelines that exemplify this approach. If no improvement is forthcoming after a reasonable period of time, the first-level supervisor may take further action such as retraining or disciplinary action. If the problem is severe, serious, or persistent, other alternatives may be pursued. As Box 6–2 shows, if the offending behavior continues or is unabated, there may be no other alternative except for terminating the employment of the errant employee.

Box 6–2   An Example of Policy Guidelines Regarding Progressive Discipline

I.   General Provisions.
    A.   Before taking any formal disciplinary actions, whenever appropriate, guidance and counseling will be offered.
    B.   Discipline should be corrective and constructive rather than punitive. Disciplinary actions should be utilized to motivate employees to develop good work habits and behavior which contributes to the successful operation of the department.
    C.   The need for disciplinary action may arise as a result of inappropriate actions on the part of the employee, including but not limited to:
        1.   Infractions of rules, regulations, policy or procedures, as established by the department or city government.
        2.   Offenses or misconduct violating general rules or specific state statutes.
        3.   Failure to perform one or more of the requirements of the job in a satisfactory manner.
    D.   Remedial Training.
        1.   If infractions occur, training may be offered to employees before any formal action is taken. The purpose of additional training is to assist the employee in correcting and improving his or her performance level. Training may be conducted during reasonable hours under a training officer or a supervisor. When necessary, the employee may be assigned to the Training Section for remedial training.
        2.   If for any reason an employee fails to attend or complete the remedial training in a satisfactory manner, the employee's Division Commander shall be notified and appropriate action taken.
II.   Application of Disciplinary Action.
    A.   Levels of Discipline. Although consistency in administering discipline is desirable, many factors should be considered in determining the appropriate level of discipline imposed at each step. Some of the factors involved include time intervals between offenses, effectiveness of prior disciplinary actions, willingness to improve, overall work performance, as well as behavior and disciplinary actions previously taken with other comparable employees for similar offenses. Some infractions

may be more serious in one case than in another because of the employee's responsibilities.

For example, failure to be at an assigned work station might be a more serious offense for a dispatcher than for a secretary. A repetition of the same offense or other serious offenses indicates more severe disciplinary measures are necessary. Certain offenses are of such a serious nature that immediate dismissal upon first offense is appropriate. When an employee is repeatedly violating various city/departmental policies and/or rules, progressive discipline should be administered even though the infractions may be unrelated.

B. When circumstances permit, the concept of progressive discipline will be practiced by administering gradually increasing disciplinary actions for each successive instance of employee misconduct. Each level of progressive discipline shall be fully documented for inclusion in the employee's personnel folder.

III. Types of Disciplinary Action.
A. Oral Reprimand.
B. Written Reprimand.
C. Suspension.
D. Demotion.
E. Dismissal.

Source: Tallahassee [Florida] Police Department, *Manual of Written Directives.*

THE IMPACT OF COMMUNITY POLICING ON PERFORMANCE EVALUATION

Community policing has made a radical change in police practices in this country, although its introduction has been a long and complicated process (Taylor, Fritsch, and Caeti, 1998). Not everyone agrees that the basic assumptions and goals of community policing are sound (Hoover, 1992). Perhaps part of the problem is not with the assumption and goals but with the implementation of community policing at the local level. Trojanowicz and his associates explain that, while community policing is

> widely, almost universally said to be important, it means different things to different people—public relations campaigns, shop fronts and mini-stations, re-scaled patrol beats, liaison with ethnic groups, permission for rank-and-file to speak to the press, Neighborhood Watch, foot patrols, patrol-detective teams, and door-to-door visits by police officers. Community policing on the ground often seems less a program than a set of aspirations wrapped up in a slogan. (1998, pp. 2–3)

Community policing "challenges basic beliefs that have become the foundation for traditional policing" (Trojanowicz et al., 1998, p. 3). To fully implement community policing, an agency must rethink its organizational structure, redefine the role and job tasks of line officers and management, and encourage members to change their way of thinking substantially.

A number of philosophical changes must be implemented before one can revamp the existing police organization into the model of community policing. Trojanowicz et al. (1998, pp. 283–284) advise departments to revise their personnel evaluation procedures to ensure adherence to the new values. As we saw earlier in this chapter, traditional evaluation methods may give some indication of how the police are combating crime. However, they give no hints as to how well a collaboration between the police and the community is working.

Community policing invokes an entirely new set of standards. For one thing, all people deserve a say in how they are policed, regardless of who they are or what position they hold in society. People are not only a vital resource, they are the raison d'être for policing. To do their job, the police must have access to average people. The populace no longer is the passive recipient of police service. Instead, citizens are transformed into important partners in the policing process. People have a right to decide both the means and objectives of the police. A critical component of this thinking is whether citizen input is included in the agency mission statement and objectives. Failure to make room for citizen input precludes full implementation of the community policing model.

Next comes the realization that ordinary people—not the police—have the ultimate power to control crime, enhance their own safety, and improve the overall quality of life in the community. Community policing must empower groups that previously wielded less power and control. These people become important arbiters who determine the relative success or failure of local initiatives. They also have a new role to play in supervising and assessing police performance. As a result, department evaluations should include measures of how often and how well its members are empowering groups to collaborate with each other and with the police to solve problems.

Finally, police officers must be retooled to see themselves as community problem solvers not just crime fighters. The administration must encourage street officers to move beyond responding to calls as isolated incidents and initiate ways to identify and alter the underlying dynamics that created the problem in the first place. Executives must demonstrate their commitment to this new philosophy by delegating power and control beyond their inner circles. Leadership must shift to emphasizing trust while maintaining accountability. It must grant officers the freedom and autonomy to move beyond merely responding to calls as isolated incidents to managing social problems (Trojanowicz et al., 1998).

The implementation of community policing is different from one place to another. This variability occurs because community policing makes sense only within the context of the partnership bond formed between the police agency and the citizenry it serves (Police Executive Research Forum, 1996). It follows, then, that any performance assessment must take into account the overall mission and goals of the organization.

Evaluating Individual Performance

Individual performance evaluations probably are easier to modify to fit the community policing model than overall agency assessments. Trojanowicz and Bucqueroux (1998, pp. 89–90) offer several recommendations for altering individual performance evaluations. Supervisors should document an individual officer's performance and compare the behavior against a job description or task inventory. This fit between behavior and expectation should serve as a foundation for establishing future performance goals and goal-directed activities. In addition, one should not overlook performance evaluations as a rich source of data for devising effective strategies and tactics for police problem solving. Supervisors should identify, document, analyze, and disseminate information about useful avenues that their officers have employed so that other members can benefit from this institutional memory. This process also is valuable for calling attention to ideas that did not work or to warn others of potential pitfalls they might encounter.

Individual performance evaluations can be part of the overall agency performance evaluation. Individual evaluations contribute data to assessments of the impact and effectiveness of the changes made to implement community policing. They help assess individual and collective training needs and provide a foundation for promotional consideration. They can be used to assess progress in specific projects which contribute to the overall goals and mission of the agency. Finally, individual performance evaluations help the employee gauge his or her progress in making a positive difference in the community, through leadership, community building, and problem solving (Trojanowicz and Bucqueroux, 1998, pp. 89–90).

A good example of individual performance evaluations designed in partnership with the fundamental concepts of community policing can be found in the implementation of Neighborhood Oriented Policing in Houston, Texas, in 1986. The Houston Police Department redesigned its personnel evaluation process through a two-stage process. First, a group of officers and first-line supervisors collected data relevant to the process. Then, a group of volunteers from within the department developed a new evaluation protocol. Six new forms were designed to elicit data and provide feedback (Wycoff and Oettmeier, 1994).

Sergeants use the first form, The Patrol Officer's Bi-Annual Assessment Report, to evaluate police officer performance based on 22 specific criteria. Written comments regarding work assignments, work progress, and overall and special recognition are encouraged. The evaluation criteria reflect the department's expectations regarding officer performance in the neighborhood-oriented policing program.

The second form, The Patrol Officer's Monthly Worksheet, was designed to document officer actions during a designated tour of duty. Police officers have the opportunity to use this form as input into their performance appraisals. Using this form, officers could provide data on different types of projects or programs they have worked on during the evaluation period and document their progress.

The third form built on the interaction between a police officer and citizens, an integral part of the community policing philosophy. This particular document, The Community Information Form, elicits information from citizens who worked on projects with specific officers. The information requested is very specific and provides additional insight into what the officer is trying to accomplish and how he or she is going about doing it.

The fourth evaluative device is the Calls for Service–Citizen Feedback Form. The most frequent source of officer-citizen interaction are calls for service. This form is designed to gather information on the quality and nature of the contact. Citizens are asked a few questions by sergeants. The responses are made a part of the record and are factored into the overall evaluation. Sergeants are expected to use this form at least once a month. Some police agencies take citizen feedback a step further. They randomly select a number of calls for service, contact the reporting party, and ask the citizen a few questions about how he or she feels the call was handled and what could be done to improve police services (Trojanowicz et al., 1998).

Since all police officers are expected to conduct high-quality criminal investigations, the fifth form is the Investigator Questionnaire. Even though the information contained in an investigative report provides a critical database for case managers, the officer's immediate supervisor seldom reviewed this material. The function of the Investigator's Questionnaire is to obtain information from investigative sergeants concerning an officer's knowledge and the quality of performance in both preliminary and follow-up investigations. Just as before, the officer determines whether or not to submit the form for consideration.

The sixth and final form is the Officer's Immediate Supervisor Assessment Form. Officers are given an opportunity to evaluate their immediate supervisors on a variety of dimensions related to supervision. While the feedback is fairly general in nature, the form is returned to the sergeant's superior. This information helps identify significant trends in the relationship between the sergeant and subordinate personnel (Wycoff and Oettmeier, 1994).

Obviously, this evaluation strategy represents a new look at individual performance evaluation strategies. Although some would argue that we should, we no longer can afford to use the old, traditional methods of evaluation, which were built on the paramilitary, bureaucratic method of policing. Community policing, with its paradigm shift in the way agencies think about themselves and operate, requires a corresponding change in individual performance evaluation strategies.

Evaluating Agency Performance

There also is a need to change the methods of evaluating agency-based performance. While a traditional police department may be satisfied with utilizing methods such as crime rates, arrests, clearances, and response time, we have seen that these measures are not sufficient. It is imperative to evaluate the agency as a whole, particularly in light of its mission and stated goals. The mission statement is the beginning of the evaluation process for an agency. Goals are derived from the mission statement and they generate measurable objectives. Analysis of these objectives give administrators an indication of how an agency is performing.

Watson, Stone, and DeLuca (1998) isolate five components critical for an organizational evaluation: organizational structure of the department, community involvement, quality of service, citizen satisfaction, and employee satisfaction. These five factors must be examined in light of the agency's mission statement, goals, and objectives. Only then will the department have a clear picture of what it *is* doing, rather than what it *says* it is doing for the community.

The transition from a traditional to a community police agency does not eliminate the need to assess the effectiveness, efficiency, or equity of services. It does require, however, that the department assess these concepts from the standpoint of the department and the citizenry.

CONCLUSION

Herein lies the nagging question: How do we know if community policing is working and working well? The answer, quite simply, is to ask the people who should know: the police and the community. One caveat, however, is in order. Once we embark on a process to really evaluate police agency performance from both the internal and external perspectives and take pains to avoid falling into what Longmire (1992) calls the "activity trap," we must be willing to take the next step. J. T. Walker (1997) argues that technological changes have forced a "re-blueing" of law enforcement practices as they relate to technology. In the same vein, we must be prepared to make changes in the way we evaluate both agency and individual performance and include measures of community input. Otherwise, we will never know whether community policing works.

According to Alpert and Moore (1997), police administrators have three major tasks ahead of them when reforming performance measures. First, they must reorient the agency to the community. Existing measures can be improved. New measures should be linked to the community. Police should encourage, not discourage, calls for service. The evaluative focus should be on quality, not quantity, of service. Second, departments should encourage proactive problem solving. They should reward officers who actively court community members to resolve problems. Although problems come in different sizes, they can be measured in terms of amount of time needed, importance to the community, or the number of specialized resources needed to solve. Finally, police administrators must manage the transition to community policing. Regardless of all the planning involved, there will be hard times in the transition and some recalcitrants will want to revert to the old ways of doing business, particularly since they are familiar and relatively easy to accomplish. New systems of evaluation always take longer to implement than first thought.

Holden (1994) maintains that police management must change because past practices have been a failure. This statement is particularly true when we consider that no handbook for implementation of community policing sets out concrete guidelines. Since there is no single style of police organization, there can be no single style of implementing or evaluating community policing. Roberg and Kuykendall (1997) recommend that police managers increase their reliance on research and evaluation. Since the problem-solving emphasis of community policing requires line officers to scan, analyze, respond, and assess, management should become more analytic and diagnostic. Roberg and Kuykendall conclude:

> In the final analysis, if police departments are to adapt appropriately to their environments, police managers must be willing to look to the future and use creative management methods that are supported by contemporary research rather than to the past and the status quo. . . . In this way, police departments should be able to implement significant change and become more adaptable, thus increasing the satisfaction levels of their employees and citizens alike. (1997, pp. 423–424)

Ultimately, police managers who do not use comprehensive evaluative techniques and reject citizen input will fall back into the "activity trap." Those who fail to use scientific research as a basis for decision making and policy reformulation are likely to repeat past failures. This stubborn steadfastness will further drive the police apart from the citizenry they serve and destroy many of the gains made by true collaboration between the police and the community to solve problems and reduce the impact of crime in the community.

DISCUSSION QUESTIONS

1. How do different implementations of community policing require different evaluation strategies?
2. How has evaluation of police agencies changed during the 20th century?
3. What are some of the barriers that keep police managers from adopting new personnel evaluation strategies? New agency evaluation strategies?
4. Suppose you are invited to be part of a citizen's group that will evaluate the protective services agency on your campus. What would you consider to be important?
5. How will improved performance strategies assist in the implementation of community policing in a community? What about improved personnel evaluation strategies?
6. Imagine that you are an officer in a traditional police agency. On what dimensions would you expect to be evaluated? Now imagine that you are in an agency that emphasizes a community policing orientation. How would you expect your evaluation to differ?

REFERENCES

Alpert, G. P., and M. H. Moore. "Measuring police performance in the new paradigm of policing." In R. G. Dunham and G. P. Alpert (eds.), *Critical Issues in Policing*, 3rd ed., pp.
265–281. Prospect Heights, IL: Waveland Press, 1997.

Bennett, W. W., and K. M. Hess. *Management and Supervision in Law Enforcement*, 2nd ed.
Minneapolis, MN: West Publishing Company, 1996.

Black, D. J. "Production of crime rates." *American Sociological Review* 35, no. 5 (1970), pp.
733–748.

Bopp, W., and P. Whisenhand. *Police Personnel Administration*, 2nd ed. Boston: Allyn and
Bacon, 1980.

Boydstun, J. E., M. E. Sherry, and N. P. Moelter. *Patrol Staffing in San Diego*. Washington,
DC: Police Foundation, 1977.

Britt, D. W., and C. R. Tittle. "Crime rates and police behavior." *Social Forces* 54, no. 2
(1975), pp. 441–451.

Carter, D., and L. Radelet. *The Police and the Community*, 6th ed. Upper Saddle River, NJ:
Prentice Hall, 1999.

Cloninger, D. O., and L. Sartorius. "Crime rates, clearance rates, and enforcement effort: The
case of Houston, Texas." *American Journal of Economics and Sociology* 38, no. 4
(1979), pp. 389–402.

Cordner, G. W. "The effects of directed patrol." In J. J. Fyfe (ed.), *Contemporary Issues in
Law Enforcement*. Newbury Park, CA: Sage Publications, 1981.

_____ and G. L. Williams. "Community policing and accreditation: A content analysis of
CALEA standards." *Police Forum* 5, no. 2 (1995), pp. 1–10.

_____ and G. L. Williams. *Community Policing and Police Agency Accreditation*. Washington, DC: National Institute of Justice, 1997.

Crowe, T. D. *Policy: A Manual for Improving Productivity*. Washington, DC: Office of Juvenile Justice and Delinquency Prevention, 1988.

Deakin, T. J. "The police foundation: A special report." *FBI Law Enforcement Bulletin* 55, no.
11 (1986), pp. 1–10.

Decker, S. H. "Official crime rates and victim surveys: An empirical comparison." *Journal of
Criminal Justice* 5, no. 1 (1977), pp. 47–54.

Federal Bureau of Investigation. *Crime in the United States*. Washington, DC: U.S. Government Printing Office, 1992.

_____. *Crime in the United States*. Washington, DC: U.S. Government Printing Office, 1996.

Gaines, L. K., V. E. Kappeler, and J. B. Vaughn. *Policing in America*, 2nd ed. Cincinnati:
Anderson Publishing Company, 1997.

Goldstein, H. *Policing a Free Society*. Cambridge, MA: Ballinger Books, 1977.

Greenwood, P. W., J. M. Chaiken, and J. Petersilia. *The Criminal Investigation Process*. Lexington, MA: D. C. Heath, 1977.

Hindelang, M. J. "The uniform crime reports revisited." *Journal of Criminal Justice* 2, no. 1
(1974), pp. 1–17.

Holden, R. N. *Modern Police Management*, 2nd ed. Englewood Cliffs, NJ: Prentice Hall,
1994.

Hoover, L. T. "Police mission: An era of debate." In L. T. Hoover (ed.). *Police Management:
Issues and Perspectives*, pp. 1–30. Washington, DC: Police Executive Research Forum,
1992.

Iannone, N. F. *Supervision of Police Personnel*, 5th ed. Englewood Cliffs, NJ: Prentice Hall,
1994.

Inciardi, J. "The uniform crime reports: Some considerations on their shortcoming and utility." *Public Data Use* 6, no. 6 (1978), pp. 3–16.

Kelling, G. L., T. Pate, D. Dieckman, and C. E. Brown. *The Kansas City Preventative Patrol Experiment*. Washington, DC: Police Foundation, 1974.

Kerner Commission. *Report of the National Advisory Commission on Civil Disorders*. New York: Bantam Books, 1968.

Kohfeld, C., and J. Sprague. "Demography, police behavior, and deterrence." *Criminology* 28, no. 1 (1990), pp. 111–136.

Landy, F. J., and C. V. Goodin. "Performance appraisal." In O. G. Stahl and R. A. Staufenberger (eds.), *Police Personnel Administration*, pp. 165–184. North Scituate, MA: Duxbury Press, 1974.

Latham, G. P., and K. N. Wexley. *Increasing Productivity through Performance Appraisal*. Reading, MA: Addison-Wesley, 1981.

Longmire, D. L. "The activity trap." In L. T. Hoover (ed.), *Police Management: Issues and Perspectives*, pp. 117–136. Washington, DC: Police Executive Research Forum, 1992.

MacNamara, D. E. J. "August Vollmer." In W. G. Bailey (ed.), *The Encyclopedia of Police Science*, pp. 657–659. New York: Garland Publishing Company, 1989.

Manning, P. K. *Police Work*, 2nd ed. Prospect Heights, IL: Waveland Press, 1997.

Maxfield, M. G., D. A. Lewis, and R. Szoc. "Producing official crimes: Verified crime reports as measures of police output." *Social Science Quarterly* 61, no. 2 (1980), pp. 221–236.

McShane, M. "Federal commissions and enactments." In W. G. Bailey (ed.), *The Encyclopedia of Police Science*, pp. 194–200. New York: Garland Publishing Company, 1989.

More, H. W., and W. F. Wegener. *Effective Police Supervision*, 2nd ed. Cincinnati: Anderson Publishing Company, 1996.

National Institute of Law Enforcement and Criminal Justice. *Response Time Analysis: Executive Summary*. Washington, DC: U.S. Government Printing Office, 1978.

O'Brien, R. M. *Crime and Victimization Data*. Beverly Hills, CA: Sage Publications, 1985.

———. "Police productivity and crime rates: 1972–1992." *Criminology* 34, no. 2 (1996), pp. 183–207.

Pate, T., R. A. Bowers, A. Ferrara, and J. Lorence. *Police Reponse Time: Its Determinants and Effects*. Washington, DC: Police Foundation, 1976.

Police Executive Research Forum. *Themes and Variations in Community Policing*. Washington, DC: Police Executive Research Forum, 1996.

President's Commission on Law Enforcement and Administration of Justice. *The Challenge of Crime in a Free Society*. Washington, DC: U.S. Government Printing Office, 1967a.

———. *Task Force Report: The Police*. Washington, DC: U.S. Government Printing Office, 1967b.

Roberg, R. R., and J. Kuykendall. *Police Management*, 2nd ed. Los Angeles: Roxbury Publishing Company, 1997.

Schwartz, A. T., and S. N. Clarren. *The Cincinnati Team Policing Experiment: A Summary Report*. Washington, DC: Police Foundation, 1977.

Sheley, J. F., and J. H. Hanlon. "Unintended effects of policy decisions to actively enforce laws: Implications for analysis of crime trends." *Contemporary Crises* 2, no. 3 (1978), pp. 265–275.

Sherman, L. W., and R. Berk. "The specific deterrent effects of arrest for domestic assault." *American Sociological Review* 49, no. 2 (1984), pp. 261–272.

Sherman, L. W., C. H. Milton, and T. V. Kelly. *Team Policing: Seven Case Studies*. Washington, DC: Police Foundation, 1973.

Skogan, W. "The validity of official crime statistics: An empirical investigation." *Social Science Quarterly* 55, no. 1 (1974), pp. 25–38.

Swanson, C. R., L. Territo, and R. W. Taylor. *Police Administration: Structures, Processes, and Behavior*, 4th ed. Upper Saddle River, NJ: Prentice Hall, 1998.

Taylor, R. W., E. J. Fritsch, and T. J. Caeti. "Core challenges facing community policing: The emperor still has no clothes." *ACJS Today* 18, no. 1 (1998), pp. 1–5.

Trojanowicz, R. *An Evaluation of the Neighborhood Foot Patrol Program in Flint, Michigan.* East Lansing: Michigan State University, 1982.

_____ and B. Bucqueroux. *Community Policing: How to Get Started*, 2nd ed. Cincinnati: Anderson Publishing Company, 1998.

_____, V. E. Kappeler, L. K. Gaines, and B. Bucqueroux. (1998). *Community Policing: A Contemporary Perspective*, 2nd ed. Cincinnati: Anderson Publishing Company, 1998.

Uchida, C. "The development of the American police." In R. G. Dunham and G. P. Alpert (eds.), *Critical Issues in Policing*, 3rd ed., pp. 18–35. Prospect Heights, IL: Waveland Press, 1997.

United States Commission on Law Observance and Enforcement. *Report on Lawlessness in Law Enforcement.* Washington, DC: U.S. Government Printing Office, 1931a.

_____. *Report on Police.* Washington, DC: U.S. Government Printing Office, 1931b.

Vollmer, A. *The Police and Modern Society.* Berkeley: University of California Press, 1936.

Walker, J. T. "Re-blueing the police: Technological changes and law enforcement practice." In M. L. Dantzker (ed.). *Contemporary Policing: Personnel, Issues, and Trends*, pp. 257–276. Boston: Butterworth–Heinemann, 1997.

Walker, S. *A Critical History of Police Reform.* Lexington, MA: Lexington Books, 1977.

_____. *The Police in America: An Introduction.* New York: McGraw-Hill Book Company, 1992.

Walsh, W. F. "Patrol officer arrest rates: A study of the social organization of police work." *Justice Quarterly* 2, no. 3 (1985), pp. 271–290.

Watson, E. M., A. R. Stone, and S. M. DeLuca. *Strategies for Community Policing.* Upper Saddle River, NJ: Prentice Hall, 1998.

Whitaker, G. P. *Understanding Police Agency Performance.* Washington, DC: U.S. Government Printing Office, 1984.

Whitaker, G. P., S. Mastrofski, E. Ostrom, R. B. Parks, and S. L. Percy. "Performance measurement." In W. G. Bailey (ed.), *The Encyclopedia of Police Science*, pp. 384–388. New York: Garland Publishing Company, 1989.

Wilson, J. Q. *Varieties of Police Behavior.* New York: Anthenum Books, 1976.

_____ and B. Boland. "The effects of the police on crime." *Law and Society Review* 12, no. 3 (1978), pp. 367–390.

Wilson, O. W. *Police Administration.* New York: McGraw-Hill Book Company, 1950.

_____ and R. C. McLaren. (1977). *Police Administration*, 4th ed. New York: McGraw-Hill Book Company, 1977.

Wren, D. *The Evolution of Management Thought*, 3rd ed. New York: John Wiley and Sons, 1987.

Wycoff, M. A., and T. N. Oettmeier. *Evaluating Patrol Officer Performance Under Community Policing: The Houston Experience.* Washington DC: National Institute of Justice, 1994.

Chapter 7

Civil Liability: Executive Preparation

Damon D. Camp, Jr., Georgia State University

Police executives in today's litigious environment live under the constant threat of civil litigation. Each year, thousands of plaintiffs file civil suits claiming injury at the hands of law enforcement (Kappeler, 1997). Claims range from allegations of wrongful death when an officer runs down an innocent bystander during a high speed chase, to violations of Fourth Amendment rights when a detective mistakenly searches a drug dealer's car without probable cause, to violations of the First Amendment by police supervisors of their subordinates' rights to engage in political protests (Vaughn, 1997b).

Chief executives often are dragged into these lawsuits vicariously, due to the nature of their jobs, or personally, because they were involved in the transgression. Two requirements must be met to name a supervisor or police executive under the principle of vicarious liability. First, action on the part of the supervisor must amount to more than mere negligence—the federal standard is "deliberate indifference" (*McClelland v. Facteau*, 1979). Second, there must be evidence present (probable cause) that the supervisor engaged in conduct or omitted action which led to the harm suffered by the plaintiff (*City of Canton v. Harris*, 1989). With elected sheriffs, a less stringent standard is used: respondeat superior. This common law principle that the master is responsible for the servant applies to deputies who serve at the discretion of the sheriff. Cities can be held liable under this principal when they have waived their immunity (*Mary M. v. City of Los Angeles*, 1991). Law enforcement executives also can be subjected to liability because they themselves acted negligently or violated somebody's rights.

Much has been written about police civil liability in general and some of these efforts have included material on the liability of law enforcement executives. Training courses on executive liability abound, but very little material addresses the personal liability of police chiefs and sheriffs. This chapter attempts to fill that gap by examining the various ways executive liability comes into play. It focuses on those aspects of civil liability where personal accountability may be affixed. After examining the attachment of liability in general, we review the two major areas where executive liability is most commonly found. We also consider solutions for avoiding this problem in the first place. Included here is an exploration of liability under state tort law, which involves not only intentional acts but also negligence. This chapter also looks at liability under federal law, which deals with statuary obligations as well as legal responsibility for constitutional violations. Finally, potential solutions to these problems are explored. Included here is a review of the various legal defenses available along with suggestions for shifts in policy.

THE CIVIL LAWSUIT ARENA

A lawsuit is not an unfamiliar occurrence to the average law enforcement chief executive. Silver (1996) suggests that law enforcement agencies face more than 30,000 suits each year. However, the true number of lawsuits filed each year is unknown, and the results of these actions is an even greater mystery. While several attempts have been made to document the outcomes of published cases (del Carmen, 1981; Kappeler, Kappeler, and del Carmen, 1993), little is known about the number and nature of cases that are settled out of court.

This lack of available information is due, in part, to the nature of the typical lawsuit. When individuals feel that they have been civilly harmed because of an intentional or negligent act or a breach of contract, they often will go to the alleged offending party to redress their grievances. If the results of this initial contact are unsatisfactory, they may resort to the courts. Once a cause of action is found (discussed in more detail later), the dissatisfied plaintiff then files a complaint in the proper court. This pleading provides details as to the purported wrongdoing, who the supposed offenders are, and what measures (monetary or injunctive) will be required to satisfy the grievance. The complaint must be filed before the end of the statute of limitations and served on each defendant who, in turn, must file an answer in a timely fashion. The defendant, in turn, can file a motion to dismiss and claim a lack of jurisdiction or a failure to state a proper complaint. If this motion is not filed or is denied, then the defendant must file a response. If a defendant does not file an answer, then a *default judgment* can be entered, which means that the plaintiff wins outright.

In most cases, once the pleadings have been made (and amended, if necessary) and discovery has commenced, both sides usually request that the court issue a *summary judgment* in their favor. Here, the judge examines all of the filed documentation and looks at the motion in a light that is most favorable to the nonmoving party. After this review, if no material fact is in dispute, then the court should rule on who should win the suit as a matter of law. If no one is victorious at the pleadings stage, then the court may pressure both sides to reach a settlement. If this effort is unsuccessful, then the parties go to trial. Often the trial commences years after the alleged injury took place (Cound et al., 1989).

Most lawsuits never make it past the pleadings stage because they are settled early. It is estimated that some 90% of all cases filed result in a dismissal or settlement (Haydock and Sonsteng, 1991). This trend to settle is motivated by a wide range of factors, and many defendants calculate that fighting a lawsuit is far more expensive than settling it. When the parties to a civil action settle, they often impose *nondisclosure requirements* on the other side. In other words, neither party can reveal the terms of the settlement. As a result, little is known about the rationale for settlement. On the other hand, when a party loses at trial or, better still, at the pleadings stage, the door is opened for an appeal. The decision rendered on appeal is a matter of public record and, therefore, open to review and analysis.

Extensive research has been done concerning law enforcement civil liability utilizing appellate court decisions of this type as a foundation for analysis. The material in this chapter relies heavily on these decisions as well. They not only provide background as to the types of alleged misconduct taking place but also guidance as to how future conduct will be viewed. The leading scholars in this area (e.g., del Carmen, Kappeler, Silver, and Vaughn) have written extensively on the nature of police civil liability. Some journals, such as *Criminal Law Bulletin*, emphasize liability issues as well.

Despite the amount of research done in this area, the primary emphasis focuses on officer or agency liability. Very little work has explored the direct impact of litigation on law enforcement executives or how to prepare them for civil liability lawsuits. To develop a clearer understanding of the challenges presented by this problem, we first examine the attachment of liability then analyze the major issue areas where police executives may face personal liability.

ATTACHING LIABILITY

The first thing potential plaintiffs must do before filing suit is to find a *cause of action* (C/A). To litigate for misdeeds, the injured party must locate the key to the courthouse door. This key can come from a variety of sources. However, unless a plaintiff is willing to break new ground and "create" case law by constructing a C/A out of brand-new cloth, the injured party must find an acceptable way currently available to hold the transgressor accountable. Normally, one can find C/As in the annals of common law (case law) or in the statutes.

While numerous C/As are available to potential plaintiffs, law enforcement executives generally need to be most concerned about three basic categories: state torts, federal torts, and constitutional violations. Lawsuits seldom are simplistic. Legal actions often are filed utilizing a shotgun approach, where defendants are showered with a plethora of allegations. In *Dobos v. Driscoll* (1989), for example, the family of a motorist who died while in the custody of a Massachusetts State Trooper sued the trooper for a civil rights violation under Section 1983 (42 U.S.C. §1983). The family also sued the trooper under state tort law for assault and battery, intentional infliction of emotional stress, and false imprisonment. Furthermore, the family also sued the trooper's supervisors under §1983 and the commonwealth for negligence.

The *Dobos* case illustrates the wide array of C/As available to prospective plaintiffs. State actions generally involve either *intentional torts* (e.g., assault and battery, intentional infliction of emotional stress, and false imprisonment) or *negligence torts* (failure to take appropriate action). Federal C/As in the law enforcement field normally involve a *Section 1983 claim* (civil rights violations). However, they also may include things like violations of fair employment laws, such as Title VII, as well as Constitutional infringements, such as a violation of First Amendment rights.

Once a C/A has been found, most plaintiffs look for "deep pockets" to assuage their suffering. In virtually every suit where claims are made that an injury was caused by someone in law enforcement, an attempt will be made to have the governing body named as a defendant in the suit (Silver, 1996). The advantages behind this move are obvious. The police officer who allegedly caused the death normally has few personal assets compared to the government and its coffers. Attaching responsibility to the city, however, is not so easy to identify and may be even more difficult to prove (*Bryan County v. Brown*, 1997). Generally, governmental entities are made parties to lawsuits either directly (e.g., through the implementation of problematic policy or custom) or vicariously through the acts of supervisors (Vaughn, 1994).

According to Avery and Rudovsky (1995), a number of ways can be used to bring municipalities directly into a suit. First, local governmental agencies can be held liable for problematic policies, regulations, and ordinances (*Monell v. Department of Social Services*, 1978). For example, a city can be held liable for an arrest made under an unconstitutional ordinance (*Buffkins v. City of Omaha*, 1990). Second, local governments can also be named in a suit because of an affirmative policy or custom. Such was the case in *Lusby v. T.G. & Y. Stores* (1984), where the city had a policy of arresting suspects designated as shoplifters by local merchants. Third, local governments also can be held liable for acquiescing to unconstitutional policies, such as allowing the use of excessive force to go uncorrected (*Fundiller v. City of Cooper City*, 1985). Finally, cities have been sued successfully because of problematic hiring and retention practices, inadequate training, and improper supervision and discipline.

Local governments can also be held accountable indirectly though the actions of their supervising employees. Avery and Rudovsky (1995) suggest that supervisors are named (through vicarious liability) for a number of reasons in lawsuits involving actions of their subordinates. For example, supervisors generally are better able to satisfy judgments than subordinates. More likely, however, agencies are more inclined to assume judgment responsibility for supervisors.

While the federal circuit courts vary in their interpretations of the extent of supervisory responsibility, most agree on several theories of liability. Courts have held supervisors liable when they were present at the scene or directed an action by a subordinate that later was challenged (*Maclin v. Paulson*, 1980). They have also held supervisors legally accountable for their failure to train, direct, supervise, and correct subordinates (*City of St. Louis v. Praprotnik*, 1988). Chief executives can be drawn into the fray because of their role as policy makers. Here, the lower courts have tended to interpret *Monell* to mean that department heads, such as chiefs and sheriffs, are responsible for making policy and, thus, can subject the local government to liability (*Pembaur v. City of Cincinnati*, 1986).

These very actions also may subject chief executives and their supervising subordinates to liability. Furthermore, plaintiffs may find it advantageous to name supervisors and chief executives personally responsible, as well as accountable in their official capacities, for several reasons. For one thing, plaintiffs may find that it is easier to prove wrongdoing on the part of an individual captain or police chief than to prove the city responsible. In addition, punitive damages can be assessed against an individual but not a municipality (Avery and Rudovsky, 1995). For these and other reasons, it is important for police executives to be wary and to develop an understanding of where and how they can become liable for conduct that may give rise to civil liability. This liability generally surfaces in two areas: under state tort law and under federal law.

AN OVERVIEW OF MAJOR ISSUES

Law enforcement executives face potential personal legal liability from two sets of plaintiffs who can attack on three fronts. Most suits are filed by citizens who claim they were injured by an officer. The chief or sheriff is named either directly (because of personal involvement or supervision) or vicariously (because of a policy-making role). The other type of plaintiff is the employee or would-be employee who claims injury due to an employment-related decision promulgated or blessed by the chief executive.

The three fronts most commonly used are state tort actions, federal statutes, and constitutional violations. Provided next is an extensive discussion of lesser known state tort law as it relates to law enforcement executive liability. Also presented is an overview of the more commonly discussed federal law in this area. Included here is a review of several federal statutory C/As, as well as an examination of selected constitutional issues.

CIVIL LIABILITY UNDER STATE LAW

Tort law involves a claim of injury to person or property that is not a breach of contract (del Carmen, 1991). State torts can be found in statute books or in common law. *Statutory torts* normally include causes of action specifically singled out by a state legislature for attention. *Common law* torts embody a range of conduct not specifically identified by statute but actionable nonetheless because the courts have found the conduct to be sufficiently objectionable to warrant damage compensation (Keeton, 1984).

The purpose of tort law is to provide recompense for injured parties when they have suffered damages. It also can be used as a tool to inflict punishment of sorts, through the use of punitive damages, to discourage certain behavior. In law enforcement, defendants often are the individual officer involved in the conduct, the officer's supervisor(s), the agency head, and the host government. Plaintiffs can be citizens, perpetrators, or even employees. Torts can be divided into two basic categories: intentional torts and conduct involving negligence.

Intentional Torts

Intentional torts are grounded in the idea that liability stems from conduct that is socially unreasonable. Conduct here usually involves a three-part concept. That is, the defendant acted unreasonably, intentionally causing the plaintiff's consequences (Keeton, 1984). It could be argued further that intentional torts involve conduct where

- The defendant's actions caused *consequences* to the plaintiff.
- These actions were *intentional*.
- They amounted to an *unreasonable* interference with the interest of the plaintiff.

With most intentional torts, the "unreasonable interference" is the tort at issue. For example, with the tort of trespassing, it is thought that to use someone else's land without the owner's permission is an unreasonable interference with the owner's interest in the land. The notion of "intent" is a little less concrete. While a law enforcement officer must have intended to engage in the conduct that led to the injury, the defendant need not have intended to cause the plaintiff harm (Kappeler, 1997). Rather, the issue is whether the defendant's actions were intentional and, further, whether the consequences of these actions were foreseeable. In the trespassing example, the issue is not whether the defendant intended to trespass on the plaintiff's land but rather whether there was an intentional entry onto the land.

The focal point of most intentional torts is the results or the "consequences" of the conduct. The critical issue is whether the specific consequences of a particular case constitute an unreasonable interference. In the case of a trespass, the question might be whether a team of officers invading a home armed with a search warrant for a neighbor's house would constitute an unreasonable interference with the homeowner's property interest.

There are eight primary areas in the field of law enforcement where intentional torts tend to surface. They include abuse of process/malicious prosecution, assault and battery, defamation, excessive force, false arrest/imprisonment, intentional infliction of emotional distress, invasion of privacy, and wrongful death. Attaching liability to the chief executive for these torts tends to fall into three broad categories.

Direct executive liability is somewhat limited in the first category unless the chief or sheriff specifically is involved in the conduct that culminated in the lawsuit. Action for intentional acts, such as assault and battery, use of excessive force, and wrongful death often fall into this classification. Liability almost always can attach if the chief or sheriff participated in the incident.

Under the second category, the executive can incur liability if he or she simply authorized or directed the tortuous activity. For example, liability for false arrest or imprisonment can attach if the chief directed that a defendant be arrested or taken into custody. Likewise, the chief who authorizes a knowingly bogus prosecution is liable. Less clear is whether an administrator can be held liable for setting the tone or creating an atmosphere whereby officers are not discouraged from ignoring certain criminal procedures (*Savannah v. Wilson,* 1994).

The third area of tortuous conduct often is linked directly to the chief executive. Here, executive liability attaches when the actions involve activities normally associated with the duties of a chief or sheriff. It also can attach where policies and procedures promulgated by the top administrator result in harm to a plaintiff. Examples of torts that often fall into this classification include defamation, invasion of privacy, and intentional infliction of emotional distress.

Defamation involves the plaintiff's claim that a law enforcement action has caused damage to his or her reputation by the publication of false material that was injurious to his or her reputation (*Harris v. News-Sun,* 1995). Either printing the material (libel) or speaking it to someone other than the subject (slander) can form the basis for defamation. Claims of slander or libel can result from erroneous statements made about suspects to the press or from false accusations made in the presence of others. However, the truth is an absolute defense to charges of defamation. Plus, the criminal justice system enjoys some degree of privilege through absolute immunity in judicial proceedings and qualified immunity during certain pretrial stages (Keeton, 1984).

A relatively new C/A has surfaced in the law enforcement field that relates to the invasion of privacy. Courts have allowed actions stemming from certain invasions based on the notion that people have a right to be left alone and to keep their lives private. For example, the publication of a rape victim's picture could be such an intrusion. In addition, some states have allowed plaintiffs to collect when unwarranted strip searches were performed. However, the Maryland Court of Appeals declined to allow an invasion of privacy claim after juveniles were arrested under a bogus curfew law (*Ashton v. Brown,* 1995).

Defamation, as well as invasion of privacy, can involve the actions of the police executive. Chiefs and sheriffs often make remarks to the press, and libel suits can emanate from these contacts. They also may be responsible for strip search policies or other invasive directives that overtly intrude into the privacy of citizens.

Intentional infliction of emotional distress, often combined with other tort claims, is a common catchall for many civil actions. It is hard to prove damages (a required element in most tort allegations) in a general civil case. It is particularly difficult in an action involving law enforcement where even the most innocuous encounter can cause emotional distress. The courts generally try to protect people from intentionally outrageous or reckless conduct. Normally, an isolated event will not be sufficient to provide a judgment (*Smith v. Holeman,* 1994). Rather, the plaintiff normally must prove a pattern or practice over a period of time.

As to executive liability in this area, chiefs and sheriffs can contribute to the emotional distress on an individual basis and in other ways as well. For example, executives can foster an atmosphere of intimidation within the agency or they can allow subordinates to browbeat and frighten those who wish to lodge complaints against the department or one of its officers.

Negligence in General

Negligence, the other major branch of tort law, is based on the assumption that people have an obligation to exercise due care when they act. Here the defendant's state of mind is unimportant because intent in not required. The concept revolves around the idea that when a person breaches a recognized duty and this breach causes an injury, the careless party, and not the injured one, should bear the brunt of the damages involved. It is based on the standard of what under the circumstances a reasonably prudent person would do in a given situation.

The typical negligence case has four fundamental elements. The first involves *duty.* Here the question is whether the defendant had an obligation to behave in a certain fashion. Lawyers often refer to this to as a *legal duty.* In the case of a law enforcement officer, legal duties derive from laws, policies, customs, judicial decisions, and the like (Kappeler, 1997). These duties can include the safe operation of police equipment, firearms, or motor vehicles, and the duty to provide protection or assistance.

Once a duty is established, then the plaintiff must prove that a *breach* of this duty has occurred. Generally, this means that the defendant acted in such a way as to create an unreasonable risk to the plaintiff. This breach of duty must result in *damages* that are both real and proven: real in the sense that they are actual and substantial enough to interfere with the plaintiff's well-being, and proven in that they must have occurred and do not represent potential damages. Finally, the breach must be causally linked to the damages. In other words, the breach must be the *proximate cause* of the damages suffered.

While duties may be specifically identified in the law, the concept that a particular defendant was negligent in exercising that duty on a specific occasion is decided on a case-by-case basis. Courts generally try to determine if the defendant behaved like a reasonably prudent person would under similar circumstances.

Negligence in the law enforcement field can surface almost anywhere and chief executives can find themselves defending against a host of charges of negligence. For example, sheriffs can be held negligent for allowing jailhouse cooks to carry and discharge firearms (*Roberts v. Benoit,* 1992). Chiefs can be made responsible for officers who use vehicles to run over would-be suspects who reach at waistbands (*Guzman v. City of San Antonio,* 1989). However, they may be able to duck liability for negligent preparation for special events when isolated occurrences lead to injuries (*Darrow v. Schumacher,* 1993).

Three major areas where negligence claims are typical include negligent operation of a motor vehicle, negligent failure to protect, and negligent failure to prevent suicide. Administrative negligence based on §1983 violations is reserved for later discussion.

Negligence and Motor Vehicles

Negligence in the operation of motor vehicles can surface in three primary areas. The first relates to routine driving. Here, law enforcement personnel are afforded no real privileges. If an officer on patrol or a police chief on the way to a routine meeting has an automobile accident, then damages are litigated just as if the driver were a citizen. Executives have little to fear from vicarious liability claims unless they allow one of their officers, who is known to be a reckless driver or has a suspended license, to operate an agency vehicle. Cities, on the other hand, may be held liable under the theory of respondeat superior.

The second area concerns vehicle maintenance and is handled in a similar fashion. Provided the department has policies and procedures in place to deal with maintaining vehicles properly and identifying those that are unsafe, chief executives should be able to avoid liability.

The third area, however, receives special treatment from the courts and recently this treatment has been somewhat harsh. High-speed pursuits have troubled law enforcement agencies since the early 1900s when police departments first began using the automobile in traffic enforcement (Kappeler, 1993). Generally, state law governs the operation of emergency vehicles. In most instances, it provides limited immunity to drivers permitting them to violate traffic laws. Just what constitutes an emergency often is litigated, however, and immunity many times turns on whether the officer had reason to believe that a true emergency existed. In high-speed pursuit cases, the real issue quite often rests with the departmental policy governing chases and, thus, resides squarely on the shoulders of the chief executive.

The U.S. Supreme Court recently addressed the problem of high-speed pursuit in *County of Sacramento v. Lewis* (1998). In this case, two police officers on a traffic stop attempted to pull over a fast approaching motorcycle carrying two people. When the driver (who was under 18) failed to stop and sped away, one of the officers gave chase. Shortly thereafter, the bike tipped over and the passenger was killed. The family of the victim sued in federal court alleging a violation of the substantive due process clause of the Fourteenth Amendment. The Supreme Court ruled that police officers do not violate substantive due process by causing the death of someone through deliberate or reckless indifference to life in a high-speed automobile chase aimed at apprehending a suspected offender. While this is an important decision, it should be noted that the case was filed under 42 U.S.C. §1983 and applies to federal, not state, liability. At the district court level, the judge ruled that the officers enjoyed immunity from state tort liability because of a California statute. That may not necessarily be the case in other states.

Negligent Failure to Protect

For decades, the courts shied away from the area of "failure to protect or respond." They were reluctant to recognize this area as a duty, except under extreme circumstances. Even the U.S. Supreme Court refused to hold a county department of social services responsible under §1983 when it failed to remove a four-year-old boy from a known abusive father after repeated signs and warnings (*DeShanney v. Winnebago County Department of Social Services*, 1989). However, there are some cases when a duty to protect or to respond has been recognized, normally via statute or a departmental policy or custom.

Two particular areas have received a great deal of attention over the past several decades. The first involves the failure to remove drunk drivers from the roads. Here, courts are reluctant to blanket officers with traditional immunity for discretionary decisions, reasoning that a decision not to remove a drunk driver is not optional. Therefore, officers have a duty at least not to allow known or suspected intoxicated drivers to remain behind the wheel of a vehicle and any breach of this duty could be actionable (*Jean W. v. Commonwealth,* 1993). Chief executive liability here generally is limited to direct knowledge or a pattern or practice of allowing officers to escort drunk drivers home or allowing certain influential people to escape apprehension.

The second area involves law enforcement duties that are created when special relationships exist. In Georgia, for example, the state Supreme Court recognized such a duty in *City of Rome v. Jordan* (1993). The court established a three-part test in *Jordan* whereby a special relationship exists if the following conditions are met:

- an explicit assurance by the municipality, through promises or actions, that it would act on behalf of the injured party;
- knowledge on the part of the municipality that inaction would lead to harm; and,
- justifiable and detrimental reliance by the injured party on the municipality's affirmative undertaking. (*City of Rome v. Jordan,* 1993, p. 867)

The court reviewed the facts in *Jordan* (which dealt with a sexual assault after the police were called but did not respond promptly) and determined that the test was not met. Law enforcement chief executive liability here can be traced directly to a policy or practice. For example, if a department has a custom of assuring citizens of some degree of protection (or of lack of a need to "worry") about a potentially dangerous situation knowing that potential danger could arise from inaction and a citizen is injured due to relying on those assurances, then the chief executive could be held liable.

Negligent Failure to Prevent Suicide

The concept that a law enforcement agency can be held liable for failing to prevent a suicide stems from the idea that a special duty of care exists when somebody is in custody. When a prisoner commits suicide, the custodial agent is scrutinized for liability (Kappeler, Vaughn, and del Carmen, 1991).

The courts have found reason to hold agencies and their leaders responsible for suicides under state tort law in four general categories. The first involves any rule violation that results in lack of proper attention or supervision. The second deals with a supervision void itself. The third concerns the overall safety of a facility or the existence of potentially dangerous policy (such as allowing inmates to retain belts). The final category is failure to rescue an inmate who attempts to commit suicide. In all these areas, chief executives could be held liable particularly if policy or procedures were ignored.

CIVIL LIABILITY UNDER FEDERAL LAW

Police executives find themselves in court most often for alleged violations of federally guaranteed rights. By and large, the vast majority of cases involve some purported violation of a right actionable under 42 U.S.C. §1983. In addition, employment-related claims, which are tied to Title VII of the Civil Rights Act of 1964 or a host of other statutory protections, also are lodged against chiefs and sheriffs. Finally, law enforcement administrators have found themselves increasingly under fire for alleged constitutional violations, normally filed by employees under the aegis of §1983.

Plaintiffs flock to the federal courthouse when they feel wronged at the hands of a public official. This attitude is due, in large part, to the ease of using the federal statutory scheme. Two main avenues exist and each presents a different, but equally alluring, promenade for atonement. The first is Title 42 U.S.C. §1983, which originally was enacted in 1871 by Congress to combat the Ku Klux Klan and rampant post-Civil War constitutional violations. The carrot here is not so much that plaintiffs can collect huge awards but that the plaintiff's lawyers can collect "reasonable attorney fees" if they prevail. In other words, even though the damages incurred may be nominal, the attorney can be paid handsomely (42 U.S.C. 1988, 1997). Federal employment related actions have an additional lure. Here, not only can attorneys collect reasonable fees, but plaintiffs gain a government financed advocate (the Equal Employment Opportunity Commission) who will accompany them to court under certain circumstances (42 U.S.C. §2000). In this section, these two broad categories (citizen suits and actions by employees) will be reviewed briefly and specific applications will be examined.

Claims Made by the General Public

Federal lawsuits lodged by members of the public normally are filed under §1983. Usually they stem from actions on the part of an officer of the law that resulted in the injury of a citizen. For example, plaintiffs have been successful suing the police for unconstitutional strip searches (*Fuller v. M.G. Jewelry,* 1991), for shooting someone in a dark house without identifying themselves as police (*Yates v. City of Cleveland,* 1991), and for releasing an attack dog on a misdemeanant (*Marley v. City of Allentown,* 1991).

To be successful in a §1983 suit, plaintiffs must prove three primary elements. First, they must show that the defendant was acting under the "color of law" when the injury occurred. Generally, this refers to the state of affairs where an officer's actions, under normal circumstances, would fall within the normal confines of assumed duties. However, the officer misuses this power that is possessed only by virtue of law (*Monroe v. Pape*, 1961). According to Vaughn and Coomees (1995), the courts often look to how much official authority has been invoked to determine when an officer has been acting under the "color of law."

The second requirement is that the questionable conduct must amount to a violation of a constitutional or federally protected right. The right must be clearly established, such as the right to counsel but not a cursory search of a jail employee (*Androw v. Johnson*, 1985). Normally, the actions must constitute a violation of a recognized right protected by the U.S. Constitution or guaranteed by federal statute. For example, a §1983 violation could arise because an officer falsely imprisoned someone or arrested somebody without probable cause (*Smith v. Holeman*, 1994). Federally protected rights usually refer to statutory provisions, such as the Title VII of the Equal Employment Act. Here, an employee claiming that she was sexually harassed by her supervisor can sue not only under Title VII but also under §1983 (*Gares v. Willingboro Township*, 1996).

A third requirement is that the alleged violation represents a significant violation of constitutional proportions (Kappeler, 1997), such as actions which result in a serious injury (del Carmen, 1991). Here, plaintiffs need to show that the injury was more than minor or that the violation was sufficiently significant as to be constitutional in nature. In other words, a slight push would not be actionable, but a beating to extract a confession would easily reach the required level.

Executive liability in this area generally is limited to situations where there is personal involvement or the executive assumes the role of a policy maker. If the chief or sheriff is personally involved, then the rules applying to individual officers come into play. A new set of conditions surface when the role is that of policy maker. Here, the plaintiff claims "administrative negligence" has occurred where the injury was caused not only by the officer involved but also by the supervisor or executive who had a hand in overseeing the officer. Two main areas of concern arise here: wrongful employment and improper supervision. This oversight could be direct if the chief executive participated in the actual employment or supervision of the officer involved. Or it could be indirect, as in the case where subordinate supervisors are acting on policy promulgated by the chief. Under the latter condition, the agency is likely to be held accountable and the chief may escape personal liability. In the former setting, personal accountability may be at issue. The conditions surrounding some of the specific practices that can lead to liability are discussed next.

Claims of wrongful employment cover a wide range of activities, including hiring practices, training, and retention policies. Negligent hiring generally occurs when an unqualified individual is hired who then engages in prohibited §1983 conduct. It entails three elements. The employee must be unfit for the job, this unfitness must be or should have been known to the chief, and the employee's act was foreseeable (*J.H. by D.H. v. West Valley City*, 1992).

The standard used is deliberate indifference or gross negligence. For example, in *Mon v. City of New York* (1990), the court found that the city could be held liable for an off-duty shooting by an officer it had hired. This officer had a criminal history of disorderly conduct and had been involved in a revenge-related shooting against a previous employer. The city knew of this past and could be considered deliberately indifferent in its failure to investigate further. Administrators normally can avoid problematic hiring by having a preemployment screening program that includes a thorough background check.

In failure to train cases, the plaintiff must show that the chief executive neglected to train the officer involved, that this failure was linked to the act in question, and that the failure amounted to deliberate indifference (*City of Canton v. Harris,* 1989; *Collins v. City of Harker Heights,* 1992; *Hinshaw v. Doffer,* 1986). In *Thompson v. City of Lawrence* (1995), the court found that the Lawrence, Kansas, police chief was not liable under §1983 for allegedly failing to train his officers when they made a questionable arrest of a bail bondsman. The federal district court found differently in *McQurter v. City of Atlanta* (1983). Here, the city and its police commissioner (along with several officers and supervisors) were sued for the death of an arrestee who died as the result of an improperly administered choke hold. The court found the police commissioner liable for the victim's death because he promoted supervisors who were not adequately trained in the use of deadly force.

Training issues can also arise in First Amendment claims. This was the case in *Mackinney v. Nielsen* (1995), where officers arrested a man for writing on the sidewalk. Mackinney and a friend used chalk to declare "A police state is more expensive than a welfare state—we guarantee it." The court found the city liable for not training its officers to be sensitive to First Amendment rights. Chief executives can generally avoid liability in this area by providing officers with current, documented training on the nature of First Amendment rights (Vaughn, 1996).

As to wrongful retention, plaintiffs usually pursue one of three avenues. First, they sue when a chief fails to dismiss someone who has a history of problems, such as mental instability (*Narney v. Daniels,* 1992). Second, they may prevail when an officer who has a history of instability is not controlled (*Dobos v. Driscoll,* 1989). Finally, plaintiffs may win if a police chief fails to correct problems and retains an officer who has violated the rights of others in the past. Liability for problematic retention usually is not attached when civil service regulations intervene and when progressive discipline is utilized.

Claims of improper supervision normally encompass five areas: wrongful assignment, failure to supervise, failure to direct, negligent entrustment, and failure to discipline. Wrongful assignment usually entails assigning an employee to a job without ascertaining competency and ability. The head of the agency has an affirmative duty to properly assign personnel on the basis of competency. Failure to do so is a breach of this duty. If the breach leads to an injury, the chief can be sued. If the executive is unaware of a defect, then liability can be avoided (*Mulhern v. City of Scottsdale,* 1990).

In failure to supervise cases, the chief executive must be aware of misconduct and then either approve or acquiesce to that conduct (*Dobos v. Driscoll,* 1989). Actual knowledge is not required. Rather, if the chief knew or should have known of the problem or created a climate where the problem could continue, then liability may be assessed. If knowledge on the chief executive's part does not exist, then liability normally can be avoided (*Mackinney v. Nielsen,* 1995).

Failure to direct cases usually emerge when a chief or sheriff fails to instruct or inform officers of problems or issues (*Ford v. Breier*, 1974) or where he or she fails to establish needed policies or guidelines (*Dewell v. Lawson, 1974*). As Chapter 1 explains, a good defense to a failure to direct suit is a current, accurate, and comprehensive policy manual.

Negligent entrustment often involves the failure to oversee the use or care of equipment. Here, the test for liability is deliberate indifference: The officer was ill-prepared to use the equipment and the chief was aware of this fact but allowed the usage anyway (*Roberts v. Benoit*, 1992).

Cases dealing with failure to discipline usually involve situations where the chief executive overlooks complaints against officers or fails to discipline employees who engage in misconduct. However, to be held liable, this failure must amount to gross misconduct (*Santiago v. Fenton, 1989*). Clear procedures that are routinely followed can be the executive's best defense.

In addition to the areas just outlined, law enforcement leaders can be sued under §1983 for alleged constitutional violations by their employees as well as the citizenry. (Some of these issues are discussed later.) Also, an increasing number of plaintiffs are litigating §1983 claims in state court, which presents a host of different forums (Steinglass, 1994).

However, the U.S. Supreme Court sent a clear message in 1997 that, except under limited circumstances where an outcome was clearly predictable, plaintiffs must show the chief's or sheriff's actions were based on something other than a single, isolated event. In *Bryan County v. Brown* (1997), Sheriff Moore had hired his nephew's son, Stacy Burns, without adequately investigating his background. Burns had a long history of driving infractions and a conviction for simple assault. Before receiving any formal training, Burns was involved in a traffic stop where he permanently injured a passenger in the vehicle. The plaintiff sued for use of excessive force, negligent hiring, and failure to train. She prevailed at the district and appellate court levels. The Supreme Court reversed the lower courts. It ruled that liability could not be assessed for a single isolated incident because the plaintiff had not demonstrated that these decisions reflected a conscious disregard for a high risk that Burns might resort to excessive force.

Claims Made by Employees

Historically, employment has been viewed as an "at will" relationship where hiring, firing, and resignations are treated as a matter between the employer and the employee unless the basis for an adverse action involves a constitutionally protected matter (Zimmer, Sullivan, and Richards, 1988). This relationship is controlled, for the most part, by contract law. In the case of civil servants and teachers, statutes also play an important role. Beginning in the 1960s, the federal government began to take an active role in the statutory control of certain aspects of employment law by passing a series of fair employment laws. Law enforcement employees have used these laws as well as §1983 to litigate grievances against their employers and these two areas are discussed next.

Employment Discrimination Claims. The passage of the fair employment acts to counteract discrimination began with the Equal Pay Act of 1963 (29 U.S.C. §206(d)). This act prohibits wage discrimination based on gender. It was followed the next year with Title VII of the Civil Rights Act of 1964 (42 U.S.C. §1000(e)), which bans general employment discrimination on the basis of race, color, religion, gender, and national origin. The Age Discrimination in Employment Act of 1975 (29 U.S.C. §621), which parallels Title VII for persons 40 years of age and older, followed some eight years later. Finally, the Americans with Disabilities Act of 1990 (42 U.S.C. §12101) provides a wide range of protections for the disabled. In addition, most states have fair employment laws (so-called Mini Title VIIs) such as Georgia's Fair Employment Practices Act of 1978 (O.C.G.A. §45-19-22), which covers race, gender, national origin, handicap, and age.

In law enforcement, many employment conflicts arise out of Title VII disputes. Employers with 15 or more employees (as well as employment agencies and labor organizations, regardless of size) are banned from discriminating on the basis of race, color, religion, gender, and national origin. Normally, the primary issues that have arisen revolve around hiring and promotion customs, compensation practices, and employment conditions. However, former employees can sue former employers for discriminatory acts. Such was the case in *Robinson v. Shell Oil Company* (1997), where the U.S. Supreme Court granted a former employee standing to sue his previous employer for giving him a poor letter of recommendation, allegedly based on his race. While the basis for employment discrimination may vary (e.g., Title VII, age, disability), the case law governing enforcement tracks well across areas.

Procedurally, an employee (an actual, would-be, or fired employee) who suffers an adverse employment action must first file a complaint with the Equal Employment Opportunity Commission (EEOC) of the U.S. Justice Department within 180 days of the injury. The EEOC investigates and may hold hearings. If the dispute is unresolved after the investigation and evidence of discrimination found, the EEOC should issue a "right to sue" letter to the plaintiff. If it finds "outrageous behavior" on the part of the employer, then it may either join the plaintiff's suit or file on its own behalf. This independent action normally occurs if the plaintiff has settled with the employer (Zimmer et al., 1988).

Generally speaking, the employee must prove either "disparate treatment" or "disparate impact" to prove discrimination. *Disparate treatment* involves intentional discrimination directed either toward an individual employee or evidenced by systemic practices. *Disparate impact* refers to nonintentional practices that appear on the surface to be neutral but have discriminatory results.

Cases involving individual disparate treatment may be the easiest to prove. Here, the employer acts in a discriminatory manner against an individual and there is either direct proof or circumstantial evidence of discrimination. For example, in *Mann v. City of Albany* (1989), a police major was told in writing that he could not be promoted to the open position of assistant chief because he was not black. To prove systemic disparate treatment, plaintiffs have the burden of showing that they were a member of a protected class, that they applied and were qualified for the position, that they were rejected and that the position remained open or was filed by someone who was not a member of a protected class. The burden then shifts to the employer to prove that there was a legitimate, nondiscriminatory reason for the employment decision. The plaintiff then can try to rebut this position as a "mere pretext" (*McDonnell Douglas Corp. v. Green*, 1973).

To hold a police administrator responsible, the plaintiff must show that the decision maker was the final policy maker (*Randle v. City of Aurora*, 1995). Here, the question is whether the official is meaningfully constrained "by policies not of that official's own making," whether the decisions made are final, and whether the purported policy decision is within the realm of the official's grant of authority (*St. Louis v. Praprotnik*, 1988).

Systemic disparate treatment involves intentional ongoing treatment of employees where the system used for hiring, promotion, and the like is discriminatory in nature. This type of discrimination is evidenced by outright discrimination, where a practice is discriminatory on its face or via "pervasive practices." An example of an outright discriminatory practice might be the prohibition of employment to non-U.S. citizens or a retirement plan that costs more for women than men (*Los Angeles Department of Water & Power v. Manhart*, 1978).

Pervasive practices often entail situations where discrimination is part of a "pattern or practice" where factors, such as seniority preferences, result in discrimination against a protected class (*Teamsters v. U.S.*, 1977). Here, employers may offer the statutory defense of *bona fide occupational qualification* (BFOQ) and argue that a job requirement has caused the discrimination. The requirement must be bona fide, in good faith, and reasonably necessary in the normal operation of the particular occupation involved. It can include restricting female correctional duties in an all-male maximum security prison (*Dothard v. Rawlinson*, 1977) and limiting peace officer status to U.S. citizens but cannot be grounded in race or ethnicity.

Disparate impact involves activities that, on their face, appear to be nondiscriminatory in nature but have an adverse impact on protected classes. Cases in this area are difficult to prove and usually entail the use of statistical measures to show that discrimination is not the result of mere chance (*Griggs v. Duke Power Co.*, 1971). Once the plaintiff has shown a disparate impact, the employer has the opportunity to prove the difference was based on a "business necessity" or resulted from some job-related difference (*Ward's Cove Packing Company, Inc. v. Atinio*, 1989).

While cases based on racial discrimination have produced most of the landmark decisions in this area, recently a highly litigated topic has been sexual harassment. Generally, four categories of this type of sexual discrimination are recognized: quid pro quo situations, where a supervisor demands sexual favors; special treatment, where rewards (such as promotions) are given based on sexual accommodation; sexual harassment of employees by outsiders; and hostile work environments.

Police chiefs and sheriffs have found themselves named as defendants in sexual harassment cases numerous times. For example, in *Gares v. Willingboro Township* (1996) a police chief, while he was a captain, subjected a female employee to continued harassment over a seven-year period. During this time, he called her sexually offensive names, such as "bimbo," "bimbette," "tramp," "mere woman," "trollop," "dumb blonde," and "Township slut," in the presence of her fellow employees; openly condon[ed] degrading conduct against female employees by other male employees under [his] direct supervision; permitt[ed] the open display of pornographic material in the office; encourag[ed] the public telling of obscene jokes; and touch[ed the plaintiff] in an unwelcome[d] and degrading manner, including at one point taunting her by holding her badge up out of her reach and pinning her body against the wall of his office with his own body. (*Gares v. Willingboro Township*, p. 723, 1996)

She was awarded damages against the township, as well as against the chief in his individual capacity. Chief executives often can avoid liability by taking quick action to thwart harassment. In *Munn v. City of Savannah* (1995), the chief of police was able to avoid liability because he took swift, albeit non-policy-consistent, action in response to a complaint.

The U.S. Supreme Court has ruled recently on several key sexual harassment issues. In *Burlington Industries, Inc. v. Ellerth* (1998), the Court ruled that an employee could sue for sexual harassment even though she was never treated adversely for refusing her supervisor's advances. Here, the plaintiff complained of "repeated boorish and offensive remarks and gestures . . . [and] comments 'which' could be construed as threats to deny her tangible job benefits" (p. 4229). The Court ruled that when an employee is subjected to such a hostile environment that has been created by an immediate supervisor, the employer can be held vicariously liable to the victimized employee. It ruled similarly in *Faragher v. City of Boca Raton* (1998), where a female lifeguard claimed that her supervisors created a sexually hostile environment by repeatedly subjecting her and other female lifeguards to "uninvited and offensive touching, by making lewd remarks, and by speaking of women in offensive terms" (p. 4228). The Court in both instances, however, held if the employee suffered no tangible adverse employment treatment, then the employer may raise an affirmative defense. "The defense comprises of two necessary elements: (a) that the employer exercised reasonable care to prevent and correct promptly any sexually harassing behavior, and (b) that the plaintiff employee unreasonably failed to take advantage of any preventive or corrective opportunities provided by the employer or to avoid harm otherwise" (p. 4276). Finally, in a third major case in this area, the Court expanded Title VII to include same sex harassment under certain circumstances in *Oncale v. Sundowner Offshore Services, Incorporated* (1998).

Much of the case law in this area has focused on discriminatory action based on race or gender. However, other forms of discrimination have been litigated as well. Title VII also protects the practice of religion and here there is a special statutory duty (§701(j)), which requires employers to "accommodate" employees. The U.S. Supreme Court has found that an employer cannot dock an employee's pay for religious holidays (*Ansonia Board of Education v. Philbrook*, 1987). However, "super special" arrangements, like guaranteeing an employee every Sunday off, are not required (*TWA, Inc. v. Hardison*, 1977). Transversely, statutory provisions allow for some special considerations for alienage and national origin issues. Here, police can restrict employment as certified officers to U.S. citizens (§701(h)), but discrimination based on an accent can be actionable (*Carino v. University of Oklahoma Bd. of Regents,* 1984).

As to other non–Title VII issues, the Age Discrimination in Employment Act (ADEA) protects individuals age 40 or over in the hiring, promotion, and retention/retirement processes. Generally, law enforcement is exempt from certain provisions if an age limit is imposed by state law and there is a bona fide retirement plan. Recently, the U.S. Supreme Court refined the definition of *age* in *O'Connor v. Consolidated Coin Caterers Corporation* (1996). The Court ruled that the 57-year-old plaintiff who had been replaced by someone who was also covered by the act (here a 40-year-old) had standing to sue.

The Americans with Disabilities Act (ADA) covers, among other things, people and situations. Workers who have a physical or mental impairment that substantially limits a major life activity, or have a record of such impairment, or are regarded as having a disability are protected. Recently, the U.S. Supreme Court added nonsymptomatic HIV-positive status to the physical and mental conditions covered by the ADA (*Bragdon v. Abbott,* 1998). It also ruled that state prisons are covered by the statutory definition of *public entity* and, therefore, come under the provisions of the ADA (*Pennsylvania Department of Corrections v. Yeskey,* 1998).

Law enforcement cases in this area are wide ranging. For example, when an African-American police officer sued under Title VII for discriminatory termination from the job, the court ruled that the officer's destruction of police contraband was a legitimate, nondiscriminatory reason for his discharge (*Murray v. City of Sapulpa,* 1995). A Tampa police detective was able to force his reinstatement with back pay under ADA after he was transferred to patrol because his hearing aids were thought to be a "health hazard" (*Kemp v. Monge,* 1996). Employment discrimination also can arise over pay issues, as it did in *Welch v. Laney* (1995). Here, a female employee of an Alabama sheriff's department was able to make a successful claim of discrimination when she proved that she was paid less than a male counterpart in violation of the federal Equal Pay Act. Finally, gender discrimination can also be raised via the equal protection clause of the Fourteenth Amendment. However, to be successful, the plaintiff must be able to provide specific evidence that the individual defendants involved were motivated by the improper desire to discriminate against the plaintiffs because of their gender (*Morrison-Tiffin v. Hampton,* 1995).

Other Employee Claims.   Other lawsuits filed by employees against their employers (usually, but not always under §1983) normally involve allegations of constitutional violations. The rights most often litigated include those covered by the First, Fourth, Fifth, and Fourteenth Amendments to the U.S. Constitution.

Police executives face employee charges that they allegedly engaged in conduct violating the First Amendment in two primary areas. The first deals with politically related activities and the other with personal conduct. As to political activities, in *Cromer v. Brown* (1996), a black captain in a sheriff's department successfully fought a demotion allegedly because he spoke out about racial discrimination in the agency. Likewise, a Boston police officer successfully sued the police commissioner and others for harassing him in retaliation over his exercising First Amendment rights as a union representative (*Broderick v. Roache*, 1993). Retaliation suits over political activity have also been filed by plaintiffs who supported other officers over the city mayor and his family (*Morro v. City of Birmingham*, 1997; Vaughn, 1997a) and where officers have declined to participate in electoral politicking (*Nessel v. City of Northlake*, 1994). However, such claims were not upheld when an officer engaged in political activity (participated in debate over the propriety of gun control legislation) while he was in uniform (*Thomas v. Whalen*, 1995).

On the personal side, officers also are successful litigating certain First Amendment rights. For example, the right to freedom of association can be successfully argued when intradepartmental marriage is at issue (*McCabe v. Sharrett*, 1994). However, chief executives can enjoy qualified immunity when the free speech involves a possible degradation of the departmental image (*Thomas v. Whalen*, 1995). Employees can utilize § 1983 and First Amendment claims to protect their careers. In *Darnell v. Ford*, (1990), a state trooper successfully sued a post commander under the First Amendment over disciplinary action that supposedly was motivated by a desire to mar the plaintiff's record and keep him from being promoted. In addition to these First Amendment claims, law enforcement employees litigate freedom of religion infringements.

Employees also have invoked their Fourth Amendment right to protection against unreasonable searches and seizures. Here, cases often stem from either conflicts over drug testing or litigation concerning searches of employee belongings. The U.S. Supreme Court ruled in *Skinner v. Railway Labor Executives' Association* (1989) that public agencies could conduct random drug testing. Most of the cases in this area have dealt with the accuracy of the tests (*Brown v. The City of Pompano Beach*, 1997) or collective bargaining disputes (*Beattie v. City of St. Petersburg Beach*, 1990). As to searches, in *O'Connor v. Ortega* (1987), the Court ruled that employers do not need to obtain a warrant or even have probable cause to search incident to an investigation of employee misconduct or for a noninvestigatory search that has a work-related purpose. Litigation by law enforcement officers in this area has been limited. However, in *Walker v. Darby* (1990), a postal worker sued his supervisor over surreptitious electronic eavesdropping of his conversations at work.

Fifth Amendment claims deal with self-incrimination. Here, employees sometimes are faced with answering questions that could have a condemnatory impact or severe sanctions from their employers. The general rule in an administrative investigation is that police officers can be compelled to provide information directly related to official duties but the results cannot be used in criminal proceedings (del Carmen, 1991; *Garrity v. New Jersey*, 1967; *Gardner v. Broderick*, 1968). If coerced to testify in an internal affairs investigation under threat of firing, officers should be able to invoke a *Garrity*-type immunity (*Benjamin v. City of Montgomery*, 1986). Another concern in this area relates to the use of the polygraph. Police officers have objected to its use on Fifth Amendment grounds and on the basis of a constitutionally protected property right of continued employment (*Hester v. City of Milledgeville*, 1984).

Police officers also may invoke Fourteenth Amendment protections against violations of due process and equal protection. Normally, cases arise over procedural due process claims as it did in *Everett v. Napper* (1987). Here, an Atlanta firefighter was suspended without pay for refusing to submit to a drug test. The Eleventh Circuit Court ruled that this was a violation of his Fourteenth Amendment procedural due process rights. On the other hand, the U.S. Supreme Court ruled that a public employee was not entitled to a hearing before being suspended for being arrested on a drug charge (*Gilbert v. Homar*, 1997).

Finally, a word about the Fair Labor Standards Act (FLSA) is in order. While this highly litigated topic is beyond the scope of this work, it should be noted that law enforcement executives often encounter controversy over wage issues, such as overtime. Section 7(k) of the act provides police, fire, and correctional agencies with a partial exemption from the overtime provisions. Nonetheless, conflicts still arise.

The FLSA was at issue in *Jones v. City of Columbus* (1997), where the dispute was whether the performance of emergency medical services by firefighters was included under "firefighting" duties and, therefore, would be considered under that aegis for overtime purposes. In a massive action against the City of Talladega, Alabama, Police Department, four sets of almost 60 plaintiffs sued to recover for overtime and meal breaks under the FLSA and for breach of contract over promises made in the department's policy manual (*Avery v. City of Talladega*, 1994). Plaintiffs litigated over the calculation of overtime (*Spires v. Ben Hill County*, 1993) and the application of the FLSA to collective bargaining agreements where private corporations are providing public safety to governmental entities (*Lee v. Flightsafety Services Corporation*, 1994). They also have claimed the right to overtime pay for police roll-call time and detective on-call time (*Birdwell v. City of Gadsden*, 1992) and sued over canine transport time (*Bolick v. Brevard County Sheriff's Department*, 1996). Finally, the Federal Eleventh Circuit Court of Appeals ruled that Miami SWAT team members could not collect under the FLSA for overtime spent on physical fitness (*Dade County, Florida v. Alvarez*, 1997).

PROBLEMS AND SOLUTIONS

While this chapter has presented a wide ranging discussion of executive liability, the principal problem to be addressed deals with liability on the part of the chief executive. Law enforcement leaders can find themselves liable in two capacities: personally and professionally. Personal liability normally attaches when chiefs and sheriffs exceed their authority and deviate from their recognized duties for personal gain. Personal liability also can attach statutorily. For example, the Fair Labor Standards Act (discussed previously) and the recently passed Family Medical Leave Act (which was beyond the scope of this chapter) both hold the policymaker personally liable for violations of the act. Personal liability means just that. A police chief or a sheriff can be held personally responsible for the payment of a judgment.

Professional liability, on the other hand, attaches to the job or office. Here, chiefs and sheriffs are held liable in their official capacities. As a policymaker or executive in a governmental entity, defendants found liable in their official capacities actually make the agency or entity liable. Any judgments assessed, therefore, should be the responsibility of the city or county involved.

Being found legally responsible in either capacity is neither pleasant nor career enhancing. While liability at the "official" level may not cost a chief or a sheriff personally, it may cost the executive his or her job. Solutions to these problems come in two varieties. First, a number of very effective defenses are available that can assist an executive in escaping liability. In addition, several simple preventive steps can be taken that may obviate the problem in the first place.

Defenses

While it may seem that the law enforcement community is under the constant threat of a civil lawsuit, it must be remembered that certain defenses and privileges are available in many circumstances. For example, in assault and battery, excessive force, and wrongful death cases, *self-defense* can be used to ward off judgments. Claims of abuse of process, malicious prosecution, and false arrest or imprisonment can be countered with a *probable cause* defense. Here, the defendant must show that even though an arrest might have been nullified later, probable cause existed at the time. *Consent* of the plaintiff can be a very effective defense against most claims as well. A claim that the action was *necessary* can be made when the action that caused injury was required to prevent a crime or a greater harm. The *public duty* doctrine also provides protection from judgment when an individual plaintiff might be harmed as a result of some negligent failure to protect on the part of police. *Contributory negligence, comparative negligence,* and *assumption of risk* can operate as defenses as well. Here, the plaintiff lessens or negates the defendant's liability by acting negligently or assuming responsibility for injurious actions. Finally, defendants can claim they were acting under the *authority of law* when the plaintiff sustained injury.

This last defense, commonly referred to as *qualified immunity,* generally is available if the defendant was carrying out discretionary duties and acting in "good faith." Similar defenses are available in §1983 actions. Qualified immunity is available, particularly to chief executives in their individual capacity, as are the defenses of *probable cause* and *good faith.* However, these latter defenses have specific limitations and conditions.

The concept of immunity stems from the notion that the Crown can do no wrong and, therefore, should not be subjected to suit. This *sovereign immunity* technically is available to states and counties, as well as the federal government. However, most states have waived this immunity by passing state tort acts that allow citizens to sue cities, counties, and the state under certain conditions (*Mullins v. Friend,* 1994; *Gilbert v. Richardson,* 1994). Municipalities and chief executives sued in their official capacities enjoy no immunity in §1983 actions (*Monell v. Department of Social Services,* 1978; *Owens v. City of Independence,* 1980), but executives often will be found to have "qualified immunity" against individual capacity suits.

The test for qualified immunity in §1983 actions was set forth in *Harlow v. Fitzgerald* (1982). It was based on the notion that

> government officials performing discretionary functions generally are shielded from liability for civil damages insofar as their conduct [did] not violate clearly established statutory or constitutional rights of which a reasonable person would have known. (p. 818)

Discretionary acts are covered by qualified immunity whereas ministerial acts are not. This is based in part on the unwillingness of courts to second-guess a discretionary decision where, by definition, more than one avenue was available. Ministerial acts, on the other hand, carry no official immunity. Here, the officer is acting according to policy but should be able to escape personal liability because the acts in question were mandated by policy.

To distinguish between the two, the decision of a chief of police to fire an officer normally is discretionary and, therefore, immunity often is available. On the other hand, the process that must be followed to terminate someone's employment is set by policy and is ministerial. Therefore, to qualify for immunity, the chief executive must be acting within the scope of employment, performing a discretionary act that could not have been reasonably foreseen as unlawful at the time of the act.

The Court clarified the issue of what is a "clearly established right" in *Anderson v. Creighton* (1987) when it ruled that "[t]he contours of the right must be sufficiently clear that a reasonable official would understand that what he is doing violates that right" (p. 640). Most federal circuits have decided that if a law enforcement officer or chief asserts a claim of qualified immunity from liability, the court must determine two factors: Was the law governing the conduct clearly established and could a reasonable officer have believed the conduct was lawful (*Act Up!/Portland v. Bagley*, 1993)? Whether a chief executive may be held personally liable for an allegedly unlawful official action generally turns on the "objective legal reasonableness" of the action in question.

Other defenses to §1983 actions include acting on probable cause, operating in good faith, and acting within the scope of employment. All three of these rejoinders have one common denominator: The defendant in question reasonably believes that the actions taken were justifiable under the law. Either there was probable cause to conduct a search or make an arrest, or the action was based on a "good faith" belief that a policy or regulation was valid at the time, or the act clearly fell within the actor's duties as a law enforcement official.

Preventive Measures

While police chiefs and sheriffs obviously want to avoid being held liable, preventive measures can be alluding. Chief executives are under tremendous pressure to control crime, budgets, and personnel simultaneously. However, in the long run, it is cheaper, easier, and fairer to everyone involved to try to circumvent litigation than to defend against charges of misconduct. Preventive measures can be divided into four broad categories. Three deal with active measures and the last concerns a shift in mind set.

First, police executives should try to forestall litigation by keeping up-to-date. Here, training and education are key elements. They also can guard against litigation by soliciting input from reliable subordinates and experts. In addition, administrators can thwart lawsuits by taking a proactive approach. Here, creating sound, defensible policy and following it up are key factors.

Chiefs and sheriffs also can engage in better damage control. Once a problem has been uncovered, it should be dealt with swiftly and accurately. Here, effective training programs can be an excellent defense. The last thing an executive should do is ignore the problem in the hopes that it will never be noticed.

The third measure deals with situations where actions have been filed and liability admitted or adjudged. In correcting problems after the fact, chief executives should follow court orders carefully, even going back to the court for clarification if need be.

Finally, in today's highly litigious environment, it is best for law enforcement administrators to keep three idioms in mind:

- Plaintiffs don't sue loved ones.
- Winning a lawsuit can be a terrible thing to do.
- Understanding the law is far better than knowing it.

The first platitude, on the surface, appears to be a falsehood. Husbands sue wives, wives sue husbands, children sue parents, neighbors sue each other, and so on. However, seldom will you find a "loved one"—someone who cares deeply for you—on the other side of the Bailey. When we love someone, we try to work out the difficulties or we live with them. We do not file suit.

There are not many loved ones in law enforcement. While a chief or sheriff has many so-called friends, few of them could be characterized as endearing in nature. However, the nature of most of these relationships is under the control of the chief executive. Employees who are treated fairly and given the opportunity to express their opinions and disagree without fear of reprisal often will be happier, more productive, and less litigious than their counterparts.

When the citizenry believes in its law enforcement agency and the agency head, it will provide support and assistance. Nothing will eliminate the possibility of a lawsuit from a disgruntled employee or an irate citizen. Nonetheless, if this disgruntlement is based in laziness or an attempt to "beat the system," and if the "irateness" really is just retaliation for evenhanded enforcement, then the executive has little to fear from the courts. Great fear can sweep over a chief or sheriff when model employees and respected citizens resort to lawsuits. But if they are "loved ones," it is much more likely that they will try to work things out rather than sue.

The second idiom presents its own set of contradictions. It implies that one should try to lose a lawsuit. That is not only ridiculous but illogical. However, lawsuits often can be just the catalyst needed to spawn improvements and increase equity in an unequal process. This is particularly true in law enforcement and other criminal justice agencies. When budgets are tight and needs are great, a lawsuit can bring things into focus. A settlement can provide the punch for the much-needed change, championed by both sides.

On the other hand, when a law enforcement agency is able to escape unscathed from a lawsuit, it often misinterprets victory as endorsement. Seldom will a suit make it past the pleadings stage without the existence of judicable facts. In civil suits, injuries have been claimed and a culprit has been identified: a public law enforcement agency in this case. When litigation over the behavior of one or more officers results in a judgment for the defense, this should not necessarily be interpreted as a ratification of that behavior, as it often is. Rather, it should cause the top administrator to scrutinize practices that led to the lawsuit to determine how the disagreement and subsequent litigation could have been avoided.

The third platitude is not a redundancy: Law enforcement officers and executives alike know the law and can even cite the case that stands for a certain principle. However, all too often they do not really understand the law and why or how it developed. While the first two idioms are quite important and deserve attention, this third theorem is the focus of this chapter. Here, we examined the nature of civil liability for law enforcement executives and explored the primary areas of major concern. The purpose was to acquaint the reader with the myriad of problems surrounding the issue of liability and illustrate how to (and not to) deal with these problems.

CONCLUSION

While law enforcement executives may have to live under the constant threat of civil litigation, they do not have to live in ignorance of the law or its parameters. This chapter explores the nature of civil litigation and discusses the attachment of liability. To file a lawsuit, a prospective plaintiff must find a cause of action in either the statutes or common law. In addition, police leaders field threats of civil litigation from two sets of plaintiffs (the citizenry and employees) and these would-be opponents can attack on three fronts: state torts, federal statutes, and constitutional violations.

State torts come in two varieties. One type includes intentional torts, which involve purposeful action. The other kind contains negligence, which, by definition, is accidental. At the federal level, lawsuits can be filed utilizing a variety of statutes, including §1983 and a host of fair employment laws. Furthermore, citizens, as well as employees, can file for alleged violations of the U.S. Constitution.

Finally, police chiefs and sheriffs can be sued in their personal, as well as their official, capacities. When sued personally, they can become individually liable for judgments. But certain defenses and privileges are available and certain preventive measures can and should be taken to avoid or deal with liability problems. While these measures may not work all the time, the chief executive who treats employees fairly, provides the citizenry with solid, evenhanded enforcement, and prepares for litigation by becoming better educated and informed most likely will be able to live peacefully under this constant threat of litigation.

ACKNOWLEDGMENTS

I would like to express my appreciation to Michael Vaughn, Georgia State University, and Dale Mann, Georgia Public Safety Training Center, for their suggestions and helpful comments.

DISCUSSION QUESTIONS

1. What is a "cause of action" and why is it important to the initiation of a lawsuit?
2. Explain the difference between an intentional tort and negligence. What are the elements of each? How do they differ in their treatment of intent?
3. Compare and contrast the state tort of negligent failure to protect and the federal §1983 claim of negligent failure to train. Could a police chief or sheriff do both at the same time? Explain why or why not.
4. Discuss the concept of chiefs and sheriffs being held liable in their professional capacity and compare this to personal liability.
5. Explain how a police chief or sheriff can use qualified immunity to avoid liability. Is it fair for a sheriff to avoid responsibility they way Sheriff Moore did in *Bryan County v. Brown* (1997)?
6. What measures can a police chief or sheriff take to prevent liability? Does he or she have more to fear from employees or citizens? Why?

REFERENCES

Act Up!/Portland v. Bagley, 988 F.2d 868 (9th Cir. 1993).
Age Discrimination in Employment Act of 1975 (29 U.S.C. §621).
Americans with Disabilities Act of 1990 (42 U.S.C. §12101).
Anderson v. Creighton, 483 U.S. 635 (1987).
Androw v. Johnson, 623 F.Supp. 1085 (N.D. Il. 1985).
Ansonia Board of Education v. Philbrook, 479 U.S. 60 (1987).
Ashton v. Brown, 660 A.2d 447 (Md. 1995).
Avery v. City of Talladega, 24 F.3d 1337 (11th Cir. 1994).
Avery, M., and D. Rudovsky. *Police Misconduct: Law and Litigation.* Deerfield, IL: Clark, Boardman, Callaghan, 1995.
Beattie v. City of St. Petersburg Beach, 733 F.Supp. 1455 (M.D. Fla. 1990).
Benjamin v. City of Montgomery, 785 F.2d 959 (11th Cir. 1986).
Birdwell v. City of Gadsden, 970 F.2d 802 (11th Cir. 1992).
Bolick v. Brevard County Sheriff's Department, 937 F.Supp. 1560 (M.D. Fla. 1996).
Bragdon v. Abbott, 1998 U.S. LEXIS 4212.
Broderick v. Roache, 996 F.2d 1294 (1st Cir. 1993).

Brown v. The City of Pompano Beach, 969 F.Supp. 1317 (S.D. Fla. 1997).
Bryan County v. Brown, 520 U.S. 397 (1997).
Buffkins v. City of Omaha, 922 F.2d 465 (8th Cir. 1990).
Burlington Industries, Inc. v. Ellerth, 1998 U.S. LEXIS 4217.
Carino v. University of Oklahoma Bd. of Regents, 750 F.2d 815 (10th Cir. 1984).
City of Canton v. Harris, 489 U.S. 378 (1989).
City of Rome v. Jordan, 426 S.E.2d 861 (Ga. 1993).
City of St. Louis v. Praprotnik, 485 U.S. 112 (1988).
Collins v. City of Harker Heights, 503 U.S. 115 (1992).
Cound, J. J., J. H. Friedenthal, A. R. Miller, and J. E. Sexton. *Civil Procedure,* 5th ed. Saint Paul, MN: West Publishing Company, 1989.
County of Sacramento v. Lewis, 118 S. Ct. 1708 (1998).
Cromer v. Brown, 88 F.3d 1315 (4th Cir. 1996).
Dade County, Florida v. Alvarez, 124 F.3d 1380 (11th Cir. 1997).
Darnell v. Ford, 903 F.2d 556 (8th Cir. 1990).
Darrow v. Schumacher, 495 N.W.2d 511 (S.D. 1993).
del Carmen, R. V. "An overview of criminal and civil liabilities of police officers and departments." *American Journal of Criminal Law* 9, no. 1 (1981), pp. 31–36.
_____. *Civil Liability in American Policing.* Englewood Cliffs, NJ: Brady/Prentice-Hall, 1991.
DeShanney v. Winnebago County Department of Social Services, 489 U.S. 189 (1989).
Dewell v. Lawson, 489 F.2d 877 (10th Cir. 1974).
Dobos v. Driscoll, 537 N.E. 2d 558 (Mass. 1989).
Dothard v. Rawlinson, 433 US 321 (1977).
Equal Pay Act of 1963 (29 U.S.C. §206(d)).
Everett v. Napper, 833 F.2d 1507 (11th Cir.1987).
Fair Employment Practices Act of 1978 (O.C.G.A. §45-19-20).
Fair Labor Standards Act (29 U.S.C. §201).
Faragher v. City of Boca Raton, 1998 U.S. LEXIS 4216.
Ford v. Breier, 383 F.Supp. 505 (E.D. Wis. 1974).
Fuller v. M.G. Jewelry, 950 F.2d 1437 (9th Cir. 1991).
Fundiller v. City of Cooper City, 777 F.2d 1436 (11th Cir. 1985).
Gardner v. Broderick, 392 U.S. 273 (1968).
Gares v. Willingboro Township, 90 F.3d 720 (3rd Cir. 1996).
Garrity v. New Jersey, 385 U.S. 493 (1967).
Gilbert v. Homar, 117 S.Ct. 1807 (1997).
Gilbert v. Richardson, 452 S.E.2d 476 (Ga. 1994).
Griggs v. Duke Power Co., 401 US 424 (1971).
Guzman v. City of San Antonio, 766 S.W.2d 858 (Tex. App. 1989).
Harlow v. Fitzgerald, 457 U.S. 800, 818 (1982).
Harris v. News-Sun, 269 Ill.App.3d 648 (1995).
Haydock, R., and J. Sonsteng. *Trial: Theories, Tactics, Techniques.* Saint Paul, MN: West Publishing Company, 1991.
Hester v. City of Milledgeville, 598 F.Supp. 1456 (M.D. Ga. 1984).
Hinshaw v. Doffer, 785 F.2d 1260, 1263 (5th Cir.1986).
Jean W. v. Commonwealth, 610 N.E.2d 305 (Mass. 1993).
J.H. by D.H. v. West Valley City, 840 P.2d 115 (Utah 1992).
Jones v. City of Columbus, 120 F.3d 248 (11th Cir. 1997).
Kappeler, V. E. *Critical Issues in Police Civil Liability.* Cincinnati: Anderson Publishing Company, 1993.

_____. *Critical Issues in Police Civil Liability*, 2nd ed. Cincinnati: Anderson Publishing Company, 1997.

_____, S. V. Kappeler, and R. V. del Carmen. "A content analysis of police civil liability cases: Decisions of the federal district courts." *Journal of Criminal Justice* 21, no. 4 (1993), pp. 325–337.

_____, M. S. Vaughn, and R. V. del Carmen. "Death in detention: An analysis of police liability for negligent failure to prevent suicide." *Journal of Criminal Justice* 19, no. 4 (1991), pp. 381–393.

Keeton, W. P. *Prosser and Keeton on the Law of Torts*, 5th ed. Saint Paul, MN: West Publishing Company, 1984.

Kemp v. Monge, 919 F.Supp. 404 (M.D. Fla. 1996).

Lee v. Flightsafety Services Corporation, 20 F.3d 428 (11th Cir. 1994).

Los Angeles Department of Water & Power v. Manhart, 435 US 702 (1978).

Lusby v. T.G. & Y. Stores, 749 F.2d 1423 (10th Cir. 1984).

Mackinney v. Nielsen, 69 F.3d 1002 (9th Cir. 1995).

Maclin v. Paulson, 626 F.2d 83 (7th Cir. 1980).

Mann v. City of Albany, 883 F.2d 999 (11th Cir. 1989).

Marley v. City of Allentown, 774 F.Supp. 343 (E.D.Pa. 1991).

Mary M. v. City of Los Angeles, 814 P.2d 1341 (Cal. 1991).

McCabe v. Sharrett, 12 F.3d 1558 (11th Cir. 1994).

McClelland v. Facteau, 610 F.2d 693 (10th Cir.1979).

McDonnell Douglas Corp. v. Green, 411 U.S. 792 (1973).

McQurter v. City of Atlanta, 572 F.Supp. 401 (N.D. Ga. 1983).

Mon v. City of New York, 557 N.Y.S.2d 925 (A.D. 1 Dept. 1990).

Monell v. Department of Social Services, 436 U.S. 658 (1978).

Monroe v. Pape, 365 U.S. 167 (1961).

Morrison-Tiffin v. Hampton, 451 S.E.2d 650 (N.C. 1995).

Morro v. City of Birmingham, 117 F.3d 508 (11th 1997).

Mulhern v. City of Scottsdale, 799 P.2d 15 (Ariz.App. 1990).

Mullins v. Friend, 448 S.E.2d 227 (N.C. 1994).

Munn v. City of Savannah, 906 F.Supp. 1577 (1995).

Murray v. City Of Sapulpa, 45 F.3d 1417 (1995).

Narney v. Daniels, 846 P.2d 347 (N.M.App. 1992).

Nessel v. City of Northlake, 1994 WL 685511 (1994).

O'Connor v. Consolidated Coin Caterers Corporation, 517 U.S. 308 (1996).

O'Connor v. Ortega, 480 U.S. 709 (1987).

Oncale v. Sundowner Offshore Services, Incorporated, 118 S. Ct. 998 (1998).

Owens v. City of Independence, 455 U.S. 622 (1980).

Pembaur v. City of Cincinnati, 475 U.S. 469 (1986).

Pennsylvania Department of Corrections v. Yeskey, 118 S. Ct. 1952 (1998).

Randle v. City of Aurora, 69 F.3d 441 (10th Cir. 1995).

Roberts v. Benoit, 603 So.2d 150 (La. 1992).

Robinson v. Shell Oil Company, 519 U.S. 337 (1997).

Santiago v. Fenton, 891 F.2d 373 (1st Cir. 1989).

Savannah v. Wilson, 214 Ga.App. 170 (1994).

Section 1983 (42 U.S.C. §1983).

Silver, I. *Police Civil Liability*. New York: Mathew Binder, 1996.

Skinner v. Railway Labor Executives' Association, 489 U.S. 602 (1989).

Smith v. Holeman, 212 Ga.App. 158 (1994).

Spires v. Ben Hill County, 980 F.2d 683 (11th Cir. 1993).

St. Louis v. Praprotnik, 485 U.S. 112 (1988).

Steinglass, S. H. *Section 1983 Litigation in State Courts.* Deerfield, IL: Clark, Boardman, Callaghan, 1994.

Teamsters v. U.S., 431 US 324 (1977).

Thomas v. Whalen, 51 F.3d 1285 (6th Cir. 1995).

Thompson v. City of Lawrence, 58 F.3d 1511 (10th Cir. 1995).

Title VII of the Civil Rights Act of 1964 (42 U.S.C. §1000(e)).

TWA, Inc. v. Hardison, 432 US 63 (1977).

Vaughn, M. S. "Police civil liability for abandonment in high crime areas and other high risk situations." *Journal of Criminal Justice* 22, no. 5 (1994), pp. 407–424.

_____. "Police civil liability and the first amendment: Retaliation against citizens who criticize and challenge the police." *Crime and Delinquency* 42, no. 1 (1996), pp. 50–75.

_____. "First amendment civil liability against law enforcement supervisors for violating their subordinates' rights to engage in overt political expression." *Policing: An International Journal of Police Strategies and Management* 20, no. 2 (1997a), pp. 270–291.

_____. "Political patronage in law enforcement: Civil liability against police supervisors for violating their subordinates' First Amendment rights." *Journal of Criminal Justice* 25, no. 5 (1997b), pp. 347–366.

_____ and L. F. Coomees. "Police civil liability under Section 1983: When do police officers act under the color of law?" *Journal of Criminal Justice* 23, no. 5 (1995), pp. 395–415.

Walker v. Darby, 911 F.2d 1573 (11th 1990).

Ward's Cove Packing Company, Inc. v. Atinio, 487 U.S. 1232 (1989).

Welch v. Laney, 57 F.3d 1004 (11th Cir. 1995).

Yates v. City of Cleveland, 941 F.2d 444 (6th Cir. 1991).

Zimmer, M. J., C. A. Sullivan, and R. F. Richards. (1988). *Cases and Materials on Employment Discrimination,* 2nd ed. Boston: Little, Brown and Company, 1988.

Chapter 8

Wellness: A Matter of Health

Richard H. Martin, Elgin Community College

We all have seen at least one police officer whose belly hangs over the gun belt and who looks like, if he walked too fast, let alone had to run, he would not get very far. For many years, a lack of fitness was a common sight among older police officers. In more recent years, fewer officers appear to be badly out of shape or unfit. One reason for this change has been the adoption of the idea that a fit officer is a better officer, who is less of a liability to the community and the organization. This idea has risen to the creation of "wellness" programs.

The term *wellness* refers to "the active process of becoming aware of and making choices to create a healthier life, in all of life's dimensions" (Donatelle, Snow-Harter, and Wilcox, 1997, p. 7). Other writers explain that a wellness program "relies on individual fitness regimes prescribed according to the individual's specific needs, with the goal of maintaining or enhancing fitness over a period of time" (Copay and Charles, 1998, p. 416). Police officer wellness, an attempt to reach and maintain optimum health, is an emerging managerial concern. As you know, policing can be stressful and hazardous. A fit officer will be in a much better position to tackle job tasks and cope with occupational pressures. As we see in this chapter, police organizations are beginning to realize a wide range of benefits is to be had simply by concentrating on the theme of employee wellness.

Certain topics immediately spring to mind when people talk about health and wellness. They include exercise, eating habits, nutritional diets, and healthy lifestyle choices, such as refraining from drugs, alcohol, and tobacco. Changes in these areas can help ward off or reduce stress and the accompanying chemical reactions within the body when it responds to a threat. In addition, medical experts agree that reaching and maintaining a healthy body weight reduces the risk of high blood pressure and other cardiovascular disorders. Furthermore, weight maintenance can improve blood sugar utilization, lower cholesterol levels, and decrease coronary disease. Stress also can be reduced by improving job skills.

One skill that will be addressed in this chapter is self-defense. Defensive tactics, even before using the option of deadly force, may be necessary to save officers' lives. Generally, self-defense and stress control through martial arts are not considered for a departmental fitness program. Traditionally, people look for running and weight lifting programs at health clubs for exercise. Not only can self-defense be a complete exercise program, it can hone skills and develop confidence to control stress during many stressful job functions. It is hoped that administrators will see the value of developing fitness programs and encourage wellness.

The reality that policing contributes to a precipitous decline in one's health and fitness is no secret. The job itself is very sedentary. Officers spend a great deal of time sitting behind the wheel of a patrol vehicle. Shift-work, rotating assignments around the clock, stress, convenient fatty fast foods, heavy smoking, drinking, and sudden physical exertion all are lethal ingredients. Every year more officers die from a heart attack while on duty than are killed during a physical attack (Rachlin, 1996). Premature heart disease is higher among officers than civilians of similar ages in other occupations. The Institute of Aerobic Research (Rachlin, 1996) states that police officers over the age of 30 frequently are less physically fit than the general population. In short, the profile of a police officer, which includes poor aerobic conditioning teamed with sudden strenuous exertion, requires attention.

Since policing contributes to the decline of one's health and abilities even though fitness and abilities are required for the job, police administrators need to make changes for their personnel. Studies have shown that fitness is required to perform the functions of policing. Some common physical requirements of police work include wrestling, running, pulling, pushing, climbing, twisting, bending, and running. Any of these activities can be used to save a life. If an officer cannot perform any of these functions, somebody's life may be lost. Couper (1983) concludes that police departments should enforce minimum fitness standards to include those pertaining to general health and physical fitness. A balanced diet and routine physical exercise provide officers the ability to perform duties of the job and control negative stress physically and emotionally (Couper, 1983). In *Parker v. District of Columbia* (1988), an officer could not subdue a suspect and shot him. The court ruled that liability could be imposed on a municipality if it showed indifference toward adequate training of officers. The officer in this case had to resort to his firearm because he was physically unable to subdue the suspect.

In this chapter, we look at how tobacco, alcohol, and poor physical conditioning in general affects the mortality and morbidity of police officers and their ability to control stress in their lives and jobs. We see how police officers are in poorer physical condition than the general public and how stress can lead to idleness, the need to rely on excessive force, and increased liability to agencies. Good conditioning will decrease the costs of police downtime from illness and injury. We approach the concept of wellness from a holistic viewpoint, illustrating that not only the traditional methods of fitness programs, such as running, weight training, and diet, but also self-defense training and martial arts are alternative approaches to wellness. We see how stress plays an important part of the deterioration of police officer health and how stress management can be controlled by learning exceptional skills in dealing with the functions of the job. In short, the position taken in this chapter is that self-defense training, good nutrition, and aerobic exercise will decrease the liability of agencies and improve the effectiveness of officers.

THE HEALTH TOLL OF POLICE WORK

Being physically fit offers many advantages. Increased health benefits, better self-esteem and confidence, and less loss of self-control because of stress are a few benefits that immediately come to mind. Cardiovascular efficiency not only helps the heart but also aids in reduced recovery time after an injury, illness, or stress. Enhanced muscle tone, increased strength, more flexibility, and higher endurance levels translate into better daily functioning, more stamina, and fewer injuries from pulls and strains. Higher levels of fitness strengthen the immune system, reduce infections and chronic disease, and promote better stress management. Better stress management, in turn, will lead to fewer citizen complaints against officers and their agencies and reduce situations of liability. All these are very important issues for police officers and police administrators, especially the relationships between fitness and heart aliments and between stress and agency liability.

According to Collingwood (1988), research about the physical fitness of police officers indicates the capacity for low-work, a high incidence of early retirement and disability, a high mortality rate, and higher than average health risk. The International Association of Chiefs of Police (IACP) found in a two-year study that police have a heart attack risk higher than the general population, resulting from high job stress and sedentary work, smoking, and poor diets (Collingwood, 1988).

Aging results in a decline in the heart's ability to pump blood and deliver oxygen while removing metabolic waste products. The components of cardiovascular pump performance are the maximal heart rate that can be achieved, the size and contractibility of heart muscles, and the stiffness or flexibility of the vessels (Seiler, 1996). Heart rate ranges between 220 for young children to about 180 for men age 60 or more. The heart rate decreases due to aging. There is no strong evidence to suggest that training can influence the decline in the heart rate. Although heart size in active older adults has been shown to be similar to that of active youth, it is larger than their sedentary, same-aged peers. Maximal stroke volume of blood pumped by the heart appears to decrease because of a reduction in physical training and a loss in the elasticity of the vessels, which increases the peripheral resistance and elevates blood pressure. Increased peripheral resistance produces a decrease in maximal blood flow to working muscles (Seiler, 1996). Good breathing techniques, such as *qi gong*, help oxygenate the muscles (cardiopulmonary efficiency) during training and while at rest.

Research on *qi gong* breathing techniques shows an increase in lung capacity over others in that age group who are not using the techniques. The two-year research also illustrated that although lung capacity generally declines in the early to mid-30s, those involved in the experiment did not decline. The test group included subjects between the ages of 30 and 65 (Massey et al., 1993). Since aging affects the heart's efficiency, it is imperative that a regimen of regular exercise for officers be implemented to help the heart maintain efficiency superior to that of their sedentary peers of the same age group.

Numerous studies in China and Japan have been conducted on the effects of *qi gong*. It is an energy-based exercise but does not focus on defensive tactics like tai chi. *Qi gong* concentrates on breathing and cardiopulmonary functioning. *Qi gong* has been used in clinical settings to improve health and wellness. It has proven to bring positive results with high blood pressure, stroke, cardiovascular efficiency, bone density, sex hormone levels, cancer, and even early stages of senility (Seaward, 1997). Data indicate that *qi gong* can be a significant factor in promoting health. Similar studies in the United States are taking place with support by the National Institute of Health's Office of Alternative Medicine (Seaward, 1997).

After age 25, aerobic fitness declines each year at a rate of 1% per year. Without aerobic fitness, the decline is much faster (Donatelle et al., 1997). The prevalence of obesity in the American adult population is 27% for women and 24% for men. One in three people over age 45 is obese, mostly because of reduced physical activity. Only 25% of the variability of body fat on the body is genetic. Therefore, officers can control how much body fat they carry and how much they weigh by the amount of exercise and how much food they eat (Donatelle et al., 1997).

Research comparing police victims of heart attacks with the number of officers killed in the line of duty shows the number of officers killed feloniously was minuscule. This finding led the Nassau County (New York) Police Department to begin a voluntary fitness program in 1994. Of the 3,100 officers in that agency, 1,500 are striving to achieve better health (Rachlin, 1996). Administrators first worked with union leaders and informed them that the new fitness program was intended to reduce heart attacks and that it was strictly voluntary. No one would lose his or her job for not participating. It was also pointed out that officers dying of heart attacks while lifting or chasing were not treated the same as those who were killed in the line of duty (Rachlin, 1996).

In addition to preventing heart disease, fitness programs can do much to help reduce back injuries. According to the American Association of Occupational Health Nurses (Pucetti, 1995), 85% of all adults suffer from back pain at some point in their lives. The annual cost for back problems, which includes compensation benefits, medical treatment, and pensions, topples the $14 billion mark. In 1992, for example, more than 800,000 disabling back injuries were related to work. Back injury to people below the age of 45 is the leading cause of disability in this country. The ITT Hartford Life Insurance Companies estimate that 8% of a company's payroll goes to covering disability costs (Puccetti, 1995). Obviously, prevention can be less expensive and result in more productive employees.

Yoga and tai chi exercises are used in the treatment of back problems at the Alexian Brothers' Medical Center in Elk Grove Village, Illinois. Although scientific research has been scarce, it is now beginning to emerge. The clinic, Alt-Med, offers a successful alternative treatment to surgery. In three years, the clinic has had over a 90% pain-resolution success rate for persons with chronic and acute back pain who have not had back surgery (Karuhn, 1994). The same exercises can be used in a fitness program to prevent back problems.

Police administrators need to provide fitness programs in an effort to cut down worker compensation claims. Over a two-year period, officers in the Elgin (Illinois) Police Department (EPD) filed 110 workers compensation claims. The EPD roster contains 159 sworn personnel. The claims represent 30% and 38% of the officers for each of the two years, respectively. During fiscal year 1996–97, 49 EPD officers incurred $112,475 in workers compensation claims. That figure reached $229,803 for 61 worker compensation claims in fiscal year 1997–98. To put these dollar amounts into a meaningful context, the annual in-service training budget for the entire EPD hovers at the $100,000 mark (Sarro, 1998). While one can only guess how many claims a fitness program could have prevented, it is pretty clear that changes would be welcomed.

Research into the physical fitness of police officers finds a low capacity for physical activity, a high incidence of early retirement, greater disability rates, an excessive mortality rate, and a higher-than-average health risk in this group (Collingwood, 1988). The IACP-sponsored study indicates that police officers have a heart attack risk that is higher than the general population. Much of this debilitation is attributed to high job stress and sedentary work, smoking, and poor dietary habits (Collingwood, 1988). As you can see, health issues ought to be of paramount importance to police administrators.

THE REALITY OF POLICE WORK

According to Alpert and Dunham (1998), relatively few police officers are killed in the line of duty. However, around 15% of all police officers are assaulted every year and approximately 21,000 officers sustain injuries from these incidents. Most assaults stem from an attempt to escape custody (Doerner, 1998, pp. 201–203). As one might imagine, the constant threat of violence has a corrosive emotional impact on officers (Alpert and Dunham, 1998).

These figures are instructive because they indicate that physical confrontations are a foreseeable event in police work, making physical fitness an imperative. One good argument in favor of fitness standards being job related comes from an understanding of the people with whom the police have contact. Men between the ages of 16 and 24 are responsible for the majority of crime in this country. This profile does not change much from one year to the next. For our purposes, this observation boils down to the fact that the police are fighting criminals who generally are in better physical shape than they. It stands to reason, then, that physical fitness is not a luxury for police officers; it is an absolute occupational necessity.

Given this information, one would think that police officers should, and would, want to better their conditioning. For example, Copay and Charles (1998) report that incoming police academy recruits tend to register average fitness scores. Krajick (1979) also finds that officers between the ages of 21 and 35 were in average physical condition, which medical doctors readily admit is terrible. Furthermore, officers between the ages of 36 and 52 are in worse shape than their counterparts in other occupations. Additional proof comes in the form of *life expectancies*, how long one can expect to live. The average police officer does not live long enough to enjoy the "golden years." The typical police officer is dead by age 60. When compared to the general population, the average police officer can expect to have 15 fewer years of life.

COST OF ABSENTEEISM

Exact workers compensation costs charged to the police sector are not readily available. However, one can arrive at an estimate for these expenditures. Suppose that the average yearly salary is $40,000 for all levels of officers under the position of chief. This figure works out to approximately $20 per hour. An annual downtime of ten days spells a staggering cost for police organizations. For example, if there are 21,000 injuries to officers annually (Maguire and Pastore, 1998) and these officers are off-duty for an average of five to ten days, the total cost lies somewhere between $16 and $33 million in lost productivity ($20 per hour multiplied by an eight-hour workday equals $160 per day, which when multiplied by five days yields $800, which is then multiplied by 21,000 for a grand total of $16.8 million). An emphasis on defensive training, in addition to physical fitness, will help deflect these costs, let alone the untold costs stemming from lawsuits involving excessive force. As you can see, it is in the best interest of police managers to encourage defensive tactics training as part of a departmental total wellness program.

TRENDS IN POLICE FITNESS REQUIREMENTS

By now, you are well aware that a number of perils are associated with policing. The debilitating consequences of such risks as heart disease, diabetes, high blood pressure, colon cancer, depression, and anxiety are well documented. Given this background, what exactly are police agencies doing to combat this problem?

Just about every law enforcement agency in this country requires incoming personnel to demonstrate some level of fitness prior to being hired. These entrance standards range from checking cholesterol levels to heart monitoring to demonstrations of physical capability. Unfortunately, in-service practices do not always mirror preservice requirements. Regulations or policies addressing postacademy fitness are noticeably absent in many agencies. Garner (1997), for example, surveyed 63 municipal police agencies and sheriffs departments in Texas. Only three agencies had a mandatory fitness program for officers. Almost two-thirds of the departments had no directives at all pertaining to officer conditioning.

A police fitness program should consist of a uniform system for wellness management, provide standards that promote the attainment and retention of good health and physical fitness, and enhance the overall effectiveness of the agency. Departments that have been successful in requiring ongoing fitness standards for employees also have disciplinary measures in place for those not meeting the standards. Furthermore, as Professor Camp explains in Chapter 7, negligent failure to train can cost an agency severely. Usually, litigation against agencies for failure to train flows from two sources. The first are citizens whose rights have been violated by an officer who lacks proper training. The second source are subordinates who suffer injuries in the course of duty because of insufficient training (del Carmen, 1994).

One pocket of resistance to mandatory in-service fitness standards are collective bargaining units. It can be extremely difficult to get unions to conform voluntarily with fitness standards. As Professors Hunter and Merritt explain in Chapter 10, the purpose of a bargaining unit is to protect job rights. Consequently, these units are quite reluctant to grant agencies further grounds for employee dismissals.

Another reason for the lack of fitness standards stems from the Americans with Disabilities Act (ADA). According to the ADA, fitness performance tests must be relevant to the job. The standards must be constructed in such a way that failure to perform at a certain level will be detrimental to discharging the tasks of the job. As the next section explains, there are some very valid ways to measure fitness that can transcend these objections.

Measuring Fitness

The Cooper Center for Aerobics Research in Dallas is a good source to validate benefits of police fitness because of its research involving defensible, job-related standards. The Cooper Test measures fitness through four different trials: a timed $1\frac{1}{2}$ mile run (cardiovascular stamina), the number of push-ups a person can perform (upper body strength), the number of sit-ups one can do (abdominal strength), and the sit and reach (determines flexibility by inches reached beyond the knees). Fitness in these categories measure fitness for the job; flexibility also helps reduce injuries. Flexibility of back and legs, more than any other aspect, helps prevent back injuries (Anderson, 1996; Pucetti, 1995).

Boards of police commissioners set police hiring and promotion standards in Illinois. They also conduct hearings to discipline and dismiss officers. These boards require police applicants to take several tests to earn a spot on an eligibility list. One such requirement is a physical ability test called the POWER test. Recruits must pass the POWER test during the first week of attendance at the academy or they are dismissed. The POWER test is a modified version of the Cooper Test. It measures flexibility (sit and reach), cardiovascular stamina (a $1\frac{1}{2}$ mile run), upper body strength (bench press), and abdominal strength (sit-ups). The four categories are separated by gender into age standards. Some academies also use a weight threshold.

Typical height-and-weight charts, while used in some locales, do not take muscle mass into account. Because of this shortcoming, the Palatine (Illinois) Police Department measures excessive body fat in addition to administering the POWER test. The U.S. Department of Defense also uses a height-and-weight chart, along with a body fat measurement.

One study reports that over 80% of responding police agencies say they use a physical ability test for employment qualification (Swanson, Territo, and Taylor, 1998). Before the enactment of Title VII in 1972, the principal physical requirement used in officer selection was based on height-and-weight charts. Because these standards discriminate against women and some ethnic groups with small body size, they no longer are used as hiring criteria unless the agency can show that these factors relate to actual job performance.

Some departments abandoned height-and-weight charts and adopted obstacle courses. However, these agencies quickly learned that they could not defend their reliance on an obstacle course when challenged by women who had a disproportionate failure rate. In *Harless v. Duck* (1980), the court struck down physical agility requirements because the job did not specify how much strength was needed. Another department was challenged successfully when it required candidates to scale a 6-foot fence, but the city had an ordinance that limited fences in its jurisdiction to 5 feet (Swanson et al., 1998).

Failure to Comply

Some agencies now require officers to maintain their fitness after basic training. Altamonte Springs (Florida) Police Department has had such a mandatory fitness program since 1987. Minimum standards are required, with rewards for those who exceed the standards. In yet another example, the Mobile (Alabama) Police Department uses the minimum physical ability test established by the Alabama Peace Officers Standards and Training Commission. It incorporates a graduated sequence of discipline for officers who fail to comply with the wellness standards requirements (Mobile, Alabama, Police Department, 1998). As Box 8–1 shows, discipline ranges from the first step, an observation, up to the sixth step, which is a three-day suspension for noncompliance. Officers who demonstrate progress toward meeting the fitness standards, even though they do not actually satisfy the standards, are not disciplined.

Box 8–1   An Example of Graduated Disciplinary Guidelines

Violation 1: Performance observation.

Violation 2: Letter of reprimand.

Violation 3: Letter of reprimand and officer/cadet will not be considered for promotion.

Violation 4: Extra job privileges, voluntary overtime privileges and/or where applicable, take home car privileges are suspended.

Violation 5: Officer will be declared ineligible for scheduled merit raise.

Violation 6: Three-day suspension.

Source: Mobile [Alabama] Police Department, *Manual of Written Directives*.

The Mobile Police Department has a sophisticated mandatory wellness program and holds each officer or cadet responsible for his or her own fitness. Training is the responsibility of the unit commanding officers, including supervisors. The department tests officers annually for compliance with the physical standards. Officers who fail are subject to the disciplinary provisions that Box 8–1 outlines.

Just as in high school physical education classes, sometimes a forced fitness program will produce real injuries, feigned injuries, officers with doctors' excuses to circumvent the program, and officers who are just reluctant to participate. Many agencies uses monetary incentives to prod officers into compliance. The California Highway Patrol (CHP), for example, provides a cash incentive of an extra $130 per month to participants. This supplement actually saves the CHP millions of dollars a year from workers compensation claims, lawsuits, and dismissals. The CHP also has an attractive disability retirement incentive that produces a tidy financial savings (McDermott, 1987, pp. 18, 23).

The Americans with Disabilities Act and the Civil Rights acts make it difficult, but not insurmountable, to implement fitness standards for police officers. Some administrators are afraid that fitness requirements will violate these statutes so they take the easy way out and ignore the issues. But the civil liability inherent in negligent hiring, training, and retention makes it difficult to deploy unfit police officers who are unable to perform life-saving duties. This failure to protect the public with professional police services is indefensible. If it can be illustrated that an officer who satisfies minimal physical fitness standards could have effected an arrest without injury to the suspect, then the department might become liable through "negligence to train" theory. This analysis suggests that agencies that sidestep the issue of physical fitness are flirting with a considerable risk. However, physical well-being is more than just being in shape through exercise. It also includes monitoring other health-related factors, such as tobacco and alcohol use.

THE HAZARDS OF TOBACCO INGESTION

The World Health Organization (1998b) estimates that tobacco products are respon-sible for 6% of all deaths throughout the world. Closer to home, over 400,000 deaths in this country were attributed to tobacco and over 100,000 deaths to alcohol in 1991 (World Health Organization, 1998a). Tobacco causes more deaths than all other forms of substance abuse combined. Effective medical intervention rarely is possible for most tobacco-related illnesses.

Available data suggest that, globally, approximately 47% of men and 12% of women smoke. The health consequences from this tobacco epidemic in both developed and developing countries are devastating. Since the middle of the 20th century, tobacco products have killed more than 60 million people in developed countries. Currently, tobacco is responsible for 3.5 million deaths worldwide every year.

Tobacco is known to be the probable cause of about 25 diseases. The sheer scale of the impact tobacco has on disease throughout the United States still is not fully appreciated. For example, tobacco is the leading cause of lung cancer. According to

---

Box 8–2   An Example of Policy Guidelines Regarding Smoking While on Duty

The use of tobacco products while on-duty shall be as inconspicuous as possible at all times. In no event will a member or employee smoke a tobacco product in any public or private place where smoking is prohibited by state law or city ordinance.

Source: Tallahassee [Florida] Police Department, *Manual of Written Directives.*

---

the World Health Organization (1998a), it also kills even more people through many other allied diseases. Tobacco also is instrumental in cancers at other sites, heart disease, stroke, emphysema, bronchitis, lung fibrosis, and other chronic lung diseases. Lifetime smokers have a 50% chance of dying from tobacco-induced ailments. A quarter of these consumers will die about 22 years earlier than the normal life expectancy.

Tobacco cessation produces positive health benefits. For example, the risk of coronary heart disease decreases by 50% one year after quitting. Within 15 years, the risk of dying from coronary heart disease approaches that of one who has never smoked. Furthermore, according to the World Health Organization (1998a), 10–14 years after cessation of smoking, the risk of mortality from cancer decreases to nearly that of those who have never smoked (World Health Organization, 1998c).

Police work exposes officers to situations that compromise their physical and mental well-being. Some officers resort to tobacco products as a mechanism to relieve this stress. However, it already is evident that smoking and chewing tobacco exert a detrimental effect upon a person's health. In recognition of this unhealthy effect, some agencies have banned tobacco ingestion. Other agencies restrict tobacco usage for merely cosmetic reasons. As Box 8–2 displays, some agencies appear to worry more about the public appearance than the health of their employees. Regardless of why the policy may be in place, the truth remains that tobacco usage is detrimental to one's health, and by controlling or even eliminating its use among officers, both individuals and their agencies reap the benefits.

THE HAZARDS OF ALCOHOL INGESTION

Excessive drinking leads to more than 100,000 deaths annually in the United States (Doyle, 1996). In 1992, drunken driving accidents made up 25% of this number. Alcohol-related homicide and suicide accounted for 11% and 8%, respectively. Cancers that are partly attributable to alcohol, such as those of the esophagus and larynx, contribute an additional 17%. About 19% resulted from alcohol-related strokes. Another major contributor is a group of 12 ailments wholly caused by alcohol, such as alcoholic cirrhosis of the liver and alcohol dependence syndrome. These 12 ailments represented 18% of all alcohol-related deaths in 1992.

According to the ADA, a person who uses alcohol regularly suffers from a disability. An employer may have to make an accommodation if the alcoholic is qualified to perform the essential functions of the job (Moriarity and Field, 1994). But, if an employee uses alcohol in a manner that affects job performance or conduct so that he or she is not qualified to do the job, then an employer may discipline, fire, or deny employment. In fact, some agencies have adopted a "zero tolerance" toward officers who report for duty in a less than optimal condition. Unfortunately, alcohol consumption, like tobacco use, is difficult to govern because for many officers, both items work as stress reducers. Still, existing data on the negative impact of these products offer support for police agencies willing to implement, for health reasons, policies against the use or consumption of both products.

USE OF FORCE AND STRESS

Earlier in this chapter, I explain that assaults resulting in injuries to police officers represent a formidable outlay for police departments. No doubt, the emotional toll from this potential danger also generates negative stress. While physical fitness may be one way to control the problem, another option is self-defense training. Proper preparation will increase self-confidence in handling attacks and lessen the possibility of injury to the officer and the suspect.

Stress also can cause officers to overreact to situations, especially in less-than-lethal confrontations where the officer wants to maintain the upper hand. Uncontrolled stress can lead to verbal abuse or excessive use of physical force, which invites claims of police misconduct and brutality. Reiss (1968) found that most complaints of police brutality in Chicago turned out be mostly verbal abuse. However, officers are more likely to strike out or lose composure when they are angry or frightened rather than when they are collected and self-assured. Being able to control stress helps officers maintain composure. Poise gained through self-confidence in self-defense training, for example, does not make an individual more violent or aggressive. Rather, fear, insecurity, and a lack of confidence elicit the poor decision making that leads to violence. The positive implications for management are fewer lawsuits by citizens and injured officers, fewer citizen complaints, and less downtime for officers because of injuries.

The term *self-defense* usually is used in a very narrow context. The training actually is more encompassing than just punching and kicking. It involves taking care of oneself both mentally and physically, protecting against sickness and disease. Self-defense training should include an approach of total wellness, with a goal of absence of disease and disease-producing manifestations, such as negative stress. It includes a lifestyle of exercise and good nutrition that promotes health. It is important to develop consistency of personal daily routines that foster a healthy, confident lifestyle that helps control stress, thereby reducing inappropriate police behavior.

Police officers encounter three categories of stress in their personal and professional lives: eustress, neustress, and distress. *Eustress* (positive stress) comes from pleasant and desirable things or events, such as a vacation or a promotion. *Neustress* is neutral and does not affect a person either negatively or positively; it has no significant impact on an individual. *Distress*, or negative stress, can lead to potentially serious consequences, such as excessive force and ill health if not controlled. This negative stress can be broken down into two other types: acute and chronic. *Acute distress* is intense and usually causes physiological changes and altered perception. However, it is not ongoing and usually subsides after the confrontation ends. Physically attempting to subdue a resisting suspect would be one such example. *Chronic distress* is not as intense, but may last over an extremely long period of time. Going to work every day to face an unbearable supervisor (Seaward, 1997) or the anticipation of a possible physical confrontation during a call for service would fit here.

Negative stress originates in unpleasant situations that threaten personal well-being. Negative stress can be prolonged and trigger inappropriate responses. The application of excessive force when arresting a driver after a high-speed pursuit would be one such example (Conroy and Hess, 1992). Since police officers cannot always avoid contact with negative stress, they must learn how to control it. Several factors can aggravate negative stress. Poor nutrition, lack of exercise, and lack of self-confidence are just a few. Poor control during negative stress situations can be prevented by a healthy diet, staying physically fit through exercise, stress control techniques, and having self-confidence when dealing with negative stress situations, especially during confrontations where there is the potential of being physically injured or killed.

CONTROLLING STRESS

Several institutionalized methods are used to prevent detrimental consequences of negative stress, including exercise, meditation, flexibility and breathing (yoga), martial arts (*qi gong,* tai chi, *tai su,* etc.), and other relaxation techniques. Zorn (1994) writes about the increased health benefits of *qi* (pronounced che) *gong* breathing to reduce stress. For millions of Chinese people, *qi gong* is the only route to a long, healthy life. Some Western scientists now are studying the effects of Eastern styles of exercise.

The benefits of correct exercise are unquestioned. Almost everyone recognizes the advantages of an adequate exercise program; it is the type and amount of that exercise program that are a mystery. The documented benefits of exercise are numerous. According to Rice (1992), positive effects for an individual include increased respiratory capacity, improved muscle tone, stronger skeletal and connective tissues, heightened cardiovascular functioning, better circulation, lower LDL cholesterol and triglyceride levels, increased HDL cholesterol, more energy, improved sleep, a higher metabolic rate and lowered body fat, reduced risk of injury from slips and falls as the body becomes more resilient, and slower aging.

Some tangible mental benefits also are associated with proper exercise. They include increased feelings of self-control, independence, enhanced self-confidence and self-esteem, decreased mental fatigue from work pressure, improved mental functioning and alertness, emotional cleansing of tensions from interpersonal conflict and job stress, reduced levels of stress, and relief from mild depression (Crews and Landers, 1987). Both the physical and psychological benefits help mitigate the consequences of negative stress.

SELF-CONFIDENCE TO REDUCE STRESS

In some instances, police brutality is the result of officers not having the necessary confidence and skill to counteract suspect resistance. Their fear results in overreacting with excessive force or a continued emotional response after the suspect is subdued. Being in shape, the product of an exercise program, is necessary when confronting a hostile suspect. As you might imagine, this preparation also can help decrease liability for police administrators.

As previously noted, the astute administrator must provide ample incentives for officers to train regularly. Once there is an administrative mind set that this type of training is part of the totality of wellness, administrators will begin providing opportunities to polish the skills for confident self-defense. To become ingrained, a technique must be practiced 2,000–3,000 times. A maintenance program also is needed to maintain these acquired skills. Take, for example, a person who used to be quite active in a sport, say, basketball. Even though considerable time has passed, that person may still be able to recount how to perform movements and how to execute techniques in his or her mind. However, the body probably will lag behind without periodic practice or maintenance.

Police managers should provide in-service skill development as a means to reduce and control stress in situational conflicts. Officers should have opportunities that will foster weight reduction, stamina, flexibility, and enhance strength and coordination development. Fitness will increase productivity, reduce liability, reduce worker compensation claims, reduce complaints from the public, increase longevity, improve health, and prevent disease and stress.

CONCLUSION

Regardless of one's occupation, repeated exposure to stress, tobacco, alcohol, a sedentary lifestyle, and an inadequate diet can exert detrimental effects on a person's performance, health, and wellness. This statement is especially true for people involved in policing. What factors mold a person's wellness? Experts (Donatelle et al., 1997, pp. 7–8) mention the following as positive steps toward achieving better health and a more wellness-oriented lifestyle:

- Exercise aerobically at least three times per week.
- Engage in other forms of moderate to strenuous exercise.
- Quit smoking.
- Limit alcohol consumption to two drinks per day and seven drinks per week.
- Eat wholesome, nutritious food.
- Reduce daily consumption of caffeine.
- Practice safe sex.
- Engage in practices like meditation and deep breathing exercises to reduce stress.
- Avoid inappropriate hostile or aggressive behavior.
- Avoid inappropriate passive behavior.
- Balance your life with family, work, social, and other activities.

Wellness does not depend on a person's age, intelligence, or physical condition. One can view wellness on a continuum that ranges from negative (premature death) to positive (optimal health). Moving a few steps in the right direction on the continuum or making improvements can be more important than one's actual location on the wellness continuum. Many people believe that high levels of wellness come through adopting a holistic approach in which the interaction and balance among the mind, body, and spirit are emphasized.

The road to wellness is an individual responsibility but also should be an organizational concern. A healthier police officer lives longer, is more productive, and has fewer complaints from the public. A healthier officer takes off fewer days, has fewer disabilities, and lives longer after retirement. Obviously, one can make a coherent argument that mandated fitness standards after officers leave the basic training academy should be in place. A physically fit officer can serve the public better than an unfit officer. At the same time, management might be held liable for not providing the public with officers who can handle the job physically. Once an organizational commitment is made to a fitness program, other positive benefits will follow. These programs also can reduce stress and its accompanying pitfalls.

Police administrators should develop a well-rounded employee assistance program (EAP) and take a high-quality approach to its operation and improvement. Police executives may need to achieve support in the community, typically in form of gaining access to adequate fitness and health facilities. The cornerstone of an EAP is prevention. In other words, there must be a commitment to deliver all types of health-related programs. These efforts may include retirement preparedness workshops, a peer counseling program, an awards and recognition program to promote participation, the ability to quickly deliver professional counseling services any time of the day, "turn-around" interventions aimed at smoking cessation and cholesterol control, and access to substance abuse treatment programs.

Perhaps the Commission on Law Enforcement Accreditation (the topic of Chapter 10) needs to make its policy on fitness standards mandatory for agencies instead of optional. Furthermore, if fitness standards do become mandatory, supervisors and managers must lead by example. Are administrators ready to do this? Younger officers are eager to be physically fit when they first join the force. We need to maintain that desire and enthusiasm.

DISCUSSION QUESTIONS

1. What is meant by the totality of wellness?
2. Prepare a wellness philosophy for your department.
3. What are the benefits of developing a fitness program for your department?
4. Prepare a policy statement concerning mandatory fitness for all police officers.
5. What are some of the resistance factors in establishing a fitness requirement? Who is holding back mandatory physical fitness standards? Are administrators responsible for holding back mandatory fitness standards?
6. What is your definition of a physically fit officer? Compare that with the wellness philosophy you just prepared.

REFERENCES

Alpert, G. P., and R. G. Dunham. *Policing Urban America*, 3rd ed. Prospect Heights, IL: Waveland Press, 1998.

Anderson, A. "Marshalling your resources." *Law and Order* 44, no. 11 (1996), pp. 65–66.

Collingwood, T. C. "Implementing programs and standards for law enforcement physical fitness." *The Police Chief* 55, no. 4 (1988), pp. 20–24.

Conroy, D. L., and K. M. Hess. *Officers at Risk: How to Identify and Cope with Stress*. Placerville, CA: Custom Publishing Company, 1992.

Copay, A. G., and M. T. Charles. "Police academy fitness training at the Police Training Institute, University of Illinois." *Policing: A Journal of Police Strategies and Management* 21, no. 3 (1998), pp. 416–431.

Couper, D. C. *How to Rate Your Local Police*. Washington, DC: Police Executive Research Forum, 1983.

Crews, D. J., and D. M. Landers. "A meta-analytic review of aerobic fitness and reactivity to psychosocial stressors." *Medicine and Science in Sports and Exercise* 19, no. 2 (1987), pp. 114–120.

del Carmen, R. "Criminal and civil liabilities of police officers." In T. Barker and D. L. Carter (eds.), *Police Deviance*, 3rd ed., pp. 409–430. Cincinnati: Anderson Publishing Company, 1994.

Doerner, W. G. *Introduction to Law Enforcement: An Insider's View*. Boston: Butterworth–Heinemann, 1998.

Donatelle, R., C. Snow-Harter, and A. Wilcox. *Wellness: Choices for Health and Fitness*. New York: The Benjamin-Cummings Publishing Company, 1997.

Doyle, R. "Deaths due to alcohol: National clearinghouse for alcohol and drug information." *Scientific American* (December 1996), p. 1.

Garner, R. "Post-academy fitness programs: Part I." *Texas Law Enforcement Management and Administrative Statistics Program Bulletin* 4, no. 7 (1997), pp. 1–7.

Harless v. Duck, 629 F.2nd 611, U.S. cert. den, 449 U.S. 872 (1980).

Karuhn, C. "Martial arts defends against back pain." *Chicago Tribune* (March 24, 1994), section 2, p. 3.

Krajick, K. "Out of shape on the beat." *Police Magazine* 3, no. 5 (1979), p. 68.

Maguire, K., and A. L. Pastore. *Sourcebook of Criminal Justice Statistics 1997*. Washington, DC: U.S. Government Printing Office, 1998.

Massey, P. B., E. Thorner, W. Preston, and J. S. Lee. "Increased lung capacity through qi gong breathing: Techniques of chung moo quan." *Journal of Asian Martial Arts* 2, no. 3 (1993), pp. 71–72.

McDermott, B. *What Will Be the Future of Police Fitness Programs by the Year 2000?* Sacramento: California Commission on Peace Officer Standards and Training, 1987.

Mobile, Alabama, Police Department. At www.zebra.netI~mobilepd/wellness.htm, 1998.

Moriarity, A. R., and M. W. Field. *Police Officer Selection: A Handbook for Law Enforcement Administrators.* Springfield, IL: Charles C Thomas, 1994.

Parker v. District of Columbia, 850 F.2d 708 (D.C. Cir. 1988).

Puccetti, W. "Back injury can disarm police." *Law and Order* 43, no. 3 (1995), pp. 13–15.

Rachlin, H. "Officers and heart disease: Awards for physical fitness." *Law and Order* 44, no. 8 (1996), pp. 61–66.

Reiss, A. J., Jr. "Police brutality—Answers to key questions." *Trans-Action* 5, no. 8 (1968), pp. 10–19.

Rice, P. L. *Stress and Health,* 2nd ed. Pacific Grove, CA: Brooks/Cole Publishers, 1992.

Sarro, M. *Police Department Worker's Compensation Report from October 1, 1996 to September 30, 1998.* Elgin, IL: City of Elgin, 1998.

Scientific American. At http://www.legalize.org/global/alcohol1.htm, December 1996.

Seaward, B. L. *Managing Stress: Principles and Strategies for Health and Well-Being,* 2nd ed. Boston: Jones and Bartlett, 1997.

Seiler, S. *Aging and Cardiovascular Function.* At http://www.krs.hia.no/~stephes/hrtage.htm, 1996.

Swanson, C. R., L. Territo, and R. W. Taylor. *Police Administration: Structures, Processes, and Behavior,* 4th ed. Upper Saddle River, NJ: Prentice Hall, 1998.

World Health Organization. *Tobacco Epidemic: Health Dimensions.* At http://www.hq.who.or.jp/inf/fs/fact154.htm, 1998a.

_____. At http://www.legalize.org/global/s4.htm, 1998b.

_____. At http://www.hq.who.or.jp.inf/fs/factl54.html, 1998c.

Zorn, F. H. "Chi gong: New enthusiasm for an ancient healing/exercise discipline is filling fitness classes and piquing the interest of scientists as well." *Longevity* 46, no. 6 (1994), pp. 84, 86.

Chapter 9

Labor Relations

Ronald D. Hunter, State University of West Georgia, and
James B. Merritt, Southern States Police Benevolent Association

> The petitioner may have a constitutional right to talk politics but he has no constitutional right to be a policeman. (Justice Oliver Wendall Holmes in *McAuliffe v. New Bedford*, 155 Mass. 216, 220 (1892))

From the earliest factories to today's sports leagues, American history is replete with stories about management and labor disputes. Although for many years policing was not among those occupations in which labor relations was a concern, time and society changed that. Today, labor relations is a major element of police personnel practices.

Labor relations can be defined as the interactions between the leaders and employees making up the human resources of an organization. This is an operational definition designed to be applicable throughout this chapter. Using this definition allows us an opportunity to explain what currently is going on in the field of labor relations in general and in the field of law enforcement in particular.

LABOR RELATIONS AND ITS COMPONENTS

When one mentions the term *labor relations*, most of us immediately think of employee unions and collective bargaining. Indeed, collective bargaining and union activities dominate labor relations discussions and receive a lion's share of the attention within this chapter. However, labor relations also includes other efforts to maintain positive employee-management relations. It is important to understand that a number of other salient issues, in addition to collective bargaining, influence labor relations in the United States. For many public employees, the laws of the federal government and their respective states and communities provide protection from arbitrary and unfair behavior at the hands of their employers. This section gives a brief overview of those other issues that have an impact on labor relations before turning to a discussion of collective bargaining.

159

Civil Service

In 1883, the Pendleton Act established a merit system by which the United States government would operate. This act implemented four reforms:

- selection of civil servants based upon personal competence rather than patronage;
- prohibition banning the dismissal of employees for political reasons and against coercing employees to contribute financially to or being compelled to participate in political campaigns;
- authorization for the president to create a bipartisan Civil Service Commission; and,
- authorization for future presidents to increase or decrease the number of positions covered by the Act. (Tompkins, 1995, p. 59)

The Pendelton Act and its subsequent reforms (Classification Act of 1923, Civil Service Reform Act of 1978) have affected not only federal employees but also state and local government workers. Most state and local governments have emulated federal efforts by creating their own civil service systems. Today, many of the protections that public employees enjoy are provided by civil service systems.

Fair Labor Standards

Congress enacted the Fair Labor Standards Act in 1938. This act established minimum wages, provided for overtime pay, and regulated hours of work. Initially, these provisions applied only to private employers directly engaged in commerce. However, school, hospital, and transit employees were added to its protections in 1966 and 1974. The U.S. Supreme Court extended its application in 1985 to include state and local government employees. The result of this case was federal legislation that required government entities to pay overtime or grant compensatory time to city workers, including police and firefighters, based on an established time frame (Dantzker, 1999).

Equal Employment Opportunity and Affirmative Action

A number of important actions over the years have resulted in employee protections that are enforced by the United States government. Equal Employment Opportunity (EEO) is designed to ensure that discriminatory employment practices against women and minority-group members come to a halt. In addition to applying these laws, many state and local government entities enacted their own versions into either law or policy. Box 9–1 displays the more significant EEO actions.

Affirmative action differs considerably from Equal Employment Opportunity. Whereas EEO is designed to prevent discrimination against women and minority-group members, affirmative action seeks to remedy past and current discrimination

Box 9–1   Key Equal Employment Opportunity Landmarks

Civil Rights Act of 1866. Guaranteed to all persons the same legal rights as "white citizens."

14th Amendment to the U.S. Constitution. Applied U.S. Constitutional protections to the states. Prohibited states from depriving any person of life, liberty, or property without due process of law, or denying any person the equal protection of the law.

Civil Rights Act of 1871. Allowed citizens to sue local government officials and certain private individuals who deprive citizens of any constitutional or federal statutory rights.

Executive Order 8802 of 1941. Prohibited employment discrimination in the federal civil service and by defense contractors. Established the Fair Employment Practices Committee to investigate complaints of discrimination.

Equal Pay Act of 1963. Prohibited discrimination in compensation on the basis of sex for work requiring equal skill, effort, and responsibility and performed under similar working conditions.

Civil Rights Act of 1964 (Title VII). Prohibited employers, employment agencies and labor organizations from discriminating on the basis of race, color, religion, sex, and national origin. Since 1972, it applies to both public and private employers with 15 or more employees.

Age Discrimination in Employment Act of 1967. Prohibited discrimination on the basis of age in hiring, discharge, and the terms, conditions, and privileges of employment by employers with 20 or more employees. Also included unions and employment agencies. Was applied to state and local governments in 1974. Was amended to protect individuals 40 years of age and older in 1986.

Equal Employment Opportunity Act of 1972. Applied the Civil Rights Act of 1964 to public sector employers. Also awarded the Equal Employment Opportunity Commission enforcement powers.

Rehabilitation Act of 1973. Prohibited the federal government, government contractors and programs receiving federal financial assistance from discriminating against individuals on the basis of physical or mental disability.

Pregnancy Discrimination Act of 1978. Prohibited employers from discriminating against individuals on the basis of pregnancy, childbirth, or medical conditions related to childbirth.

Americans with Disabilities Act of 1990 (Title I). Prohibited private and public employers with 15 or more employees from discriminating against the disabled in employment and required them to make reasonable accommodation for disabilities.

Civil Rights Act of 1991. Allowed individuals to receive punitive and compensatory damages under the Civil Rights Act, Americans with Disabilities Act, and Rehabilitation Act. It also placed the burden on the employer to defend practices that adversely affected individuals in protected categories.

Adapted from J. Tompkins. *Human Resource Management in Government*, pp. 132–133. New York: HarperCollins, 1995.

by providing preferential opportunities to women and minority-group members. One of the most publicized examples of court-ordered affirmative action was the 1972 federal court ruling mandating that the Alabama Department of Public Safety hire one black person for every white person until blacks constituted 25% of state troopers. While highly controversial and often leading to charges of "reverse discrimination" against whites and men, affirmative action persists as a strategy for ensuring fair employment opportunities for women and minority-group members.

Occupational Safety and Health Reform Act of 1970

The Occupational Safety and Health Reform Act of 1970 established the Office of Safety and Health Administration (OSHA). OSHA's charge is to reduce workplace hazards for American workers (Rosenbloom, 1998). This agency focuses on ensuring that employees are not subjected to unnecessary health risks due to unsafe working conditions during the performance of their jobs.

Family and Medical Leave Act of 1993

The Family and Medical Leave Act became effective on August 8, 1993. This statute entitles workers in organizations of 50 or more employees up to a total of 12 weeks of unpaid medical leave during any 12-month period. The employer is responsible for continuing all employee benefits during this period. Furthermore, when the employee is ready to return to work, he or she must be reinstated to his or her former position or a similar one (Tompkins, 1995).

Collective Bargaining

When one talks about labor relations, the basic premise is that employees are represented by an organization that is empowered to advocate on their behalf. Collective bargaining came about because labor leaders learned it was extremely difficult to approach management on an individual basis. The odds of altering work practices increase if the workforce bands together and speaks with one voice. Presenting a solid, unified front to management commands respect (Burpo, Delord, and Shannon, 1997).

The purpose of collective bargaining is to seek justice, fairness, and equity for workers. It is the product of months of careful planning, deliberate research, and comparisons about how the membership's benefits stack up against those of similar organizations. The mission is to improve the quality of work life for the rank-and-file union member. It also is an opportunity for the union's leadership to send a message to management asking for additional benefits for workers (Carrell and Heavrin, 1995).

The term *collective bargaining* is used exclusively in labor relations to refer to the negotiations between management and labor aimed at forging an agreement about working conditions. It implies the union is of one mind, focused, and mission oriented. The very title of the process conjures solid support for what the union is asking. In reality, both management and the union may have secondary or fallback positions (Carter and Sapp, 1992). Both sides know their own goals and objectives and try not to let their adversary discover this information. Negotiators at the table usually do not have this information while they are participating in discussions. As the bargaining process continues, observers for both sides watch their opponents, translate phrases and key words, and continuously evaluate the strengths and weaknesses of the other side.

The purpose of collective bargaining is to hammer out a formal agreement. To start the process, both sides review the proposals submitted by the other party and identify those items with which they can agree. As the deliberations unfold, items with mutual agreement are removed from the head-to-head meeting. When it is time for serious negotiating, the only items left on the table are those points where management and union representatives differ.

Labor enters the room with the basic premise that it needs to return to the membership with an improvement in working conditions. Negotiators may be bargaining for increased wages, a better health care program, a stronger voice in agency operations, a better pension plan, or a host of other worker benefits. These demands may require concessions by union members to help address financial exigency or other conditions. In any event, negotiating a collective bargaining agreement is a two-way street.

The talks do not always produce an amicable ending. If the two sides cannot find a mutually agreeable solution, the negotiations may be declared to be at an impasse. An *impasse* means that neither side thinks it is possible for further talks to reach an agreement. There are two common ways to end an impasse. One route is *mediation*. Here, an independent party enters the picture, hears both side's version of the dispute, and then recommends a settlement for both sides to follow. The stronger alternative is *binding arbitration.* In this situation, both labor and management agree beforehand that they will submit to whatever the mediator decrees. In more extreme cases, either or both parties may seek a court hearing as the proper forum in which to present the issues. In any event, the actual mechanism by which an impasse is resolved ultimately depends on state laws and local ordinances regarding collective bargaining rights of public employees.

A BRIEF HISTORY OF THE LABOR MOVEMENT IN THE PRIVATE SECTOR

Labor organizations have existed in the United States since the republic was formed. Several craft groups in the Northeast formed trade societies during the 1790s to protect their interests against shop factory owners. By 1866, trade unionists managed to establish the first national trade union, the National Labor Union (Carrell and Heavrin, 1995). This short-lived organization called for the establishment of eight-hour workdays, immigration controls, and the abolition of convict labor. Like other unions that were operating at that time, the National Labor Union fell victim to poor organization and the Depression of 1873.

A number of violent events during the 1870s and 1880s delayed the union movement. As a result, America's capitalists were able to depict the union movement as both violent and criminal. The questionable convictions and executions of several infamous Molly Maguires (a group of union organizers in Pennsylvania's mine fields infiltrated by Pinkerton agents), the use of state militias to suppress the Railway Strike of 1877, along with the arrests and convictions of eight "anarchists" for their supposed complicity in the Haymarket Square Riot in Chicago suggests that unionists more frequently were the victims of violence than the protagonists (Carrell and Heavrin, 1995).

During the 1890s capitalists continued to use Pinkerton agents, state militias, and the courts to break the existing unions and deter any efforts to organize workers. The Carnegie Steel Company crushed the fledgling steelworkers' union, first in the Homestead area and then throughout Pennsylvania. The Pullman Railway Strike was ended thanks to help from the federal government, which added mail cars to all the trains so that strikers could be prosecuted for interfering with mail delivery (Carrell and Heavrin, 1995).

Not until the creation of the American Federation of Labor (AFL) in 1886 did labor organizations begin to win support. Under the leadership of Samuel Gompers, the AFL managed to distance itself from the violence associated with other organizations, such as the Knights of Labor and the American Railway Union. In addition, Gompers's focus on economic rather than political action allowed the AFL to gain an identity as a labor organization and not as a fledging political party (which prompted the demise of the National Labor Union and the Industrial Workers of the World). From this humble beginning, the AFL would go on to become the dominant union in America for skilled craftsmen.

In 1935, John L. Lewis (who had experience with the United Mine Workers and the AFL) collaborated with the Ladies Garment Workers to create the Congress of Industrial Workers (CIO). Not only did the CIO provide union benefits to unskilled workers, it also included women and African-Americans within its membership. The United Auto Workers soon joined with the CIO. Thanks to the passage of the Wagner Act (United National Labor Relations Act of 1935), the CIO grew considerably during the next 20 years. By the time it merged with the 10.9 million member AFL in 1955, the CIO had amassed over 5.2 million members (Carrell and Heavrin, 1995, p. 127).

The National Labor Relations Act of 1935 provided employees in the private sector with the right to bargain collectively. This legislation sparked worker interest and union membership peaked during the 1960s. Afterward, though, private sector interest waned and labor organizations began eyeing public employees as fertile ground for new development (Tompkins, 1995).

A BRIEF HISTORY OF THE LABOR MOVEMENT IN THE PUBLIC SECTOR

Labor organizations among skilled public workers existed as early as the 1820s in the U.S. Navy shipyards and among postal workers in the 1860s (Tompkins, 1995, p. 327). However, for most public employees, job security (civil service) was more important than being lured to a higher wage by working in the private sector. Government employment translated as security. Employees took civil service protection, trading higher salaries for job security (Salerno, 1981). Given this backdrop, it was very difficult to argue a need for union protection since civil service protections were in effect (Burpo, 1979).

Congress passed the Lloyd-LaFollette Act in 1912 and effectively overruled an earlier ban on public labor organizations by President Teddy Roosevelt. This act gave federal employees the right to organize and lobby. Following the passage of the Lloyd-LaFollette Act, a number of labor organizations clamored to represent public employee interests (i.e., the National Federation of Federal Employees, the American Federation of Government Employees, the National Association of Government Employees, as well as a myriad of teacher, police, and firefighter groups at the state and local levels). The American Association of State, County, and Municipal Employees was founded in 1936. However, this event was not very significant. Most states denied public employees the right to bargain collectively, so union benefits were very limited.

By the 1960s, a number of cities and states were permitting labor negotiations for public employees. Union membership escalated after President Kennedy issued Executive Order 10988 in January of 1962 permitting federal employees to bargain collectively. During a time when union membership was declining in the private sector, membership in public labor organizations was beginning to grow rapidly (Carrell and Heavrin, 1995).

Despite the efforts of many states and communities to prohibit public employees from participating in labor organizations, these entities continued to thrive. The Civil Service Reform Act, passed in 1978, forbade strikes but ensured that federal employees had the right to bargain collectively. Bolstered by the example of the federal government, the U.S. District Court in *Atkins v. City of Charlotte* (1969) struck down a North Carolina law that prohibited public employees from joining labor organizations. This atmosphere encouraged many states to begin easing restrictions on labor organizations for public employees (Tompkins, 1995).

Today, over 45% of all government workers are represented by unions, with the bulk being firefighters, sanitation workers, and teachers (Harrigan, 1998, p. 273). As of this writing, the American Federation of State, County, and Municipal Employees (AFSCME) has over 1.3 million members (AFSCME, 1998). In addition, traditional private sector unions, such as the AFL/CIO, are now recruiting members from all aspects of government employment. Historically, union organizing has been resisted in the South. However, even there, these large unions have begun attracting members from the public sector, including law enforcement.

Despite these advances, many public employees have seen a decline in the protections they have enjoyed because economic restrictions that previously affected only the private sector now impinge on public sector employment. For instance, government workers at all levels now are subject to layoffs, just as in the private sector. Local and state governments are deemphasizing civil service protection for employees by abolishing protections under state merit systems.

The lack of protections afforded public sector employees has become painfully obvious over the past several years (Tompkins, 1995; Rosenbloom, 1998). Government employees have discovered that they are not immune from the economic roller coasters that, in the past, beset just nongovernment workers. Recognizing that there is very little difference between public and private employment because the same economic forces are at work has brought a new realization to how employees are viewed. The impact of these forces on the future of public service labor relations is discussed later.

A BRIEF HISTORY OF THE LABOR MOVEMENT IN LAW ENFORCEMENT

The American Federation of Labor got its start in 1886 from a merger involving several craft unions. Police officers in Cleveland approached the AFL in 1897 and asked that labor group to issue them a charter. However, the AFL refused on the grounds that police officers regularly functioned as strikebreakers and issued a ban on recognizing police unions. By 1919, the AFL had received numerous requests from police officers and lifted this ban. Almost immediately, the Boston Police Social Club affiliated with the AFL and became the Boston Police Union (Gammage and Sachs, 1972).

The Boston Police commissioner refused to recognize the union and fired 19 of its leaders. These dismissals lead 1,117 out of 1,544 officers to walk off the job on September 9, 1919. The remaining 427 officers showed up for work. However, they were unable to stop the rioting and extensive looting that resulted in seven deaths and hundreds of injuries. In response to the public outrage that followed, Governor Coolidge activated the state guard and ordered it to take measures to stop the crime wave (White, 1988). Afterward, every officer who participated in the strike was fired from the job.

The results of the Boston strike had an impact on law enforcement labor relations until the 1960s (Barker, Hunter, and Rush, 1994). Several unsuccessful attempts were made throughout the country to organize police unions between 1919 and 1964. However, the prevailing public fear of unions, state laws prohibiting labor organizations, and restrictive court decisions prevented "union" organizing until 1965. In 1965, as a result of a change in Michigan's laws that now allowed the formation of public associations, the Detroit Police Officers' Association was founded. Police organizations and unions would grow quite rapidly during the next 25 years (Dantzker, 1999).

By 1965, several organizations representing police officers, but not affiliated with the AFL, were in place. The Fraternal Order of Police (FOP), for instance, escaped the bitterness stemming from the 1919 Boston police strike by establishing lodges for social activities both at the state and local levels (Burpo, 1971). Some other more prominent groups at the time included the Peace Officer Research Association of California (PORAC), the Police Benevolent Association of New York City (NYPBA), and the Florida Police Benevolent Association (FLPBA).

The question of putting together a constitution for the police union arose at a labor meeting in Omaha. A special AFL/CIO panel reviewed the charter request, and law enforcement leaders of the major associations met on November 2, 1969, to draft a constitution. This group named itself the International Brotherhood of Police Officers (IBPO). The IBPO had four basic objectives. First, there was a need to create a common philosophy and communication among the police groups in the United States. Second, it was important to present a united front in contract negotiations with municipal governments. Third, an effort needed to be established that would give police officers a strong voice in local, state, and federal legislation. Finally, organizers recognized that it was important to maintain a continuous dialogue between the union and the community (Burpo et al., 1997).

George Meany, the president of the AFL/CIO, rejected the IBPO charter in February 1971. Meany felt there was no demand or real desire for a police officer's international union (Gammage and Sachs, 1972). Despite this setback, other efforts were in progress. The American Federation of State, County, and Municipal Employees had been trying to charter police unions since the 1930s. The AFL/CIO chartered the International Union of Police Associations (IUPA) in February 1979. Since then, many local organizations have affiliated with either the AFL/CIO or AFSCME.

During this period, law enforcement officers kept a watchful eye on the tactics employed by labor and grew more aware of the gains unions were making. Maintaining the peace in and around labor disputes between management and workers was a common police function. This presence gave the police a front-row seat during these confrontations. Members of law enforcement observed the way union workers behaved on the pickets. At the same time, officers watched management use scabs (outside temporary replacements) after locking out long-time employees. All these tactics caused law enforcement employees to remain skeptical of unions (Burpo, 1971).

As the 1960s dawned, labor organizations realized that one untapped domain was the public employee sector. At the same time, awareness was growing that police officers needed more education and training to understand the social forces driving the rising crime rates. The federal government, through the Law Enforcement Assistance Administration (LEAA), emphasized the need for college-level courses and began funding educational opportunities. As a result, both in-service and aspiring law enforcement officers began attending college.

This opportunity created the avenue for police officers to learn more about personnel management, public administration, and other aspects. They soon found out how to do research and organize self-help associations. This emphasis on self-help associations, rather than traditional labor unions, stemmed from the early experience with unions and a recognition that law enforcement was an emerging profession (Burpo, 1971).

During the 1990s, the AFL/CIO rediscovered public employees, especially police officers, as an untapped market. Other unions, such as the Communication Workers of America (CWA), unveiled an active recruiting effort in the South. One of the CWA's first efforts pitted it against the Florida PBA in 1996 in a bitter contest to represent correctional officers. CWA won that election and later expanded its efforts by funding a state organization, the Georgia Coalition of Police and Sheriffs.

As you can see from this short presentation, a wide range of labor groups has been interested in representing law enforcement officers. Each has its own orientation, philosophy, and perspective. To get a better picture of these efforts, the next section visits some of the more prominent police labor organizations.

POLICE LABOR ORGANIZATIONS

A number of organizations or forums are available to members of the criminal justice system. The attraction to join a particular group can range from professional development to fulfilling an altruistic concern. In any event, looking at several common dimensions will give a fuller understanding of what these organizations encompass. For example, we can look at who the members are, the services the organization provides, the source of income for the group, and the kind of political activity each group promotes. Box 9–2 contains a brief listing of selected Internet sites for those who wish to take a closer peek at some police organizations.

Note that these organizations involve police employees in a myriad of activities. The nature of some of those activities may or may not be considered "labor relations." For instance, the first three types of organizations that we discuss are not labor unions, in the sense that they do not engage in collective bargaining. The fourth type of organization may or may not do so. However, because their activities (particularly those of management organizations) can exert a profound impact on labor relations, they warrant inclusion here. In fact, they often are the mechanisms by which opposition to or cooperation with other police labor organizations is initiated.

Box 9–2   Selected Internet Sites Pertaining to Police Labor Organizations

Management Organizations
International Association of Chiefs of Police: www.theiacp.org
National Sheriff's Association: www.sheriffs.org

State Peace Officers Associations
Combined Law Enforcement Associations of Texas: www.cleat.org
National Association of Police Organizations: www.napo.org

Job Assignment Organizations
American Federation of Railroad Police: www.pipeline.com
International Association of Auto Theft Investigators: www.iaati.org
National Association of School Resource Officers: www.rt66.com/nasro/
index.html

Fraternal Organizations
Illinois Fraternal Order of Police: www.fop.org

Unions
Boston Patrolman's Association, Inc.: www.bppa.org
International Union of Police Associations: www.sddi.com/iupa
Missouri Union of Law Enforcement: www.mule57.org

Self-Help Professional Organizations
Florida Police Benevolent Association: www.flapba.org
New York City Police Benevolent Association: www.nycpba.org
New York State Correctional Officers and Police Benevolent Association:
www.nyscopba.org
Southern States Police Benevolent Association: www.sspba.org

Nonunion Management Organizations

Police chiefs and sheriffs are organized at both the national and state levels. Probably the two best known groups are the International Association of Chiefs of Police (IACP) and the National Sheriffs Association (NSA). Annual dues for individual chiefs and sheriffs normally are paid for by the agency as part of the

Box 9–3   The International Association of Chiefs of Police Official
View on Collective Bargaining

Collective bargaining is the process by which labor and management
representatives negotiate the wages and working conditions for a given
employment entity. Bargaining is both an economic and political process.
As in the private sector, the bargaining power of public management
consists primarily of the ability to manipulate the economic costs of
agreement and disagreement to employees. Economic decisions in public
sector bargaining, however, have a direct relationship to political consequences. Since most government services are monopolistic and largely
nonsubstitutable, performance in the economic marketplace is not the
major consideration of public sector management. Although they may be
spared competitive economic pressures, public management is subject to
political pressures. Labor organizations can be significant political institutions because their members are taxpayers and voters, as well as public
employees. In consequence, the bargaining power of a public sector union
largely depends upon the extent to which it can influence the competitive
position of elected officials in the political marketplace by granting or
withholding support. The political power capability of these unions
becomes a function of their size, wealth, control, and influence in
community affairs.

Source: International Association of Chiefs of Police. *Critical Issues in Police Labor Relations*, p. 6. Alexandria, VA: International Association of Chiefs of Police, 1977.

executive benefit package. While other high ranking command staff members may
join these organizations, they usually are admitted as "associate members" and
cannot hold office or chair committees. These groups stand ready to provide
testimony in front of legislative or congressional committees on a wide range of law
enforcement topics. In addition, these associations provide training programs, help
manage and direct promotional examinations, conduct policy and procedure
reviews, and will oversee agency evaluations.

Each state has a separate, but parallel, organization for municipal police chiefs
and county sheriffs, which provides similar services as do the national groups. Both
organizations wield strong political power. Very often, state legislators will delay
voting on a piece of legislation until they discuss the matter with several chiefs and
sheriffs. Bear in mind that sheriffs, as elected public officials, represent a powerful
lobbying group. Therefore, legislators usually will defer to their wishes.

Also note that management organizations traditionally are vocal opponents of
rank-and-file police labor organizations. Box 9–3 reveals the International Association of Chiefs of Police view of collective bargaining.

Nonunion State Peace Officer Associations

These associations are open to persons working in the criminal justice system. Most of the membership consists of traditional peace officers who have the power of arrest. Usually, these groups sponsor a state convention and the Peace Officers Standards and Training (POST) agency will manage the convention in partnership with the association. This vehicle increases participation because attendance at the presentations counts as training that satisfies recertification requirements.

Participants are likely to receive a certificate of membership and a magazine. The magazine focuses on general articles of interest and will sidestep controversy. In many instances, the association provides a supplemental pension or insurance benefits. It is not unusual to find the president of the state peace officers' association appointed to the POST, crime commissions, and other statewide blue-ribbon committees. While they will address issues of interest to law enforcement, these organizations normally stay out of labor disputes.

Nonunion Job Assignment Organizations

Specialty associations tend to congregate around law enforcement assignments. Loosely knit associations may be devoted to robbery and homicide investigators, fraud investigators, traffic accident reconstructionists, identification technicians, canine trainers, members of narcotics units, academy instructors, training officers, and the like. The purpose behind these associations is to share information, provide specialized instruction, and establish a communication network among members. Specialty organizations also pass on confidential information about crime trends and behavioral characteristics of individual offenders. Sometimes, these groups will mail periodic newsletters to members alerting them to new developments. The only political activity they engage in is an occasional appearance in front of a legislative committee on a bill that affects their special reason for existence. However, members frequently use their special status and certifications in efforts to obtain additional recognition and benefits from their employers.

Fraternal Organizations and Local Unions

Fraternal organizations, such as the Fraternal Order of Police, emphasize the social aspects of law enforcement. The FOP, for instance, provides a lodge where members and guests can go for relaxation, fellowship, cookouts, and seasonal parties. Some of these groups represent their members in a manner similar to unions (Halpern, 1974). They handle grievances, discipline, and termination of employment but do so with much less vigor. All services must be approved by the local organization and then forwarded to the state and, in some cases, the national organization to receive financial support. While the FOP maintains a lobbying effort in Washington, similar efforts at the state level often are sporadic.

Police officer associations (POAs) also began as "social" organizations. Like FOPs, they may or may not engage in collective bargaining. In some cities, such as Fort Worth, Texas, the POA is the collective bargaining agent with the city for the rank and file. While some police officers may belong to union-affiliated chapters, most are strictly local in nature.

National Unions and Labor Federations

As mentioned earlier, union affiliates of the AFL/CIO and AFSCME have been active in recruiting law enforcement employees for many years. The AFL, for instance, began chartering police local unions in 1918. Had the aftermath of the 1919 Boston Police Strike not led to subsequent withdrawals, police unions today most likely would be dominated chapters with AFL/CIO affiliation. However, not until the 1940s did the AFL/CIO once again make inroads into chartering local chapters. While it did not become heavily involved in recruiting police membership until the 1970s, AFSCME actually chartered its first police local in Portsmouth, Virginia, in 1937 (Gammage and Sachs, 1972).

Many law enforcement unions are governed by a structure handed down from the AFL/CIO, although exceptions like the FOP do exist. Dues are set and a portion of these funds goes to the national headquarters. In return, the union represents the members' contract negotiations, grievances, and disciplinary actions. The representation may be by a coworker or a trained professional staff person. If it becomes necessary, the union may provide the member with a lawyer. The main purpose, though, is to use the *meet-and-confer process*. Here, leaders of the police association meet periodically with management to discuss problems or issues facing employees and seek a resolution. For example, concerns may be about staffing levels on the streets, equipment, transfer and promotion practices, and the like. The goal, of course, is to resolve these issues in a way that is beneficial to the officers.

Most unions are funded through dues, usually a percent of the member's monthly salary. In addition, unions can use a process whereby members are assessed an additional charge to support a special action. Suppose, for example, that a salary comparison survey is needed to demonstrate the need for a pay increase. The union may approach the membership and ask for a 10% "add on" to the normal dues. This extra money is earmarked for paying the costs of the survey. If the membership votes in the affirmative for an increase, the cost of being a union member goes up for the time being.

As mentioned earlier, local unions may belong to an umbrella organization such as AFL/CIO or AFSCME. Part of the dues going to the national headquarters ends up in a political action contribution fund. These monies are used to endorse and assist selected political candidates.

Independent Unions and Self-Help Organizations

Some law enforcement officers are reluctant to affiliate with a large conglomerate like the AFL/CIO or AFSCME. They are more comfortable addressing issues at the local level. Unfortunately, this restriction limits their effectiveness considerably. Independent police unions (whose leaders tend to think of themselves as "self-help" organizations) that extend beyond the local level bridge this gap. These groups are hybrid associations that borrow and employ strategies from a wide range of organizations. Applying labor tactics when needed and using gentle political pressure makes a unique service organization for criminal justice employees. In short, these organizations are independent unions run by police officers (the staff composed mostly of former officers) for police officers.

Examples of self-help organizations are the Florida Police Benevolent Association, the Southern States Police Benevolent Association (SSPBA), and in some cases, regionally organized FOP or POA chapters that focus on collective bargaining. The Florida PBA, which is not affiliated with any national or international organization, is the oldest example of such an independent labor organization. It has a history of representing law enforcement officers in a wide range of services. At its height, membership exceeded 30,000 officers just in the state of Florida. Currently, though, its membership is experiencing a decline due to intense competition from other groups.

The Florida PBA pioneered professional services to law enforcement officers in that state. This organization started prior to the establishment of a Public Employees Relations Commission (PERC) in Florida. In fact, PERC is the result of legislation proposed by the Florida PBA. As a result of the work done by Florida PBA, a large number of law enforcement officers within that state enjoy collective bargaining, higher salaries, as well as good retirement and pension options. Other services range from representation in grievances, discipline, and termination of employment to putting a lawyer at the scene when a member police officer uses deadly force. Also included in this potpourri are things like consultation on retirement and pension matters, salary surveys, and information exchange through newsletters and other outlets.

A prime function of these groups is lobbying. Both the Florida PBA and the Southern States PBA operate under the Internal Revenue Service rules and regulations 501(c)(5), which gives them the authority to lobby and influence legislation at all levels of government. The basic belief is that significant changes in the quality of work life for criminal justice employees are best obtained through the political process. A key tool that has proven beneficial is endorsing candidates running for political office at both the local and state levels. Support comes in the form of publicity, political action committee (PAC) funds, and personnel who set out campaign signs, stuff envelopes, make telephone calls, transport voters to the polls, and perform other pertinent activities.

One of the newest self-help organizations is the New York State Correctional Officers and Police Benevolent Association (NYSCOPBA). This group is seeking to replace the American Federation of State, County, and Municipal Employees as the labor representative for police and correctional officers within several New York communities.

MEMBERSHIP AND BENEFITS OF POLICE LABOR ORGANIZATIONS

What benefits are derived from joining a police labor organization? The answer depends on the organization. As the last section indicates, police labor organizations may or may not engage in collective bargaining. Of those that do, local unions deal solely with issues within their own police agency or immediate area. They may or may not affiliate with more traditional labor unions. Traditional labor unions, like the AFL/CIO or AFSCME, tend to have national or international organizational structures and may be affiliated with many other labor organizations. Independent unions, such as the Florida PBA, the SSPBA, and the newly formed NYCOPBA, seek to be independent from nonpolice influences. It should be noted that all these organizations engage in collective bargaining on behalf of their members.

Membership

Membership in most police labor organizations is open to employees of a general category, such as the police officers employed by a specific city or county agency. States with statutes that permit collective bargaining clearly delineate classes of employees eligible for representation by a bargaining unit. Usually, patrol officers, detectives, and other categories up to the supervisory ranks are covered. There are other units for sergeants and lieutenants in some states, since they are supervisors but not part of upper management. In general, employees at or above the rank of captain are considered management and cannot engage in collective bargaining. However, employees in a number of agencies are now challenging this "norm." As this chapter was being prepared, an Illinois court granted lieutenants and captains within the Chicago Police Department the right to belong to such organizations.

Government employees at all levels are free to form their own association. Once formed, it becomes the organization's responsibility to gain recognition through any means it can. The Alameda, California, Police Association started as a group that met for lunch each month. Later, it affiliated with the Bay Area Chapter of PORAC and now is recognized by the administration. Other law enforcement associations have followed a different strategy. Typically, a labor group will support particular candidates in an effort to change the composition of the local governing board of the city or county. After they have a majority of the council who favor the association, an ordinance is introduced that establishes the right of employees to meet and confer with the department's management, including the chief executive officer of the city or county.

Those organizations that are not traditional unions outline membership qualifications in their constitution and bylaws. Defining the entry criteria also spells out the classes of membership, such as active, associate, honorary, and so forth. Another section determines who can hold office. Usually, this privilege is restricted to employees who are not members of upper-level management.

Some managers may wish to join these associations so they can keep abreast of what is on the agenda. Usually, though, management does not interfere with this type of association's actions. Political and legal awareness leads to constraint in those associations that engage in collective bargaining. These are deliberate bodies, and ever since the Boston strike some 79 years ago, rash decisions rarely are going to be made at general meetings.

Benefits

Every organization has a constitution and bylaws that spell out the benefits members receive. These sections become the inherent reasons why a person joins the association, and a member expects this service in return for payment of dues. As you might imagine, benefits vary from one organization to another. Box 9–4 spells out the benefits members derive from joining the SSPBA.

Traditional unions, for instance, have *shop stewards* who must represent the employee during disciplinary and grievance procedures whether the member is right or wrong. Usually, the actual mechanism for such an arrangement is worked out during the collective bargaining process. Other organizations may not have a contract in place but, nevertheless, provide employees with representation during disputes (Burpo et al., 1997). Most police labor organizations provide services to members under the presumption they are being treated unfairly. If the member is unjustly dismissed and the local organization approves representation, then help is provided. If it is determined that the member violated his or her oath of office by involvement in misconduct, there is no obligation to represent the member.

Other available benefits might include salary replacement, legislative services, computer services, pension consultants, disciplinary representation with approval of the local organization, and credit union services. While traditional unions offer their members a pension plan, such activity is not allowed when members belong to the public sector because government employee retirement benefits are regulated by statute.

Probably one of the most basic gains associated with collective bargaining concerns the concept of at-will employment, embraced in many states. *At-will employment* basically means that no employee, whether in the public or private sector, can expect to have a property right in a job. *Property right* is defined as the understanding that, unless discharged for cause, the employee can expect to continue to work for his or her employer as long as he or she wishes. Essentially, at-will employment translates into a lack of job security. It means that management can fire employees for either no reason or for any reason it deems necessary with no due process protection.

The impact of at-will employment cannot be overstated. As this chapter is being written, Georgia Governor Zell Miller is preparing to leave office. Thanks to his creation of the Hope Scholarship Funds and the blessings of a good economy, Miller

---

Box 9–4   An Example of the Types of Services Offered to Members of a Police Labor Association

The Southern States PBA offers a variety of services to its members. The association:

- Pays the member's beneficiary an amount equal to his or her base salary for one year if the member is accidentally or intentionally killed, whether on- or off-duty. (The minimum payout is $20,000 and the maximum payout is $100,000.)
- Provides an attorney if members are named as defendants in civil or criminal action resulting from their duties, and represents members at the scene of all on-duty shootings or serious injuries.
- Maintains a professional staff to provide members with consultation on pension matters and to aid in obtaining legislation beneficial to the law enforcement profession.
- Upon approval of local chapter boards, will provide representation to members in cases where they have been unfairly disciplined.
- Operates a political action committee (PAC) and is involved in screening and endorsing political candidates at the local, county, state, and federal levels.
- Offers a credit union to its members. The credit union provides a full range of financial services including a specially designed, low interest rate VISA credit card.
- Maintains a 24-hour hotline for members seeking immediate assistance.

Source: Southern States Police Benevolent Association. *Membership Brochure.*

---

exits with a 85% public approval rating. However, state employees are very much aware that many public jobs were lost to privatization under Governor Miller. His legacy will be well remembered by newer state employees who find their positions to be "unclassified." *Unclassified*, like *at will*, means that workers can be released from their positions without cause and with no right of appeal.

Unless "at-will" employment is addressed explicitly by statute or in a collective bargaining agreement, most criminal justice agencies operate under this doctrine. If a collective bargaining agreement or some other mechanism is in place, then the at-will employment doctrine does not apply. As Box 9–5 illustrates, it is not difficult to imagine the advantage this concept gives employers over their workers. At the same time, it is easy to see the advantages of a collective bargaining agreement that requires termination of employment must be "for cause" and must follow proscribed administrative and legal standards of due process (Carrell and Heavrin, 1995).

Box 9–5   Examples of Actual Recent Cases Regarding "At-Will" Employment

"At the request of local attorneys for the Florida ACLU, we [the National Association of Police Organizations] became involved in the case of a Florida female Deputy Sheriff who had been fired because she married a man who had once been arrested on a marijuana charge. The Sheriff's office argued that the Deputy had violated the rules against 'association with criminals.' The Deputy pointed out that the man had successfully completed the Sheriff's office's own drug rehabilitation program and was clean and sober and a good citizen when she met and married him years later. She was fired anyway." (Source: http://www.napo.org)

"The Missouri Union of Law Enforcement AFL-CIO (MULE) has received a copy of a letter sent by Ivan L. Schraeder, Attorney-at-Law, threatening legal action against the Hazelwood Police Officer's spouse's organization, known as the SWAT Team. Schraeder accuses the SWAT Team of circulating defamatory, untrue remarks which are damaging to Hazelwood Police Chief Carl Wolf. . . . The SWAT Team has most recently criticized the chief for his testimony at . . . [a] Civil Service board hearing. His testimony given under oath, was contradicted by other officers at the hearing, leading many Hazelwood officers to believe that Chief Wolf was not being truthful in his testimony." (Source: http://www.mule57.org)

In 1997, a small town in Georgia mandated that all of its 20 plus police officers would carry OC spray and that they would all be squirted in the face with the spray as part of their OC orientation process. One officer objected, stating that he feared being sprayed and did not wish to carry OC spray. The chief of police ordered the officer to comply with the departmental policy or be fired. When the officer stated that he would go through the training and would carry the spray if ordered but would not submit to being sprayed in the face, his employment was terminated. When interviewed by news reporters about his dismissal, the officer stated, "I carry a gun, too. Does that mean I have to be shot?"

In Birmingham, Alabama, Officer Scott Bahakel arrested two young women who continued fighting at a public event after his efforts to separate them failed. One of the women involved was the daughter of Birmingham mayor Richard Arrington. The next day, the arrest records regarding the mayor's daughter disappeared. The other young woman, who had been released on bond, was discreetly told by a city official that if she would keep her mouth shut, charges against her would be dropped. Officer Bahakel was suspended for having used inappropriate force. Despite witnesses who testified that Bahakel had used only enough force necessary to separate the two women and effect their arrests, he subsequently was fired. News coverage of the events lead to police chief Artie Doitch and a couple of jail officials being tried and convicted of altering public records. While Doitch appealed his conviction, Mayor Arrington reassigned him to "special duties" in city hall. Doitch was later awarded a medical retirement for injuries suffered after he "slipped and fell on the steps" at city hall. Officer Bahakel's efforts to regain his position were unsuccessful.

A few years ago, the Alabama legislature gave serious consideration to passing legislation creating a Police Officer Bill of Rights. Anniston police chief Wayne Chandler used the agency's teletype to send out messages to all the police chiefs within the state of Alabama, urging them to contact their legislators and oppose this effort to usurp their authority. Police employees at agencies that had received the communication alerted the media to this blatant misuse of the NCIC system. When confronted by reporters about his misuse of the system and the possibility of punishment for violating NCIC regulations, Chief Chandler was unrepentant. He acknowledged having the messages sent and stated that he saw it as a proper use of the system because he was trying to prevent legislation that would have undermined law enforcement within the state.

OPPOSITION TO POLICE LABOR ORGANIZATIONS

The history of union activity and uncertainty works against the participation of law enforcement officers in traditional labor unions. There is a certain amount of reluctance among officers to take part in an organization they do not control. However, police officers also recognize they have outgrown the utility of civil service or merit systems that originated as the primary way to protect government employees from being victimized by politics. However, the changing workplace environment has compelled law enforcement officers to look for a safe harbor. Civil liability, low pay, inept supervision, lack of job security, and other poor conditions prompted the search for outside organizations that offer additional protection. However, as the following materials demonstrate, this change did not come about easily.

Government Opposition

Most employers fear third-party organizations as a source of unrest and labor difficulties (Burpo, 1971; Salerno, 1981). Managers usually view police labor groups as trying to usurp their authority. Many police administrators, who belong to their own professional associations, oppose efforts to organize employees and make a concerted effort to block such movements. An example is the official position of the International Association of Chiefs of Police, developed in 1958, which states that "police agencies are semi-military in nature, and police officers . . . are required to forgo certain personal privileges enjoyed by employees in private industry" (IACP, 1958, p. 3).

One form of government opposition is to limit the activities of police labor organizations. As the Georgia legislation depicted in Box 9–6 shows, most states have banned police officers from walking off the job and engaging in labor strikes.

Box 9–6   Georgia Laws Regarding the Right of Public Employees to Strike

45-19-2. Public Employees Not to Promote, Participate in, or Encourage Strikes.

No public employee shall promote, encourage, or participate in any strike. Provided, however, that no right to collective bargaining currently recognized by law is abridged by this act. (Ga. L. 1962, p. 450, § 1; Ga. L. 1998, p. 1155 § 1.)

45-19-3. Supervising Personnel Not to Authorize, Approve, or Consent to Strike.

No person exercising any authority, supervision, or direction over any public employee shall have the power to authorize, approve, or consent to a strike by one or more public employees; and such person shall not authorize, approve, or consent to such a strike. (GL L. 1962, p. 459, § 5; Ga. L. 1998, p. 1155, § 1.)

45-19-4. Termination of Employment, Forfeiture of Civil Service Status, Job Rights, Seniority, and Emoluments upon Violation of Code Section, 45-19-2.

Any public employee who violates Code Section 45-19-2 shall be deemed to have terminated his or her employment; shall forfeit his or her civil service status, job rights, seniority, and emoluments, if any; and subsequent to such violation shall not be eligible for appointment or reappointment or employment or reemployment in public employment for a period of three years after such violation except upon the following conditions:

1. His or her direct or indirect compensation shall in no event exceed that received by him or her immediately prior to the time of such violation;

2. His or her direct or indirect compensation shall not be increased for three years after such subsequent appointment or reappointment or employment or reemployment; and

3. He or she shall be on probation for a period of five years following such appointment or reappointment or employment or reemployment, during which period he or she shall serve without tenure and at the pleasure of the appointing or employing officer or body. (Ga. L. 1962, p. 459, § S; Ga- I.; 1998, p. 1155, § 1.)

A second form of government opposition occurs when management refuses to abide by the agreements made with labor organizations. In these situations, police administrators either ignore labor agreements entirely or consistently resist com-

Box 9–7   Minimumed Out

Approximately 20 years ago, a contract was reached between the Florida PBA and the city of Tallahassee, which sought to increase the salaries of police sergeants. A minimum salary was established for new sergeants and current sergeants were to receive salary increases of 10%. New sergeants would receive the new minimum salary and an additional 5% increase on completion of a six-month probationary period. A young sergeant who had been in rank for over two years thought the contract was fair in that, while his current salary was $19 below the new minimum, the 10% increase he would receive would place him well above the new sergeants.

When the contract took effect, the young sergeant discovered that his salary had been raised by only $19, not the sum he was expecting. When this sergeant inquired why he had not received his full 10% salary increase, the director of Employee Relations for the city of Tallahassee gleefully informed the sergeant that a strict interpretation of the contract meant that his pay had to be raised only to the minimum salary instead of a 10% increase. Within six months, the sergeant (who had received "above average" and "outstanding" evaluations ever since being promoted) was making 5% less that new sergeants who successfully completed probation. In effect, he had been minimumed out.

pliance with contractual obligations. The first two situations can be dealt with through litigation even though this approach creates difficulties for both the union and the employer. A third situation is more difficult to counter. Here, administrators try to use the contractual agreement as a means to harass union employees. They may comply with only those issues agreed on contractually and seek to avoid providing benefits that nonunion employees receive. Or, they may interpret the contract to actually deny benefits. Box 9–7 displays an example of how this tactic can occur.

Officer Opposition

Many law enforcement officers do not favor police unionization. Traditionally, police officers tend to be lower-middle class and politically conservative. In addition, because of their role as protectors of public order and property rights, some officers historically have been opponents of private sector unions (Barker et al., 1994). With the exceptions noted in prior sections, until recently, many police officers shared the general public's fear of organized labor. Some still do.

Another reason for this reluctance to become affiliated with a labor organization stems from the belief that police officers ought not to have to be unionized. Many officers are distrustful of unions. Even independent unions run by police officers are looked on as controlled by outsiders. Other officers may feel that, if they must look to a union to ameliorate workplace conditions, then they do not want to work for that agency in the first place.

Another fear is that participating in a labor organization will result in officers being forced by the union to participate in some sort of job action (strike, sickout, etc.). The worry is that this activity could prompt government officials to take punitive action that, if not job threatening, still might result in adverse treatment for all officers. An excellent example of this is the San Francisco Police strike in August of 1975. In this case, the Police Officers Association believed that Mayor Alioto was in charge and had the power to make decisions on their behalf. When the strike ended, the Board of Supervisors had the final say. As a result, the police officers lost and suffered for some time afterward (Bent and Reeves, 1978). As time went on, the governing Board of Supervisors took back some gains granted to the police and fire associations prior to the strike. The mistake here was that the police association leadership ignored the role of elected politicians. In this case, Mayor Alioto was in his last term of office and could not run again. The members of the Board of Supervisors were beginning an election campaign and two of them were running for mayor (Bopp, Chignell, and Maddox, 1977) .

The San Francisco Police strike points out the significant difference between a private sector labor organization and a similar group of government workers. The private sector union strives to identify goals and objectives while defining their public. Traditionally, police unions have not been as well focused on their goals and objectives. Even if the group identifies some goals and objectives, these not always are supported by all the members (Salerno, 1981).

Box 9–8   Don't Feel Pressured

In 1981, the sergeants and lieutenants at the Tallahassee, Florida, Police Department received the right to vote on whether they wanted the Florida PBA to represent them in collective bargaining with the city of Tallahassee. While officials at city hall did not seem to oppose the process, the chief of police took it as a personal insult. He made a point of meeting individually with many of the sergeants and lieutenants, several of whom had been promoted during his administration. In a private meeting with one young sergeant, the chief explained that the sergeant's education, intellect, and ambition had placed him "on a management track." Unfortunately, the sergeant's support for "the union" revealed a serious and disturbing lack of loyalty to the chief and the agency that, if not corrected, would preclude him from being considered for any future promotions.

The sergeant thought about the warning and then later voted for the Florida PBA contract. Despite being at or near the top of the promotion lists during the next several years, the sergeant (who continued to receive "excellent" and "above average" evaluations from his superiors) was not promoted to lieutenant and later left the department.

Probably the leading reason for officer hesitation to become involved in police labor organizations is the fear of being punished for being "disloyal" to the agency. Many officers still believe (some correctly, despite federal court rulings that state laws prohibiting union membership are unconstitutional) that, if they were to promote or participate in establishing a labor organization, they would face disciplinary action. We clearly can recall events during our own police careers where support for the union was seen as disloyalty to the organization and could result in being transferred to a lesser assignment, being denied consideration for promotion, or being fired on the spot. Box 9–8 shows what could happen.

IMPACT OF UNIONS AND LABOR RELATIONS ON LAW ENFORCEMENT

Despite strong opposition by police administrators and elected officials, police unions have developed in response to desires for better economic benefits, enhanced working conditions, fair treatment, and greater input into policy making (Roberg and Kuykendall, 1997, pp. 330–331). Today, nearly three-fourths of all American police officers are members of unions (Walker, 1992, p. 372).

As discussed previously, *collective bargaining* is the term that describes the negotiation process between the police union and the employing organization. Within the negotiation process, representatives of the union and representatives of the government entity that employs them seek to reach agreement over issues such as salaries, work conditions, job assignments, promotional policies, disciplinary procedures, health coverage, pensions, paid leave, and other relevant concerns. Once an agreement has been reached (either through negotiations or, following their breakdown, arbitration or court settlement), the parties enter into a legally binding contract that specifies the rights of both sides regarding their interaction with one another. Failure of either side to comply with the contractual agreement is dealt with administratively and, if necessary, through litigation.

In addition to collective bargaining, police unions provide representation for individual employees in disciplinary proceedings. They also represent employees who have filed grievances against supervisory actions or administrative policies that are perceived as improper or unfair. Police unions also assist in providing legal representation for members. Members participate in political campaigns to strengthen the police influence on lawmaking and government policies. They lobby local, state, and occasionally, the federal government on pertinent law enforcement issues. In addition, unions serve as social organizations, which sponsor activities for and on behalf of their members.

Police administrators and civilian reformers who see the unions as promoting employee issues at the expense of the police organization often depict police unions in a negative light. Unions are believed to impede organizational progress due to their concerns about seniority, which frequently conflicts with affirmative action and merit programs; their resistance to civilian review boards, which some people think enhance community relations; their desire to participate in decision making, which restricts managerial discretion in the achievement of the police mission; and, their concern with economic benefits, which restricts allocations that government would rather spend in other areas (Cole, 1992; Gaines, Southerland, and Angell, 1991; Roberg and Kuykendall, 1997; Walker, 1992).

However, police unions also are seen as having a positive impact on policing in that they force police organizations to become more professional. Many police administrators define professionalism as bureaucratic enforcement of strict rules and regulations. Unions have required managers to become more sensitive to employee issues and give employees greater input into departmental decision making. Involving the rank and file in decision making has improved agency effectiveness and required police administrators to enhance their own performance. Professionalism now is viewed by progressive police administrators as developing competent personnel, capable of interacting with the community to provide desired services. The sense of belonging fostered by increased participation and subsequent increased responsibility in the organization's success has heightened officer performance. Limiting the potential for administrative mismanagement has benefited not only the internal communities but external communities as well (Gaines et. al., 1991; Roberg and Kuykendall, 1997; Walker, 1992; Whisenand and Ferguson, 1989).

CONCLUSION

The previous section discusses the impact of police labor organizations on American law enforcement. The impact will continue to be felt. Police administrators increasingly will find themselves dealing with officers who expect to be treated fairly, to have more input into departmental decision making, and who want better opportunities for career advancement. In addition, officers will continue to expect to receive economic compensation and fringe benefits commensurate with the increasingly complex demands of contemporary police work. As Professor Golden explains in Chapter 6, these expectations will be heightened by community policing efforts that require the revision of traditional police organizational structures and management techniques (Barker et al., 1994).

Police agencies will have to become more humanistic or employee oriented for a number of reasons other than the effects of labor organizations. Federal and state laws that protect the rights of women, minority-group members, and employees in general must be obeyed. Also, technological advances and social changes have resulted in better educated, more professional employees, who are more likely to question the status quo and expect understanding and assistance rather than strict discipline from their employers. Police administrators will find that employee issues are increasingly complicated and the autocratic management styles that used to dominate policing are becoming passé. As in the past, those agencies that are well managed will tend to have few problems with police labor organizations (Gaines et al., 1991).

The future of police labor relations, however, is not going to be all rosy. Financial shortfalls will lead to downsizing in the public sector similar to that which the private sector has experienced. Citizen demands for leaner government that requires fewer tax dollars while providing more services are unrealistic. But as Professor Olson writes in Chapter 11, the reduction in government budgets and the demands for enhancement in accountability, effectiveness, and efficiency are very real. Like other government entities, police agencies are finding themselves being asked to "do more with less." Budget constraints will lead to greater utilization of civilians, sharing of support services among agencies, increased reliance on problem-oriented service-delivery systems, and the consolidation of smaller agencies into larger ones (Barker et al., 1994).

Police labor organizations will have to adapt to these changes. Concerns about seniority may be overridden by federal and state mandates regarding equal employment opportunity and merit programs. Civilian review boards, along with other means of enhancing community relations, will override labor relations concerns regarding autonomy. Many police administrators will try to use budget constraints and accountability demands to restrict employee input into decision making. Like their private sector counterparts, government leaders will seek to restrict or even reduce economic benefits to police employees to address other financial shortfalls.

The results of all these pressures will be that the role of labor organizations within police labor relations will change. Labor organizations still will be needed to articulate the concerns of employees, provide representation for grievance resolutions and disciplinary hearings, and advocate economic advancements. Employee protections will continue to be the focus of these organizations. But, to avoid the membership declines experienced within the private sector, police labor organizations will have to demonstrate to both police officers and administrators that they are able to provide needed services to their membership that do not interfere with the attainment of the challenging police mission.

DISCUSSION QUESTIONS

1. Define labor relations. Make a list of those issues, in addition to collective bargaining, that have an impact on labor relations.
2. Suppose you are the police chief in a local law enforcement agency. Some of your employees want to talk about the possibility of establishing a police officer labor organization. What points would you raise in an effort to dissuade the officers from proceeding further?
3. Suppose that you are a police officer in a local law enforcement agency. Some of your colleagues want to talk about the possibility of establishing a police officer labor organization. What points would you raise pro and con?
4. Continuing with the previous question, your colleagues ask you to visit the Internet sites contained in this chapter and recommend which police labor organizations they should consider joining. What recommendations would you issue and why?
5. Continuing with the previous question, suppose that you and your colleagues have affiliated with a police labor organization. You now are faced with the task of negotiating the first collective bargaining agreement between the municipality and officers. What points do you think the contract should cover?
6. Continuing with the previous question, the city balks at all the points you wish to include in the collective bargaining agreement. What strategies do you now pursue? Why?

REFERENCES

American Federation of State and County Municipal Employees. At http://www.afscme.org/about/content.htm, 1998.
Atkins v. City of Charlotte, 269 F.Supp. 1068 (1969).
Barker, T., R. D. Hunter, and J. P. Rush. *Police Systems and Practices: An Introduction.* Englewood Cliffs, NJ: Prentice-Hall, 1994.
Bent, A. E., and T. Z. Reeves. *Collective Bargaining in the Public Sector.* Menlo Park, CA: Benjamin-Cummings, 1978.
Bopp, W. J., P. Chignell, and C. Maddox. "The San Francisco police strike of 1975: A case study." *Journal of Police Science and Administration* 5, no. 2 (1977), pp. 32–42.
Burpo, J. H. *The Police Labor Movement: Problems and Perspectives.* Springfield, IL: Charles C Thomas, 1971.

_____. *Police Unions in the Civil Service Setting.* Washington, DC: U.S. Government Printing Office, 1979.

_____, R. Delord, and M. Shannon. *Police Association Power, Politics, and Confrontation: A Guide for the Successful Police Labor Leader.* Springfield, IL: Charles C Thomas, 1997.

Carrell, M. R., and C. Heavrin. *Labor Relations and Collective Bargaining: Cases, Practices, and Law,* 4th ed. Englewood Cliffs, NJ: Prentice Hall, 1995.

Carter, D. L., and A. D. Sapp. "A comparative analysis of clauses in police collective bargaining agreements as indicators of change in labor relations." *American Journal of Police* 12, no. 2 (1992), pp. 17–46.

Cole, G. F. *The American System of Criminal Justice,* 6th ed. Pacific Grove, CA: Brooks/Cole, 1992.

Dantzker, M. L. *Police Organization and Management: Yesterday, Today, and Tomorrow.* Boston: Butterworth–Heinemann, 1999.

Gaines, L. K., M. D. Southerland, and J. E. Angell. *Police Administration.* New York: McGraw-Hill Book Company, 1991.

Gammage, A. Z., and S. L. Sachs. *Police Unions.* Springfield, IL: Charles C Thomas, 1972.

Halpern, S. C. *Police Association and Department Leaders.* Lexington, MA: Lexington Books, 1974.

Harrigan, J. J. *Politics and Policy in States and Communities,* 6th ed. New York: Longman, 1998.

International Association of Chiefs of Police. *Police Unions.* Alexandria, VA: International Association of Chiefs of Police, 1958.

_____. *Critical Issues in Police Labor Relations.* Alexandria, VA: International Association of Chiefs of Police, 1977.

McAuliffe v. New Bedford, 155 Mass. 216 (1892).

Roberg, R. R., and J. Kuykendall. *Police Management,* 2nd ed. Los Angeles: Roxbury, 1997.

Rosenbloom, D. H. *Public Administration: Understanding Management, Politics, and Law in the Public Sector,* 4th ed. New York: McGraw-Hill Book Company, 1998.

Salerno, C. A. *Police at the Bargaining Table.* Springfield, IL: Charles C Thomas, 1981.

Tompkins, J. *Human Resource Management in Government.* New York: HarperCollins, 1995.

Walker, S. *The Police in America: An Introduction,* 2nd ed. New York: McGraw-Hill Book Company, 1992.

Whisenand, P. W., and F. Ferguson. *The Managing of Police Organizations,* 3rd ed. Englewood Cliffs, NJ: Prentice Hall, 1989.

White, J. R. "Violence during the 1919 Boston police strike: An analysis of the crime control myth." *Criminal Justice Review* 13, no. 2 (1988), pp. 61–68.

Chapter 10

Accreditation: Agency Professionalization

Kimberly A. McCabe, University of South Carolina

For many years reform proposals geared toward professionalizing the police focused on changing individual officers. Some plans sought to branch out and bring absent or underrepresented groups of people into the ranks. Other observers thought that hiking the entrance standards or making them more rigid would do the trick. Other unsatisfied critics turned to recruiting college-trained applicants as the crucial key. Despite all the good intentions behind these changes, similar problems kept resurfacing in the law enforcement world.

Lately, a new line of thinking, known as *accreditation*, has emerged. It emphasizes revamping police organizations as a more viable solution to ongoing problems. To promote deep-seated changes, accreditation calls for the standardization of policies and procedures to ensure fair, reliable, and consistent law enforcement and service delivery. The effort to upgrade or professionalize police agencies is the focus of this chapter.

During the 1950s, the FBI began recognizing the need for more effective police reorganization (Witham, 1991). Many other law enforcement groups came to share this outlook. Eventually, the International Association of Chiefs of Police, the National Sheriffs' Association, the National Organization of Black Law Enforcement Executives, and the Police Executive Research Forum joined forces and hatched a new proposal. In 1979, the Commission on Accreditation for Law Enforcement Agencies (CALEA) unveiled plans for a voluntary accreditation program for law enforcement agencies. The first nationally recognized standards for law enforcement were approved and released through the commission four years later. Since that time, the idea of accreditation has taken root. The number of law enforcement agencies earning accredited status through CALEA has swelled and a growing number of local agencies have expressed an interest in learning more about the accreditation process (Carter and Sapp, 1994).

The topics discussed in this chapter are intended to help develop a greater appreciation for the concept of accreditation as it is applied to law enforcement agencies. Some time is spent explaining the role of CALEA, what a standard is in the accreditation process, what an agency can expect to experience during the accreditation process, and the idea of reaccreditation and CALEA's certification program. Also included in this chapter is a general profile of nationally accredited agencies, the benefits an agency derives from accreditation, criticisms of accreditation, and empirical studies that evaluate differences between accredited and nonaccredited agencies.

There also is a brief presentation on the training and background of assessors, as well as a look at the steps taken by CALEA to maintain the objectivity of the assessment process. In addition, problems that may occur during the assessment phase are discussed from an assessor's point of view. Safeguards aimed at enhancing an agency's success with the accreditation process also are introduced.

After developing a background on national accreditation efforts, the focus will turn to activity at the state level. Some states now offer their own versions of accreditation as an alternative to national approval. State representatives maintain they can deliver a comparable and less costly program to their law enforcement constituents. In addition, spokespersons assert that, since their programs are unique to the state, they are better able to meet the needs of smaller local agencies and can address specific questions that may not be applicable at the national level. In any event, we visit recent state entries into the accreditation process and pay some attention to the benefits and criticism of the state efforts. The chapter should provide an appreciation for the basic issues that contemporary police administrators must consider when deciding if they should initiate an accreditation review.

ACCREDITATION

Accreditation involves a review of an organization's credentials by an overseeing body of independent experts to determine whether the organization complies with a set of minimum operating standards common in that field. Accreditation is a common feature in many public service sectors. Public and private educational institutions, ranging from kindergartens to universities, undergo periodic accreditation inspections. Hospitals, health-related institutions, and correctional facilities also fall under the watchful eyes of external experts. As a result, proponents argue that it is reasonable to expect that law enforcement organizations also should be held to a higher standard of expectations.

Law enforcement is a unique entity when compared to other agencies that serve the public. For instance, police officers are entrusted with the authority to use force, even deadly force. As the guardians of social control, the police also possess the legal authority to commit acts that, if done by members of the general public, would be considered illegal. For example, police have the authority to exceed posted speed limits when responding to an emergency. These powers, especially in a democratic society, amount to an awesome amount of control, which must be accompanied by a corresponding set of checks and balances. An accreditation program, which expresses appropriate standards of operations, represents another avenue by which law enforcement officials are held in check.

As Chapter 1 explains, law enforcement in this country is a highly fragmented enterprise. With over 17,000 local law enforcement agencies operating within the United States, it stands to reason that there would be some desire for uniformity and consistency. Unfortunately, there are numerous opinions as to what is the most appropriate method of law enforcement. As Whisenand and Ferguson (1978) pointed out over two decades ago, a multitude of theories and models exist for operating a productive police organization. Law enforcement accreditation may provide yet another option for addressing some of these key issues and providing up-to-date information.

COMMISSION ON ACCREDITATION FOR LAW ENFORCEMENT AGENCIES

As mentioned earlier, the efforts of nationally recognized police organizations have resulted in establishing an accreditation program for law enforcement agencies. The Commission on Accreditation for Law Enforcement Agencies, Inc., which is based in Virginia, administers this program.

CALEA has been in operation for nearly two decades. Its voluntary program provides law enforcement agencies the opportunity to enhance their mission statements by utilizing consistent procedures and policies of operations. Currently, CALEA is the only internationally recognized law enforcement accreditation program in existence. It has accredited agencies in the United States, Canada, and Barbados (CALEA, 1997). At present, approximately 20% of all U.S. law enforcement officers work in agencies involved in the accreditation process as do approximately 10% of Canada's law enforcement officers (Daughtry, 1996).

Good policy guidelines are an essential ingredient for an effective police organization. We see the corollary to this line of thinking in Chapter 7, where Professor Camp talks about the various grounds for civil litigation. That is, any agency that lacks adequate policy guidelines is a prime target for civil liability lawsuits. The absence of sound policy not only endangers the lives of officers but threatens the lives of the very citizens whom the agency is sworn to serve and protect. Therefore, policy development becomes an integral part of the professionalization strategy advocated by the accreditation process.

The standards promoted by CALEA address such areas as the role of law enforcement, personnel, operations, prisoner handling, and court-related activities. These areas provide specific foci for law enforcement policy and procedures. However, before we can discuss the accreditation process, we turn to the topic of standards, which is the foundation of accreditation.

Standards

In its original draft, the commission identified 48 topical areas to be addressed through approximately 1,000 standards. After much review and several modifications, the number of topical areas was reduced to 40 and the number of standards was streamlined to approximately 430. The standards essentially are the groundwork for the entire accreditation process, because they provide the rules and regulations that guide an agency seeking accredited status. An agency that demonstrates compliance with the applicable standards is awarded accredited status.

A typical standard is composed of three parts: the standard statement, the commentary, and the appropriate level of compliance. The *standard statement* provides the requirement(s) for the agency seeking accreditation. Some statements must be expressed in what is known as a "written directive" or an agency's policies and procedures of operation. In other words, if a standard statement requires some sort of written declaration on the use of warning shots, the agency must provide a policy that states when, if ever, a member may fire a warning shot. Other statements may require only observable compliance. In this case, a standard may stipulate that all patrol vehicles must be clearly marked and outfitted with emergency lights. This standard is satisfied simply by properly equipping all patrol cars. Still other statements may require a report or supporting evidence to document an activity. For example, personnel records can verify an agency's efforts to achieve a demographic balance in its recruitment and hiring.

The *commentary* provides some explanation of the standard or some suggestion as to how the agency may comply with the standard. These suggestions are not requirements. Depending on local needs, the agency may choose any applicable avenue that satisfies compliance. Primary emphasis is not on how an agency fulfills a standard but that the requirement is addressed in a meaningful way.

The *level of compliance* indicates how important CALEA deems the standard to be. Standards can be mandatory, other than mandatory, or not applicable for an agency. In many instances, the size of an agency (number of employees) determines the level of compliance. For example, standards that deal with safety measures most often are mandatory for all agencies. Standards that address exceptional law enforcement performance most often are stipulated as other than mandatory. For example, a small agency that has no special tactical team would not be required to provide policies regarding the operating procedures for such a squad. Standards usually are deemed not applicable if an agency does not engage in the function. Most local police departments do not operate jail or booking facilities because the sheriff's office attends to these functions. Therefore, they would be excused from this area.

A major factor related to a standard's application to an agency is its size. Agency size is broken into Size A (1–24 employees), Size B (25–74 employees), Size C (75–299 employees), and Size D (300+ employees). It is possible for a standard to be classified as not applicable to agencies of size A, other than mandatory for agencies of size B, and mandatory for agencies of size C or D. Perhaps examples of three different standards will clarify this point.

Box 10–1 provides a specific directive for an agency concerning identification of its geographical jurisdiction. The commentary suggests the use of a map to satisfy the standard. The level of compliance associated with this standard statement indicates the standard is mandatory for all four size categories.

Box 10–1　An Example of a Mandatory CALEA Standard

Standard 2.1.1: A written directive delineates the specific geographical boundary of the agency's jurisdiction.

Commentary: It is fundamental that the agency clearly describe in writing the geographical boundaries of its jurisdiction. Situations involving overlapping or ambiguous territorial jurisdiction should be avoided. A detailed official map, including the boundaries of the jurisdiction, may satisfy the requirements of this standard.

Level of Compliance: (M M M M).

Source: CALEA. *Standards for Law Enforcement Agencies*, 3rd ed., p. 2-1. Fairfax, VA: Commission on Accreditation for Law Enforcement Agencies, 1994.

Box 10–2　An Example of an Optional CALEA Standard

Standard 52.1.11: The agency compiles annual statistical summaries, based upon records of internal affairs investigations, which are made available to the public and agency employees.

Commentary: None.

Level of Compliance: (O O O O).

Source: CALEA. *Standards for Law Enforcement Agencies*, 3rd ed., p. 52-3. Fairfax, VA: Commission on Accreditation for Law Enforcement Agencies, 1994.

An example of an optional standard appears in Box 10–2. Here, the standard provides a specific directive for departments that have an internal affairs component. However, no commentary is offered and compliance is optional for an agency seeking accredited status regardless of size.

To become accredited, an agency must comply with all the mandatory standards applicable to its size and with at least 80% of the other than mandatory standards. The agency is free to select the optional standards with which it will comply. This margin creates some flexibility in the accreditation process to accommodate local law enforcement practices.

The Accreditation Process

The accreditation process encompasses five distinct phases: the application, self-assessment, on-site assessment visit, commission review, and maintaining compliance. It usually takes about two years for an agency to complete the accreditation process. However, CALEA will allow an agency three years to complete the first two phases of the process. We now look at what transpires during each phase.

Application.   Most departments initiate the application phase of the accreditation process by requesting information from CALEA. These details are free and provide basic information on the rationale behind accreditation, what the process entails, how to determine an agency's eligibility, and what technical assistance is available. Eligible agencies are any government entities charged with law enforcement responsibilities. These organizations would include state police, state highway patrol, state departments of law enforcement, county law enforcement agencies, sheriffs departments, municipal law enforcement agencies, specialized law enforcement agencies such as university or transit police, and private agencies with law enforcement entities as verified by the commission (CALEA, 1992).

Some expenses are associated with the accreditation process. CALEA charges a fee for the initial accreditation and for reaccreditation. The application costs for agencies seeking accreditation for the first time range from approximately $4,500 to $18,000 and depend on the size of the department. If the agency decides to continue, it can purchase an application package for the current price of $250. The application package contains information on the process and a questionnaire for the agency to complete and return. This survey provides CALEA with background information about the agency and identifies a contact person known as the agency's *accreditation manager.* Accreditation managers, usually senior law enforcement officers, are invited to participate in a training workshop which CALEA conducts three times a year.

Once CALEA receives the agency's fee for the information package and reviews the agency's survey, the three-year time limit for completing the self-assessment phase begins. During this period agency personnel address each standard on a point-by-point basis to assure compliance through either policy or action. The next phase, the self-assessment stage, often is the first opportunity for an explicit review of agency policies.

Self-Assessment.   During this segment of the accreditation process, the agency reviews all applicable CALEA standards and provides "proof of compliance" for each standard. The agency then completes a "mock assessment." *Mock assessment* means that the agency invites trained assessors or accreditation managers from other agencies to review work to date. The purpose of the mock assessment is to provide the agency with an objective view of its standards and proofs of compliance. In most cases, the review will identify areas that the agency may have overlooked. The goal behind this mock assessment is to allow the agency the opportunity to correct any deficiencies or shortcomings prior to the actual on-site assessment visit. Once the agency feels it has remedied any flaws, it notifies CALEA and arranges for an on-site assessment visit.

On-Site Assessment Visit. After the agency initiates its on-site assessment phase, it forwards the appropriate fees to CALEA and submits an on-site plan for the assessors. CALEA selects an assessment team of usually three assessors who will visit the agency and review its efforts to address the standards. Proof regarding compliance with a standard rests with the agency, and in some cases, an agency may be asked to provide more than one proof of compliance for each standard (CALEA, 1992). The assessment team members assess the agency's compliance or noncompliance with standards. To add to the credibility of the process and avoid any appearance of impropriety, CALEA selects assessors from a state and region outside the area in which the agency under review is located.

Assessor training is an important component of the accreditation process. CALEA schedules assessor training sessions in conjunction with its three annual conferences. Potential assessors at least must hold a baccalaureate degree, have served a minimum of five years in a law enforcement capacity, and complete the training module sponsored by CALEA. In addition to attending the workshop, new assessors learn the ropes by accompanying an actual assessment team during an on-site visit. This practical experience gives new assessors the opportunity to watch experienced members conduct an actual on-site assessment process and ask questions about the dynamics. The names and addresses of these trained assessors remain on file with CALEA for future assignments.

Usually, the most experienced assessor is designated the assessment team leader. This person submits a formal report to CALEA regarding the team's findings about the agency. If the report reveals compliance with the standards, then a commission review is scheduled. If the report does not reveal compliance, then the agency must select one of three options. The agency can attempt to correct deficiencies and ask for another on-site assessment visit, it can appeal the assessment team decision to CALEA, or it can withdraw from the accreditation process.

Commission Review. The commission examines the assessment team report and, in most cases, listens to comments from agency representatives attending the hearing. If the commission is not satisfied with the agency's compliance, then accredited status is withheld. If the commission is satisfied with the agency's compliance, then accredited status is awarded to the agency for a three-year period. Shortly thereafter, a special ceremony is held in which CALEA confers formal recognition of accreditation on the agency. A second ceremony sometimes follows in the agency's hometown so that community leaders can celebrate the agency's newly acquired status.

Maintaining Compliance. At the conclusion of the three-year period of accredited status, CALEA offers the agency the opportunity to become reaccredited. If the agency decides to continue its status, the self-assessment and on-site assessment phases are initiated once again. Approximately, nine out of every ten agencies that earn initial accreditation from CALEA undertake the reaccreditation process (Daughtry, 1996).

THE CALEA CERTIFICATION PROGRAM

The commission added certification programs to its accreditation efforts in 1993. The effort here is to encourage further agency professionalization. Agencies can participate in the certificate program without making a full commitment to meet all the standards in the regular accreditation process. An agency can seek recognition for exemplary performance in the areas of training, communications, internal affairs, and court security. The fee for an area certification is approximately $1,800 and includes the cost of the on-site assessment visit. Subsequent certificates may be earned at the reduced price of $800 for the second certificate, $650 for the third certificate, and $500 for the fourth certificate. The certificate program is a relatively new component. Approximately 20 agencies across the country currently hold one or more certificates.

CHARACTERISTICS OF ACCREDITED AGENCIES

Today, over 300 law enforcement agencies in the United States are accredited by CALEA. The three most active states, as of mid-1997, in regard to agency partici- pation were Florida (49 agencies), Illinois (32), and Ohio (37). As Table 10–1 shows, most nationally accredited agencies tend to be the relatively larger municipal agencies.

When accreditation first made its appearance, the overwhelming majority of agencies receiving accredited status were large departments (100+ employees). Today, though, that picture is starting to change. Smaller agencies now are seeking accredited status. This may be because larger agencies already "paved the way." In other words, smaller agencies often mimic or adopt what works in larger agencies. Now that they have watched the accreditation process from the outside and see that the leader agencies are satisfied, smaller agencies are willing to move in this direction. The pattern appears to be part of the normal diffusionary process associated with changes in the law enforcement community (McEwen, 1997; Weiss, 1997).

Another possibility is that smaller agencies feel more welcome because some standards are optional or not required of smaller shops. A third alternative is that smaller agencies now have administrators who originally were employed by accredited agencies. These transplanted leaders have seen accreditation firsthand and view it as necessary for a well-organized law enforcement agency. As Professor Dantzker, Deputy Chief Hauptman, and Professor Southerland explain in earlier chapters, the vision that police leaders carry and how their ideas are transmitted are vital organizational characteristics. Regardless of the rationale, agency size no longer may be a determining factor for entering the accreditation process.

Although the impact of agency size may have diminished, the type of department may be an important factor that determines agency interest in accredi- tation. Most accredited law enforcement agencies in the United States are municipal or state police departments. Less than 15% are sheriffs departments. Of course,

Table 10–1   Selected Characteristics of Nationally Accredited Agencies as of April 1997

Type of Agency	Percent	Size of Agency	Percent
Municipal Police	80	1–24	2
Sheriff's Offices	12	25–74	30
State Agencies	8	75–299	36
		300+	32
Total	100		100

Source: CALEA records.

agencies that provide only correctional and judicial services would not be interested in accreditation.

This tilt probably is best explained by the power inherent in the position of sheriff. The sheriff is an elected official who wields enormous power, since this office is endowed by the constitution in most states. Historically, sheriffs have maintained absolute control over their departments. Little or no explanation is required for their actions. Accreditation standards reverse this situation. Since the accreditation process calls for consistent policies and procedures to be in place, a sheriff's department may decide not to seek accreditation.

Another attribute deals with the succession of office holders. Sheriffs serve terms of four years. A new sheriff may win the election and, in a very short span of time, completely dismantle a department in terms of employees, policies, prior decisions, and daily operations. In addition, many of a sheriff's actions are politically motivated. If local voters are not interested in accreditation, then the sheriff probably is not interested in accreditation. For these reasons, then, the underrepresentation of sheriff's offices in the accreditation process is understandable.

BENEFITS OF ACCREDITATION

Proponents of law enforcement accreditation maintain that an agency can gain a number of benefits from engaging in this process. The most often cited advantages behind accreditation include recognition as a leader in the field, a reduction in legal liability costs, and enhanced employee development. Each of these points is examined next.

Recognition

Most discussants readily agree that achieving accredited status elevates an agency's reputation for innovativeness among its peers. This recognition means that the department has demonstrated a willingness to conform to higher-than-average expectations. In addition, many would agree that becoming accredited is a milestone that generates positive publicity.

Some commentators feel that non-law enforcement entities gain new respect for accredited agencies (Greene, 1998). City and county managers, who lack a law enforcement background in most cases, gain a greater appreciation for the agency because of its emphasis on public service. As Breslin (1978) concluded 20 years ago, the observed professional actions of the police serve to increase the confidence and public support toward the agency.

Reduction in Legal Liability Costs

With respect to financial rewards, it is thought that accredited status helps reduce liability costs. Policies, which in many cases did not exist prior to becoming involved in accreditation (Greene, 1998), help standardize employee behavior and shield an agency from huge settlements. One item in the first chapter of this book, a point Professor Camp reiterates in Chapter 7, explains that an agency with a sound set of policy guidelines in place leaves little leeway to officer discretion in high-risk situations. This restrictiveness will result in fewer procedural questions and reduce the likelihood of litigious parties groping for a courtroom resolution.

Another facet attributed to accreditation is the development and distribution of operational goals and objectives to agency members (Williams, 1989). Employees within accredited agencies are more aware of procedural requirements than employees within nonaccredited agencies. As we see in Chapter 7, failure to train is an established basis for prevailing in a negligence tort. Since proper schooling in agency policies decreases a police department's liability (Ross and Jones, 1996), accreditation is a positive step in that direction (Bizzack, 1993).

Finally, another by-product of sound policy development is that insurance carriers may offer discounted rates and reduced premiums to accredited agencies (Dickman, 1995).

Enhanced Employee Development

Another positive feature associated with accreditation is that developing job and task descriptions for various positions can signal where employee development and additional training are needed. Gianakis (1992), for example, documents that officers within accredited agencies are more likely to receive extra training than their counterparts in nonaccredited agencies. Pearce and Shortum (1983) show that well-trained officers seem to handle calls for service more expediently. Freeman's (1996) examination of police brutality concludes that legal restrictions surrounding use of force can be undermined without departmental safeguards in place. Increased training, a specific protocol, and strict accountability are all positive outcomes.

A long-term benefit of accreditation may be improved officer morale. Camp's (1994) study of job satisfaction and turnover reveals that prison employees who have higher levels of organizational commitment are more likely to stay with the organization and not seek alternative employment elsewhere. As one might imagine, the impact of reduced employee turnover cannot be overstated. One case study concludes that gaining accreditation made a decided improvement in employee morale, which helped stabilize the personnel pool (DiCenzo and Broderick, 1987).

CRITICISMS OF ACCREDITATION

Although one may see tangible benefits to accreditation, other observers contend there are definite drawbacks. For starters, some people question the picture that CALEA has about what constitutes good policing (Greene, 1998). Another reaction is that accreditation has an overly restrictive view of police behavior and its focus on reining in discretion not always is appropriate. Finally, other critics dismiss the entire process as too cost prohibitive and lengthy.

View of Policing

It has been said that "good" policing is in the eyes of those who behold it. What may be an appropriate way to handle one situation might not work under other circumstances. Generally speaking, the decision as to how to handle a call for service, especially in nonfelony situations, is left to the first officer who responds to the scene. Some officers may be content to handle a call with merely a verbal warning. Other officers might elect to pursue more formal channels. For example, take a case involving a juvenile shoplifter. One officer might decide to contact the child's parents and let them handle the case informally, while another officer might arrest and transport the child to the juvenile facility.

Accreditation mandates procedural consistency and written guidelines. This requirement makes many people apprehensive about embarking on the accreditation process (DiCenzo and Broderick, 1987; McEwen, 1997). In fact, Brown (1981) sees the process as encouraging a robotic, rather than commonsense, response. This approach does not make sense in a time when many agencies are making a concerted effort to hire more college-educated officers because of the thinking skills they bring to the job. For those officers who wish to make decisions based on the circumstances and their law enforcement experience, accreditation often is not welcomed.

Cost

Another major concern, especially to smaller agencies, is that accreditation can be quite expensive and lengthy. As stated earlier, the initial outlay requires an agency to pay $250 simply to apply for the process. The actual total cost may surpass the $10,000 mark and a number of hidden costs are easy to overlook.

Bizzack (1993) reports that over 20% of the agencies seeking accreditation incurred expenses that ballooned above the $250,000 mark. Agencies may forget to factor in the salary of their designated agency manager, secretarial assistance, the time other senior officials spend reviewing and discussing potential policy guidelines, and other incidental expenses. Since most agencies operate under limited funding, the fear here is that accreditation costs may siphon dollars away from much-needed salary raises or equipment.

Another detraction is that the accreditation process is time consuming. Many agencies dedicate years to gaining accredited status. As Professor Dantzker explains in Chapter 2, there is a worrisome degree of turnover among police executives. Incoming administrators may not be in a position to devote their full attention to accreditation. Thus, lack of continuity in leadership may jeopardize organizational commitment to this process.

ASSESSOR OBSERVATIONS

Most people think that the fate of the agency rests in the hands of the on-site assessors. From an assessor's point of view, there are some common stumbling blocks to an agency seeking accreditation. The following material suggests that quite often an agency can be its own worst enemy.

Each time an assessor visits an agency, the experience is different. In many cases, a seemingly smooth process becomes engulfed in conflict because of a lack of preparation or lack of organization by the applying agency. This "fly by the seat of your pants" approach does not work when entering a process aimed at achieving professionalization. Experienced assessors have noted many problems during on-site visits which could have been avoided if simple preparation and flexibility were observed by the agency. This narrative discusses three such actual cases.

Example 1.   An agency applying for national accreditation has spent 28 months writing policies and making changes within the department for compliance with CALEA standards. Rather than contact accredited agencies for qualified assessors to review its efforts in a mock assessment, the agency's accreditation manager reviews the standards once more himself and then contacts the commission for a scheduled on-site examination. The assessment team identifies several areas that do not satisfy CALEA's requirements. The agency does not meet the requirements of its on-site assessment.

Probably the biggest blunder in this case is the failure to conduct a mock assessment prior to the actual on-site assessment. Agencies that choose not to "practice" often learn later that they have not adequately addressed some standards. By failing to schedule a mock assessment or by scheduling a session with unqualified assessors, the agency had done itself a disservice. Not only are identifiable problems not corrected prior to the actual on-site visit, but agencies may cost themselves accredited status when these problems surface during the formal visit. In addition, if the agency decides to continue its pursuit of accredited status, the extra cost of a second on-site visit is necessary. In the same realm, agencies that schedule their mock assessments only a short time prior to the on-site review may have insufficient time or energy to remedy any identified problems.

Example 2. The assessment team arrives at the airport, but no agency representative is there to greet it. After taking a cab to the agency, the team requests three copies of the agency's policies and procedures manual and a room in which to station itself during the review process. A receptionist, surprised by the visit, offers one team member her chair. She then leaves the area to search for the chief, the accreditation manager, and a policy manual. The agency definitely has not prepared for the on-site visit. The assessment team is left waiting by the receptionist's desk for two hours until the chief eventually arrives. The accreditation manager never shows. The team finally receives one policy manual six hours after arrival.

A second problem that may occur during an on-site review is that agency members are not aware of the scheduled visit. Assessors often will ask staff members questions concerning compliance with standards, and it is unfortunate when an officer is not aware of proper procedures.

In addition, the lack of a formal schedule during the on-site monitoring creates an environment of uncertainty for both the team and the agency. Stress levels already are high for agency personnel. Preparing for assessors with a formal agenda does much to reduce tension.

Example 3. During an on-site assessment, the team leader questions the sheriff about the agency's policies for employee grievance in the event of an employee's loss of promotion or termination of employment. The sheriff responds, "Through the office of the Sheriff, there is no grievance procedure. I hire and fire, at will." Although the team leader tries to explain that there must be some documentation of these procedures, the sheriff refuses to budge. The on-site report reflects the agency's noncompliance with a mandatory standard and the commission ultimately denies the agency accredited status.

As this illustration shows, a lack of compromise makes recognition of compliance almost impossible by the assessment team. By following suggestions from the team leader, an agency might be able to correct a compliance problem prior to the end of the on-site visit. Agency officials who fail to make concessions during this process often leave the assessment team with few options.

STATE ACCREDITATION PROGRAMS

Approximately ten states have either established or are planning to start a program to accredit the law enforcement agencies within their boundaries. Some states, like Florida, are carrying out the mandate of a specific state statute. Other states, such as Washington, are responding to requests from police organizations within the state.

States are moving toward their own accreditation systems for four primary reasons. For one thing, some people think the national program is too costly. Second is a sense that a state program would better meet the needs of smaller agencies. Third,

CALEA requires agencies to address over 400 standards, which some people think is too cumbersome. Finally, laws vary from one jurisdiction to the next. As a result, some people think that the philosophy of a state program would better focus on local law enforcement needs.

Cost

In many cases, agency interest in accreditation is greater for states that have established an accreditation program than in states with no accreditation program. This may be because the state program was launched as a reaction to criticism of the national movement (as Florida did in the early 1990s or as South Carolina did in the middle 1990s) or that the state program grew because of strong interest in the national program (Washington). No matter which explanation is valid, many law enforcement agencies would elect to be recognized for exemplary service if there were no budgetary constraints.

Quite honestly, a number of agencies feel that they simply cannot afford the CALEA fee structure. State-sponsored programs can fill this void and promote professional endorsement for considerably fewer dollars. Florida, for example, charges agencies on a sliding fee structure. The actual cost, which ranges from $500 to $4,000, is determined by the number of sworn-officer positions within an agency. Other states absorb administrative costs and do not charge agencies for participating in the process. For instance, the only accreditation expenses local agencies in South Carolina incur are costs for equipment and assessor travel.

Smaller Agencies

Even though the momentum has shifted, officials from smaller agencies still perceive CALEA's program as tailored toward larger agencies. Consequently, many smaller departments are dissuaded from competing for nationally recognized accredited status.

A state program allows smaller agencies to feel as if they are on equal footing with their colleagues. Half the local law enforcement agencies in this country consist of fewer than ten employees. Furthermore, 90% of all law enforcement agencies serve populations of under 25,000 (Reaves, 1996). State-based accreditation programs can be more sensitive to these constituents and generate a "comfort zone" for these small departments.

Number of Standards

The number of standards is yet another issue when considering accreditation programs. As mentioned earlier, CALEA has identified over 400 standards it deems relevant. Many state programs encompass many fewer standards. For example, both the Florida and Washington programs articulate approximately 200 standards. This is a more manageable task for agencies without complete policy manuals to tackle. Then again, if the goal is to encourage professionalism and bring laggards up to par, requiring only 200 standards makes considerable sense.

Jurisdiction

An officer with law enforcement powers in the state of South Carolina leaves that authorization whenever he or she exits that state's borders. Law enforcement officers are certified on a jurisdictional basis. Therefore, it stands to reason that agencies would be more interested in receiving recognition for exemplary status within their own state boundaries. State accreditation programs afford them that honor; the national accreditation program may not.

Critics claim that state programs are simply a "watered-down" national program, with fewer standards and less restriction on policies and procedures. Others scoff at the ensuing lack of rigor and accuse state programs of being "rubber stamps," designed to chase reduced insurance premiums. Still others charge that state programs only reinforce the "buddy system." In other words, friends review their kindred agencies and grant accreditation based on who they know instead of what the agency is actually doing.

CONCLUSION

The concept of agency accreditation, although a recent newcomer to the field, has become one of the most widely discussed avenues for improving law enforcement performance. CALEA, which has been in operation for nearly a decade, offers a voluntary program that provides law enforcement agencies the opportunity to improve their daily activities by utilizing consistent procedures and policies of operation. Through the adoption and selective modification of CALEA standards, the professionalization of law enforcement agencies is well underway. The standards, which address a wide range of concerns, provide specific foci for agencies to develop sound written guidelines. Good policy guidelines are essential to an effective police organization and CALEA attempts to provide a solid foundation for agencies.

The actual process of accreditation is multistaged, with specific actions required by the agency to progress from one stage to the next. These phases, discussed earlier, include (1) application, in which the agency submits formal application to CALEA and begins a review to satisfy standards; (2) self-assessment, which provides the agency its first review of it efforts to comply with the CALEA standards; (3) the on-site assessment visit, which is the formal review by the CALEA assessment team; (4) commission review, where the decision to grant accredited status based on the assessment team's report is made; and (5) reaccreditation, the agency's option to maintain its status by applying for a reanalysis at the end of the three-year accreditation period. In addition, this chapter provided a brief discussion of CALEA's certification program.

Another highlight of this chapter was a profile of nationally accredited agencies along with a look at some of the benefits and criticisms of accreditation. A brief presentation also is made on the training and background of an assessor, as well as an analysis of some common problems that assessors encounter during the assessment phase.

Finally, the recent entry of state governments into accreditation is discussed with particular attention directed toward the benefits and the criticisms of state programs. Some benefits of a state program include lower costs than the national program, a sense that a state program may better serve the needs of smaller agencies within the state, and a reduced number of standards with which to comply. Criticisms include the perception that state programs basically are a watered-down version of the national program and that state reviews carry the possibility of infiltration by political influences.

Accreditation is an attempt to improve the police organization through the standardization of policies and procedures. The goal of accreditation is to produce a fair and reliable avenue for the enforcement of laws and the delivery of essential services. Current research has claimed that accredited status improves training, public support, and officer satisfaction. In addition, accredited status also seems to reduce liability issues; however, its actual extent is still in question. Finally, although accreditation increases public support, its impact on the reduction of crime is yet to be fully addressed. Accreditation, though, needs to be recognized for what it does best. That is, it is a genuine effort to heed the calls of reformers to professionalize law enforcement.

DISCUSSION QUESTIONS

1. What role has the Commission on Accreditation for Law Enforcement Agencies (CALEA) played in providing law enforcement an avenue for professionalization?
2. Whenever possible, each of CALEA's standards consists of three parts. Identify and discuss those parts.
3. Identify and discuss the five phases that take place during the national accreditation process.
4. Why is a sheriff's department less likely to enter the accreditation process than a municipal police department?
5. Talk about the benefits and criticisms of national accreditation.
6. Discuss the rationale behind state-sponsored accreditation programs for law enforcement agencies.

REFERENCES

Bizzack, J. W. *Professionalization and Law Enforcement Accreditation: The First Ten Years.* Westport, CT: Praeger Books, 1993.

Breslin, W. J. "Police intervention in domestic confrontations." *Journal of Police Science and Administration* 6, no. 3 (1978), pp. 293–302.

Brown, M. K. *Working the Street: Police Discretion and the Dilemmas of Reform.* New York: Russell Sage, 1981.

CALEA. *Assessor Manual.* Fairfax, VA: Commission on Accreditation for Law Enforcement Agencies, 1992.

_____. *Standards for Law Enforcement Agencies,* 3rd ed. Fairfax, VA: Commission on Accreditation for Law Enforcement Agencies, 1994.

_____. *CALEA Update,* No. 65. Fairfax, VA: Commission on Accreditation for Law Enforcement Agencies, September, 1997.

Camp, S. D. "Assessing the effects of organizational commitment and job satisfaction on turnover: An event history approach." *Prison Journal* 74, no. 3 (1994), pp. 279–305.

Carter, D. L., and A. D. Sapp. "Issues and perspectives in law enforcement accreditation: A national study of police chiefs." *Journal of Criminal Justice* 22, no. 3 (1994), pp. 195–204.

Daughtry, S., Jr. (1996). Time to take another look at law enforcement accreditation. *Police Chief,* 63(3), 20-21.

DiCenzo, J., and J. Broderick. "A case study of law enforcement accreditation." In D. B. Kennedy and R. J. Homant (eds.), *Police and Law Enforcement,* vol. 5, pp. 131–143. New York: AMS Press, 1987.

Dickman, T. C. "Dear law enforcement official, memo." Indianapolis: American Justice Insurance Reciprocal, 1995.

Freeman, A. P. "Unscheduled departures: The circumvention of just sentencing for police brutality." *Hastings Law Journal* 47, no. 3 (1996), pp. 677–777.

Gianakis, G. A. "Appraising the performance of police patrol officers: The Florida experience." *Journal of Criminal Justice* 20, no. 5 (1992), pp. 413–428.

Greene, J. R. "Debate section." *Policing: An International Journal of Police Strategies & Management* 21, no. 1 (1998), pp. 192–205.

McEwen, T. "Policies on less-than lethal force in law enforcement agencies." *Policing: An International Journal of Police Strategies & Management* 20, no. 1 (1997), pp. 39–59.

Pearce, J. B., and J. R. Shortum. "Police effectiveness in handling disturbance calls. An evaluation of crisis intervention training." *Criminal Justice and Behavior* 10, no. 1 (1983), pp. 71–72.

Reaves, B. A. *State and Local Police Departments, 1993.* Washington, DC: Bureau of Justice Statistics, 1996.

Ross, D. L., and M. Jones. "Frequency of training in less-than-lethal force tactics and weapons: Results of a two state study." *Journal of Contemporary Criminal Justice* 12, no. 3 (1996), pp. 250–263.

Weiss, A. "The communication of innovation in American policing." *Policing: An International Journal of Police Strategies & Management* 20, no. 2 (1997), pp. 292–310.

Whisenand, P. M., and R. F. Ferguson. *The Managing of Police Organizations,* 2nd ed. Englewood Cliffs, NJ: Prentice Hall, 1978.

Williams, G. L. *Making the Grade.* Washington, DC: Police Executive Research Forum, 1989.

Witham, D. C. "Strategic planning in the Federal Bureau of Investigation." In D. Ogle (ed.), *Strategic Planning for Police,* pp. 75–80. Ottawa, Canada: Canadian Police College, 1991.

Chapter 11

Financing Police Services

David Olson, Loyola University of Chicago

For many of the concepts we have examined so far in this book, the police do not necessarily enjoy a particularly positive position, either organizationally or socially. However, this is not quite true with respect to financing, at least in comparison with the other components of the criminal justice system. In reality, the police enjoy a great deal of public support, especially when compared to the rest of the criminal justice system. Almost 60% of Americans had "a great deal" or "quite a lot" of confidence in the police in 1997, while less than 20% indicated similar levels of trust in the criminal justice system as a whole (Maguire and Pastore, 1998, p. 117). Indeed, one third of the public goes so far as to blame the court and prison systems for recent increases in crime (Maguire and Pastore, 1995, p. 157). The average person, though, does favor spending more money on crime control activities. Over the past 13 years, more than two thirds of the citizens feel that far too little is spent on crime control (Maguire and Pastore, 1998, pp. 142–143). However, people also feel that not enough money is being spent on other issues, ranging from drug addiction to education (Maguire and Pastore, 1998, p. 141). Despite these attitudes, voters have sent a clear message to elected officials: Reduce government waste and lower taxes. This sentiment places public policy makers and government administrators in the awkward position of responding to increasing expectations with limited resources.

A common perception is that putting more police in uniform will reduce crime through deterrence or apprehension of offenders. All government units are affected by the tendency to believe that hiring more officers or sheriff's deputies is the answer to winning the fight against crime (U.S. Advisory Committee on Intergovernmental Relations, 1993, p. 141). However, most police executives realize that putting more police on the streets will not necessarily reduce violent crime. When asked to name one specific activity that would lower violent crime, 31% of police chiefs and sheriffs supported efforts to cut down on drug abuse. Only 10% felt that deploying more officers would reduce violence (Maguire and Pastore, 1995, p. 172).

The movement toward community policing also is adding pressure to the balance between fiscal limitations and public expectations. Community policing requires more resources (Sadd and Grinc, 1996, p. 18). Similarly, the information age has saddled departments with the need to acquire increasingly sophisticated and expensive information and telecommunication systems. Many agencies are moving in this direction. For example, the prevalence of laptops and mobile digital terminals (MDTs) increased dramatically between 1990 and 1993 (Reaves, 1996, p. 18). Still, only 3–5% of the typical police budget goes to purchasing communication equipment (National Law Enforcement and Corrections Technology Center, 1995, p. 1).

The desire to meet the demands of the electorate have placed law enforcement leaders in a precarious position. The U.S. General Accounting Office (1993, p. 8) concluded in its examination of state and local finance issues, "there are large disparities in the levels of services that states and cities can afford (i.e., fiscal capacity differences)." This situation has led administrators to reevaluate the services they perform and seek nontraditional or nontax sources of revenue to support these operations. In many instances, services that once were provided free of charge now result in users paying fees. The provision of some services, such as unlocking car doors, have been eliminated completely and left to the private market. Also significant changes have taken place in the extent to which intergovernment grants support police activities, a heightened interest in imposing more fees and fines, and increased attention to unlocking potential revenues from asset forfeiture efforts. Police budgeting is becoming increasingly innovative.

This chapter looks at the trends and issues police executives face as they attempt to leverage more resources to support their operations. To illustrate how revenues collected from various sources end up being disbursed, we first have to describe the general funding process. This discussion is followed by a treatment of recent trends in police expenditures by various levels of government. The mechanisms by which the federal government supports state and local policing activities are explored. In addition, we visit other nontraditional funding sources, such as intergovernment transfers, user fees and fines, asset forfeiture, and financial support from the private sector. All this boils down to the concept that police officials have to be very economically nimble and astute if they hope to achieve their goals.

THE FUNDING PROCESS

The first thing we look at is how government agencies develop, receive, and expend a budget. We start by looking at the budgeting cycle and then different types of government funds. This excursion allows us to see budgets and their composition from a much more abstract or symbolic perspective. "Because the substantive effects of policies are often difficult to predict, expenditure levels often serve as proxies for the level of effort the government is making to solve specific social problems" (Weimer and Vining, 1992, p. 104). Therefore, understanding how budgets are developed can convey a sense of priorities among policy makers and legislative bodies.

The Budgeting Cycle

The potpourri of governmental jargon and acronyms can be daunting to newcomers. Look at the term *fiscal year* for a moment. Many state governments operate their fiscal year from July 1 through June 30. However, the federal fiscal year covers the period from October 1 through September 30. Counties and municipalities, on the other hand, may run on a calendar year basis. On top of all this, some states have biennial budgets that cover a 24-month period. Administrators who find themselves caught in these webs may feel like they are in a juggling act trying to cope with different time periods and various regulations.

Although most government budgets cover a 12-month fiscal year, the actual *budget cycle* is much longer. There are four distinct stages of the budget cycle: preparation or formulation, adoption, implementation, and evaluation (Peak, 1998, p. 346; Solano and Brams, 1987, p. 143). During the first stage, projections of the next year's revenues are made and provided to the mayor, county board president, governor, or president. This information then is used to direct agency or department heads as to how to formulate their budget requests. The second phase occurs when the executive finishes the budget and submits it for approval to the overseeing body, such as the city council, county board, state legislature, or Congress. The third part of the budget cycle lasts the entire fiscal year. The adopted budget is executed and appropriated funds are spent to accomplish the agency's goals and objectives. The final stage is an evaluation of whether individual agencies accomplished their goals and objectives with the money allocated and spent. Financial audits ensure that expenditures are appropriate and within the budgetary guidelines.

For the police administrator, this process usually involves working with the mayor, city manager, or county board president to prepare the agency budget. Fielding questions from city councils or county boards about the proposed budget will establish a sense of priorities. Then, the chief or sheriff must keep an eye on the expenditures and be accountable in the review of how the money was used to further the law enforcement mission.

Funding Sources

The revenue used to support police and other government services comes from a variety of sources. Some of those sources include taxes on property, income, sales and other items; intergovernment revenues; fees, fines, and other government-generated revenues; the sale of government bonds; and a variety of other revenue flows. Table 11–1 shows that the extent to which these various sources support government services differs across levels of government.

Local government expenditures are supported by the transfer of revenue from the federal and state governments, along with property taxes and charges for services. Intergovernment revenue may take the form of *revenue sharing*. In other words, taxes collected by state or federal authorities are shared with local entities. Such money

Table 11–1   Sources of Government Revenue, 1994–1995

Source	Federal	State	Local
Intergoverment	0.3%	29.2%	38.3%
Property tax	0.0%	1.3%	28.7%
Sales tax	7.9%	26.6%	6.0%
Individual income tax	57.2%	17.0%	1.8%
Corporation tax	14.8%	3.9%	0.3%
Other taxes	2.3%	3.5%	1.7%
Charges and miscellaneous	17.4%	16.8%*	23.0%
Total general revenue	$948 billion	$739 billion	$676 billion

Note: Detailed percentages do not add up to 100% due to rounding.
* Includes charges for state run hospitals, institutions of higher education, and other fee-based revenue.
Source: Compiled from U.S. Department of Commerce, *U.S. State and Local Government Finances by Level of Government, 1994–1995*, at http://www.census.gov/govs/estimate/ 95stlus.txt, 1997, and *Government Finances: Summary of Federal Government Finances*, at http://www.census.gov/govs/fedfin/federal.txt, 1994.

can be used for any purpose the local government feels is necessary and is referred to as *unrestricted intergovernment aid*.

Intergovernment revenues also can take the form of *grants in aid*, to be spent only on specifically authorized activities. Those activities pertaining to the police are discussed later in this chapter. Finally, intergovernment revenue can take the form of reimbursement for services provided. The provision of law enforcement services by a county sheriff's department to a municipality that does not operate its own police force would be one such example.

What makes the interpretation of budgets and revenue flows difficult is that some money can be spent only on specific activities. As a result, these funds must be accounted for apart from more general revenue sources. To track expenditures by revenue sources, most government budgets include a number of subbudgets supported through specific funds or combinations of funds. A *fund* is an independent fiscal entity with assets, liabilities, reserves, a residual balance or equity, and revenues and expenditures for undertaking activities (Solano and Brams, 1987, p. 119). The majority of police services are supported through three types of government funds: the general fund, special revenue funds, and capital project/development funds.

The General Fund.   The expenditures of most local government agencies, including the police, are supported through what is frequently referred to as the *general fund*. This is the fund used to account for the receipt of most tax revenue. Expenditures from the general fund can be for just about whatever the executive and legislative body approves.

Special Revenue Funds.   Revenue raised from specific sources and designated to be spent on certain legislatively approved activities are deposited into a *special revenue fund*. People often refer to these funds as *earmarked* since the purpose of their expenditure is predetermined. Some sources of special revenue funds include asset forfeitures, specific fees or fines, and 911 surcharges. More extensive examples include the establishment of special police taxes or taxing districts to support police activities. For example, Fort Worth, Texas, created a citywide crime control district that levies a half-penny sales tax with the resulting $27 million going directly to law enforcement (Pilant, 1998). Similarly, Flint, Michigan, residents voted for a $3.5 million tax increase to continue the city's foot patrol program (Kennedy, 1993, p. 7). If proceeds from fees or fines are not earmarked or deposited in a special revenue fund, they usually end up in the general fund and are distributed across all government purposes.

Capital Project or Development Funds. Money raised through the sale of government bonds and spent to acquire major assets that will be used for a significant length of time, such as buildings, cars, and computer systems, usually are accounted for through a capital project or a development fund.

LEVELS AND TRENDS IN POLICE EXPENDITURES

Nationwide, it costs local police departments about $63,000 per sworn officer to operate annually, with smaller jurisdictions having lower per-officer operating costs and larger departments experiencing annual per-officer operating costs of $77,000 (Reaves, 1996, p. 7). Almost 80 percent of state and local police expenditures go toward payroll expenses (U.S. Bureau of Justice Statistics, 1988, p. 126). What do these numbers really mean?

Police expenditures can be considered in a number of different ways. Each method provides a unique perspective and meaning to the amount spent and offers alternative ways for assessing changes over time or differences across jurisdictions. For example, conceptualizing public spending in per-capita terms allows for the comparison of the relative effort that a government makes with respect to each of its citizens (Benton, 1983, p. 233). On the other hand, examining the proportion of total government expenditures or total justice expenditures allocated to the police can offer another interpretation. Comparing expenditures in terms of the percentage of total government spending is seen as a measure of the *priority* a particular activity receives (Benton, 1983). Simply looking at sheer dollar amounts provides a sense of the financial outlay for this critical government service. It also is useful in evaluating the revenue generating potential of alternative methods of financing these activities.

Differences in Levels of Police Expenditures Across Jurisdictions

Considerable variation in the level of police expenditures across political units remains after controlling for differences in population size and crime levels. State and local governments spent about $149 per capita for police activities in 1994 (see Figure 11–1). These per-capita figures ranged from more than $200 in Alaska, New

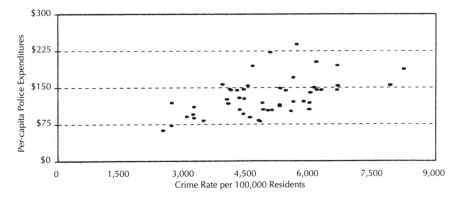

Figure 11–1   Total 1994 State and Local Police Expenditures and Index Offense Rate
(Source: U.S. Bureau of Justice Statistics, crime rate from 1995 sourcebook)

York, and California to less than $75 per capita in North Dakota and West Virginia.
States with higher crime rates tend to spend more per capita than those with lower
crime rates.

Although conceptualizing public spending in per-capita terms allows us to
compare the relative effort that a government makes with respect to each of its
citizens, it is difficult to assess what these discrepancies really mean. Since the early
1950s, policy analysts have tried to untangle the factors that lead to per-capita
differences across political units (Fabricant, 1952). The general conclusion is that
differences in fiscal capacity, public preferences, and the demand for services all
contribute to fluctuations in per-capita government expenditures. Studies that looked
at police expenditure variations report that the impact of crime is not consistent.
Some, for example, found only specific types of crime (e.g., violent index offenses or
murder) affect levels of police expenditures (Jones, 1974; Welch, 1975; Wolpin,
1978). However, differences across geographic areas with respect to police unionization, cost of living, and responsibilities of sworn officers make it difficult to draw
firm conclusions.

Some researchers have examined whether differences in police expenditures
affect crime rates. In a review of the literature on this topic, O'Connor and Gilman
(1978) found that higher levels of police resources had a slight deterrent effect on
crime. A 1% increase in police personnel or expenditures resulted in a .054–1.76%
decrease in crime. On the other hand, Greenwood and Wadycki (1973) report that an
increase in crime rates induced an increase in per-capita expenditures for police
protection and an upward movement in police expenditures boosted the level of
crime. Specifically, Greenwood and Wadycki (1973, p. 145) found that a 1% increase
in the number of police per capita resulted in a 1.3% gain in crimes against property
and a 1.7% elevation in crimes against persons. This rather unexpected relationship
was interpreted as meaning that additional police uncover crimes that otherwise
would have gone unreported. More recent assessments of the effect police
employment and expenditures have on crime rates have concluded that there is little

evidence of deterrence (Greenberg, Kessler, and Loftin, 1983; Loftin and McDowall, 1982; Uchida and Goldberg, 1986). It is fair to say that *how* police expenditures are allocated has more of an impact than *how much* is spent on police activities.

Trends by Level of Government

As Table 11–2 shows, more than $46 billion was spent nationally on police activities in 1994. That is 77% more than was spent in 1980, even after taking inflation into account. Between 1980 and 1994, federal expenditures for police activities jumped 145% in constant dollars. A similar 71% increase is found in local government expenditures for police and a 53% increase in state police expenditures.

The federal government's involvement in policing has changed over the past 14 years. During 1994, federal direct expenditures accounted for 15.9% of the nation's total police expenditures compared to 11.5% in 1980. However, despite the dramatic increase in federal expenditures and growing share of total policing expenditures, Table 11–2 shows that the majority of expenditures for police services takes place at the local level. As we see later, the extent of federal expenditures for police is even greater when transfers of funds from the federal government down to state and local police agencies are included.

Current Operating versus Capital Expenditures

Because policing is extremely labor intensive, payroll accounts for the largest budgetary item and percent of police expenditures. A relatively small portion of police resources are allocated to capital costs. During 1994, state and local police spent approximately $1.6 billion or 4.2% of their expenditures for construction, equipment, and the purchase of land. State police agencies spent a larger proportion of their total direct expenditures on capital costs than local departments (7.4%

Table 11–2   Direct Police Expenditures by Level of Government, 1980 and 1994

	1980	1994	Percent Change	Percent of 1980 Total	Percent of 1994 Total
Federal	$ 2,984,147,000	$ 7,318,000,000	+145%	11.5%	15.9%
State	$ 3,478,635,000	$ 5,324,906,000	+ 53%	13.4%	11.6%
Local	$19,557,175,000	$33,361,630,000	+ 71%	75.2%	72.5%
Total	$26,019,956,000	$46,004,536,000	+ 77%	100.1%	100.0%

The 1980 expenditures were converted into 1994 dollars to remove the effect of inflation.
Source: Compiled from U.S. Bureau of Justice Statistics, *Justice Expenditure and Employment Extracts, 1980* (Washington, DC: U.S. Department of Justice, 1983) and unpublished data obtained from Bureau of Justice Statistics.

versus 3.7%). Part of this difference is because most state police agencies are responsible for the operation of crime labs, criminal history information systems, and automated fingerprint identification systems, which require the acquisition of expensive computer systems. The proportion of total state and local police expenditures going toward capital costs has not changed much since the early 1980s.

Trends in Police Expenditures Relative to Other Government Services

The proportion of total government expenditures allocated to policing varies by level of government. The majority of police expenditures takes place at the local level. At the same time, the revenue-generating capacity and overall expenditure levels of local governments are much less than those of state or federal governments. As a result of these two conditions, it is not surprising that a larger share of the local government expenditure pie goes to police activities than at either the federal or state level.

Examining expenditures in terms of the percentage of total government spending can be interpreted as a measure of the priority a particular activity receives in the public policy arena (Benton, 1983). During recent years, the proportion of total state and local government expenditures allocated to police activities has not changed very much, hovering around the 3% mark between 1982 and 1994.

Local units of government allocate a larger share of their total expenditures to police activities than state governments. The proportion of government expenditures devoted to the police is highest at the municipal level. Table 11–3 shows that 9.5% of total direct expenditures went for police activities in 1994 compared to only 1% of total state government expenditures. The proportion of total municipal expenditures allocated to police activities in 1994 represented a slight increase from 1982. It is important to note, however, that the proportion of total expenditures allocated to police fluctuates considerably from state to state, county to county, and city to city, depending on a variety of factors. An important factor is the functions for which different levels of government are responsible and the variation in these responsibilities from one jurisdiction to the next. For example, if one municipal unit of government is responsible for funding education while another is not, obviously the latter will be able to devote a larger proportion of its resources to police activities.

Between 1982 and 1994, the relative police expenditures remained between 4.6 and 4.7% at the local level. In fact, the proportion of total local government expenditures allocated to police has stayed between 4 and 5% during the entire 20th century. So, despite the rhetoric, public pressure, and increased attention to crime, local police departments have had no substantial increase in their share of total local government resources over the past 90 years. The other way to consider this trend— or lack thereof—is that police departments are not the only government services from which the public has demanded more. Although total police expenditures have increased dramatically during the period examined, so too have all other local government activities.

Table 11–3 Proportion of Total Direct Government Expenditures Allocated to Police Activities by Level of Government

	1982	1994	Total 1994 Direct Government Expenditures
State	1.2%	1.0%	$ 551,038,917,000
County	5.4%	5.5%	$ 160,559,263,000
Municipal	8.9%	9.5%	$ 257,995,647,000
Total county and municipal*	4.6%	4.7%	$ 710,365,559,000
Total state and local	3.2%	3.1%	$1,260,643,871,000

*The total local line includes independent school districts and special districts, which are not reflected in either the county or municipal lines. Therefore, the sum of the county and municipal figures do not equal the total local.
Source: Compiled from U.S. Bureau of Justice Statistics, *Justice Expenditure and Employment Extracts, 1982* (Washington, DC: U.S. Department of Justice, 1984) and unpublished data obtained from Bureau of Justice Statistics.

Trends in Police Expenditures Relative to Other Components of the Justice System

Oftentimes, the distribution of justice expenditures across the different components of the justice system is used as a proxy or barometer of where public sentiment lies. "Governments adjust spending patterns in response to changing needs of society and shifts in the public's demand for services" (U.S. Bureau of Justice Statistics, 1988, p. 120). If one were to look at police budgets relative to the courts or corrections, it would appear that the police lost considerable ground. Figure 11–2 shows that the proportion of total state and local justice expenditures going to policing fell from more than 52% to less than 44% during the 1982–1994 period. Corrections, on the other hand, increased its market share of criminal justice resources. It climbed from 27% in 1982 to more than 36% in 1994. Courts, despite their relatively small share of justice expenditures, have managed to hold on to an average of 20% during the 1980s and 1990s.

Some readers might be tempted to interpret this trend as showing more public support for incarceration over other methods of crime control or that correctional agencies are siphoning funds from law enforcement. That is not the case. Police and correctional agencies compete for resources in different arenas. Most police appropriations and expenditures take place at the local level. About two thirds of correctional expenditures occur at the state level. However, the trend evident in Figure 11–2 illustrates how the allocation of resources across the justice system has changed in this country.

At the municipal level, only a very small proportion of justice expenditures is used to support court or correctional activities, since most of these responsibilities fall to either the county or the state. Therefore, municipal police departments pose little competition for *justice* resources, although other public agencies obviously are

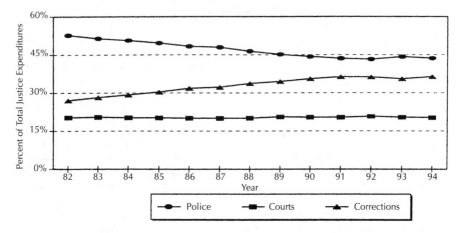

Figure 11–2   Distribution of Total State and Local Justice Expenditures, by Component, 1982–1994 (Source: U.S. Bureau of Justice Statistics)

contenders. At the county level, however, sheriff's agencies have to vie much more vigorously for resources against other components of the justice system. Depending on the state, counties may support all or part of the operation of the courts, prosecutorial agencies, public defense, county jails, juvenile detention centers, and probation and other community correctional programs. While many counties receive some financial support from the state for the provision of many of these services, most often county coffers still must support the majority of agency operations.

FEDERAL FUNDING OF STATE AND LOCAL POLICE ACTIVITIES

In addition to operating a number of specific law enforcement agencies, such as the Federal Bureau of Investigation, the Bureau of Alcohol, Tobacco, and Firearms, the U.S. Marshall's Service, and the Drug Enforcement Administration, to name a few, the federal government provides financial support to state and local units of government for various criminal justice programs. The federal government's provision of financial support for state and local criminal justice activities began in the mid-1960s. Initially, many state and local law enforcement officials felt threatened by the flow of federal funds into police departments. Although the police welcomed the possibility of additional resources, many feared that state and local law enforcement would come under the control or direction of the U.S. Attorney General (Hudzik, 1984, pp. 228–229). As Chapter 1 explains, our criminal justice system historically has operated under the belief that there should be no centralized police force. In 1965, the International Association of Chiefs of Police (IACP) went so far as to pass a resolution against "any attempted encroachment by the federal government into state or local government in the law enforcement field" (U.S. Advisory Commission on Intergovernmental Relations, 1977, p. 10).

Today, there is greater willingness to receive federal funding. But before we embark on an overview of the various types of federal aid programs, it is necessary to put the support provided by the federal government through its grant programs into some perspective. Although the dollars provided to state and local agencies each year are substantial, state and local units of government still are responsible for more than 85% of their total justice system expenditures. Still, these funds have provided state and local agencies the ability to experiment with new approaches and develop innovative ways of addressing local crime problems.

The Process of Getting Federal Funds to State and Local Police Departments

Understanding how federal funds make their way to state and local police departments is important. Embodied in the various mechanisms are different views on the federal government's role in justice system improvement and issues related to system coordination and effectiveness. Federal funds make their way to state or local police departments through three general means. The first avenue is through criminal justice block grants distributed to state administrative agencies (SAA). Usually, these awards are parceled out on needs-based allocations, competitive applications, or formulas. The second route is through block grants distributed based on a formula to individual police departments. The third mechanism is through competitive, discretionary grant programs managed by the U.S. Department of Justice.

Federal Criminal Justice Block Grants to State Administrative Agencies

Historically, most of the large federal criminal justice aid programs have provided block grants to SAAs, which in turn, pass on the funds to state and local criminal justice agencies. One of the strongest arguments for providing funds through SAAs is that it allows for better planning and coordination. Currently, a number of different federal criminal justice block grants go to individual state administrative agencies. Each has specific purposes, requirements, and varying levels of support. Although a complete description of each block grant program is beyond the scope of this chapter, a sampling of the characteristics and requirements of some major programs will provide insight into their administration, purpose, and impact on police operations.

The Edward Byrne Memorial State and Local Law Enforcement Assistance Program. The Byrne Program was authorized through the Anti-Drug Abuse Act of 1988 and has provided federal financial aid to state and local criminal justice agencies since 1989. Between fiscal years 1991 and 1998, the total amounts appropriated to this formula block-grant program ranged between $385 and $500 million. Each state receives a base award plus a proportionate share of any remaining funds computed from its percentage of the U.S. population. These funds are administered by a SAA, which allocates them across a number of different federally prescribed purpose areas. As has been the case with federal criminal justice block grants in the past, SAAs are required to "pass through" a specified minimum proportion of the total block grant receipts to local units of government.

The process by which SAAs distribute funds to local agencies varies from state to state. Some states use a competitive process, whereby local agencies submit proposals in response to a request for proposals (RFP) issued by the SAA. Others may identify areas in need of programming through data analyses and subsequent negotiation with local agencies. There is one relevant restriction. Federal funds can not support more than 75% of the total cost of each project. Therefore, subgrantees must provide a 25% match to the grant funds.

The purpose area that received the largest share of these federal block-grant funds between 1989 and 1994 was multijurisdictional task forces. The multijurisdictional task forces received 40% of all subgrant funds from the inception of the Byrne Program through 1994, while none of the other 20 federally approved purpose areas received more than 10% of the total allocations (Dunworth, Haynes, and Saiger, 1997, p. 5). Although a number of multijurisdictional task forces were in operation before the Byrne Program, including many initiated with LEAA funding, the funds undoubtedly increased the number of units targeting drug offenders and promoted interagency cooperation..

S-T-O-P Violence Against Women Act Formula Grant Funds.   The S-T-O-P (Services-Training-Officers-Prosecutors) Violence Against Women (VAWA) Formula Grant Program requires that 25% of the state block grant go to law enforcement agencies. Funds provided the police can support training, development of specialized units, development of data collection, and communications systems to more effectively identify and respond to domestic violence, sexual assault, and stalking. Agency recipients are required to provide a match so that the federal funds do not support more than 75% of the project cost.

Juvenile Justice Formula Grants.   Formula grant funds through the Juvenile Justice and Delinquency Prevention Act also are managed by state agencies, which then allocate the funds to state and local criminal justice agencies. The allocation to each state is based on each state or territory's percentage of the U.S. population under age 18, and two thirds of these funds must pass through to local units of government. Unlike other block grants, funds from the Juvenile Justice Formula Block Grant require no matching funds, unless the funds are used for administrative or construction activities; and the funds can be used for a variety of delinquency prevention and intervention programs. Congress appropriated $84 million for juvenile justice formula in federal fiscal year 1997.

The Local Law Enforcement Block Grant Program.   Police administrators have criticized the requirement that federal grants go through state administrative agencies to be distributed to the local level (Hudzik, 1984, p. 79). Their concern primarily had to do with not being consulted during the program planning or strategy development (Dunworth and Saiger, 1992, p. 39). There also was the feeling that disproportionate amounts of federal funds were going to suburban and rural communities (Hudzik, 1984). In response to these concerns, the Local Law Enforcement Block Grants (LLEBG) Program was launched in federal fiscal year 1996 to provide funds *directly* to units of local government to underwrite projects aimed at reducing crime and improving public safety.

The funds received through the grant program can be used for everything from "hiring, training, and employing . . . law enforcement officers and necessary support personnel" to "obtaining equipment related to basic law enforcement functions" to "establishing crime prevention programs" (U.S. Bureau of Justice Assistance, 1998, p. 1). More than $500 million per year has been appropriated to the LLEBG program since its inception. The LLEBG Program channels money directly to local agencies based on a two-stage formula. First, the proportion of the nation's violent offenses index accounted for by each state is applied to the total available grant dollars. Second, the state allocation is then divided among all local jurisdictions based on their relative share of the state's violent offenses index. Almost 3,400 local units of government received direct awards totaling more than $442 million during 1998.

The Community Oriented Policing Services (COPS) Program.   Probably, the most significant federal grant program designed specifically for police was a result of the 1994 Violent Crime Control and Law Enforcement Act. More than $8.8 billion was authorized over six years to assist agencies in adding community policing officers to their rosters. To administer these programs, the U.S. Department of Justice created the Community Oriented Policing Services (COPS) Office.

> Under the Community Policing Act, grants are generally available to any law enforcement agency that can demonstrate a public safety need; demonstrate an inability to address the need without a grant; and, in most instances, contribute a 25 percent match of the federal share of the grant. (U.S. General Accounting Office, 1997, p. 2)

Although the COPS Office has a number of different programs, one key character-istic is the requirement that federal funds not supplant local funds. In addition, the Community Policing Act reserves half the grant funds for police departments serving populations of 150,000 or less. Some specific programs include COPS AHEAD (Accelerated Hiring, Education, and Deployment), the COPS FAST (Funding Accelerated for Smaller Towns) Program, the COPS MORE (Making Officer Redeployment Effective) Program, and the Universal Hiring Program. Agencies receiving these funds must promise that they will continue to employ these officers after the federal grant program ends in 2000 (U.S. General Accounting Office, 1997, p. 6). Failure to abide by this stipulation means that agencies will be forced to return the grant money and will not be eligible to receive certain funds in the future.

Obviously, police agencies can attempt to obtain funding from a variety of federal sources. However, in most cases, police agencies turn to state and local sources.

STATE SUPPORT FOR LOCAL POLICE ACTIVITIES

The termination of federal general revenue sharing in 1986 stimulated interest in state aid to local government (Gold and Erickson, 1988, p. 1). However, the extent to which state governments were able to make up for the elimination of federal funds varied considerably, as did the specific activities supported. State to local aid usually takes the form of reimbursement to local governments for providing specific services.

State funding of justice activities carried out at the local level is important for a number of reasons. First, if states mandate that local governments engage in certain justice activities, they must offer some financial incentive or assistance. Second, justice system operations are becoming more centralized or under greater state control. We see remnants of this movement when Professor McCabe explains in Chapter 10 how states are becoming more involved in agency accreditation. Third, local units of government are restricted in terms of how much revenue they can generate through local sources and, therefore, must rely on the state government for financial assistance. Finally, like our congressional representatives, one reason state legislators have mobilized resources is to support a get-tough-on-crime agenda.

The extent, nature, and purpose of state aid to local police vary considerably. Some states support a portion of officer salaries if they meet certain educational requirements (U.S. Department of Commerce, 1984). Florida, for example, sends an extra $50 every month to officers who have earned a college diploma. Kentucky runs a 15% salary supplement for all local police officers whose agencies meet minimum standards, including basic and in-service training and educational incentives (Hudzik, 1984, p. 218). State aid for police also comes in the form of multijurisdictional programs or special task forces.

NONTRADITIONAL FUNDING

The constant pressure to "do more with less" has filtered down to every level of policing. That public sentiment, along with the lack of change in the police share of the "government resource pie," forces police administrators to be constantly on the prowl for ways to supplement their budgets. Some of these remedies we examine are increased fees and fines, seizing assets from criminals, and soliciting funds directly from the private sector.

Fees and Fines

Originally, fines were created as a deterrent or punishment. However, the imposition of fees and fines has turned into a lucrative source of income. As Box 11–1 shows, some cities have enacted ordinances to dun residents and business owners when the police respond to repeated false burglary alarms. Similar efforts are underway to have sports teams, sponsors of other events, or high users of police services like

Box 11–1   An Example of a Municipal Ordinance Regarding Fees for
Repeat False Alarms

Sec. 41.05. False Alarm Warning Notice; Service Fee.

1. Each time the Orlando Police Department responds to a false
    intrusion alarm due to system malfunction or when no reason can be
    determined for such false alarm, the Orlando Police Department shall
    issue a false alarm warning notice.
2. A service fee for excessive false intrusion alarms shall be charged as
    follows:
    a. No service fee shall be charged for the first three (3) false alarms
        occurring within a twelve (12) month period calculated from the
        date of the first such alarm.
    b. Each false alarm in excess of three (3) and up to and including six
        (6) within a twelve (12) month period shall result in a service fee
        of $50.00 (fifty dollars) per false alarm.
    c. Each false alarm in excess of six (6) within a twelve (12) month
        period shall result in a service fee of $100.00 (one hundred
        dollars) per false alarm.
3. No service fee shall be assessed if the false alarm is:
    a. Caused by an electrical storm, hurricane, tornado or other act of
        God where there is clear evidence of physical damage to the alarm
        system;
    b. Caused by the intermittent disruption of telephone circuits beyond
        the control of the alarm site owner;
    c. Caused by electrical power disruption or failure in excess of two
        (2) hours beyond the control of the alarm site owner; or
    d. At a location where the Orlando Police Department has installed a
        CATCH alarm.
4. All false alarm service fees are due and payable within thirty (30)
    days from date of invoice. In the event that false alarm service fees
    are not paid as required by this chapter, the Orlando Police
    Department may refer the matter to the City's Office of Legal Affairs
    for appropriate legal action.
5. A person commits an offense in violation of this chapter if such
    person suffers or permits false alarms in excess of three (3) within a
    twelve (12) month period, each such false alarm constituting a
    separate violation.

Source: Orlando [Florida] City Ordinances.

shopping malls or specific apartment buildings pay fees for officers who control traffic, crowds, or respond to frequent calls for service. Often, though, public reaction can be counterproductive. People resent these charges because they feel that they have already paid for these services through their taxes (Stellwagen and Wylie, 1985). Because some traditional services can sap understaffed squads, many departments have decided not to provide them. Unlocking car doors for stranded motorists or providing police escorts to businesses making bank deposits at night are practices now falling by the wayside.

A number of issues are involved in the imposition of fees and fines. These concerns include the amount to be charged, the likelihood of collection, the distribution of proceeds, and whether the revenue generated will be spent on specific criminal justice activities or more general government operations. In addition, the system must be prepared to respond to people who cannot, or do not, pay imposed fees or fines. Will this failure to pay result in a more punitive and expensive sanction, thus reducing the overall benefit of the fees or fine revenue? In Arizona, for example, fines imposed on convicted serious drug offenders are deposited into the Drug and Gang Enforcement Account, which is used to support drug enforcement efforts (U.S. Bureau of Justice Assistance, 1993, p. 3). In Illinois, the Traffic and Criminal Conviction Surcharge requires an additional 10% fine be imposed on a conviction for criminal or traffic offenses. These receipts have averaged around $9 million over the past few years and are used to reimburse local law enforcement agencies for half the costs related to police officer training (Olson, 1991, p. 2). So, when reviewing how fees and fines are distributed, one should consider if police are the direct or indirect beneficiaries of the funds.

Despite their apparent simplicity, fees and fines can generate problems. A major problem is the proliferation of different fees, fines, and surcharges that can be imposed depending on the class or type of offense. Some states have had to revamp their collection and distribution methods to streamline this system. For example, in 1991 Utah eliminated all fees and fines that were not part of a criminal sentence. Instead, the legislature created a uniform surcharge on all criminal fines, penalties, and forfeitures. The proceeds from this single surcharge are distributed among special revenue funds according to a predetermined formula (U.S. Bureau of Justice Assistance, 1993, p. 3).

One result of having court clerks track so many different fees, fines, and surcharges frequently means that the collected money does not make it to the appropriate fund. At one time, Florida court clerks received minimal formal guidance in how fines and fees should be distributed. This oversight resulted in fees and fines being distributed to the wrong funds and some funds received substantially less than the statutorily required amount (Hanberry, 1992).

Private Donations

The law enforcement community also turns to the general public or the private sector for support. Businesses have sponsored fund-raisers to purchase body armor for police officers (Stellwagen and Wylie, 1985). When the Crown Point, Indiana, Police Department needed new squad cars, it created the AdoptACar Program. To finance the equipment needed for each new car, local businesses were asked to make a donation in return for the inscription "This vehicle is equipped by [business name]" on the back of the patrol unit. Despite controversy over the perception that the police were selling advertising space on their cars, 29 businesses sponsored police cars and paid a one-time fee of $1,650 for the life of the vehicle (Pilant, 1998, p. 43).

The private sector supports law enforcement in other ways, too. A few years ago, areas plagued by stolen vehicles started to form Anti-Car Theft groups, many of which were funded by the insurance industry (Insurance Information Institute, 1998, p. 4). The programs are supported through fees paid by insurance companies issuing policies in the state. The extra money is channeled to enforcement efforts related to motor vehicle theft. Illinois, for example, has a $1 annual assessment on each insured passenger car (Illinois Criminal Justice Information Authority, 1997). These funds, $5.3 million annually, are distributed by a policy board that includes representatives from the insurance industry and the criminal justice system to various programs targeting motor vehicle theft, many of which are law enforcement task forces. Similar insurance industry-funded programs operate in a number of other states (Insurance Information Institute, 1998, p. 5).

Asset Forfeiture

Forfeiture is the loss of ownership of property derived from or used in criminal activity after the government has seized the tainted property (U.S. Bureau of Justice Statistics, 1992, p.156). The merit of asset forfeiture is that it reduces the profitability of illegal activity and interrupts the operations of criminal organizations. Policy makers see asset forfeiture as an opportunity to supplement law enforcement budgets without having to resort to more taxes. It also makes the law-abiding public feel better knowing that criminals are losing their illegal profits. Most state statutes dedicate seized assets to future drug control activities (Gallagher, 1988, p. 5). Thus, most forfeited assets end up in special revenue funds that support drug interdiction task forces, DARE (Drug Abuse Resistance Through Education) programs aimed at middle school children, and the like.

In addition to state and local asset forfeiture programs, a considerable amount of revenue is generated through federal law enforcement efforts. These forfeitures are deposited into either the Department of Justice Assets Forfeiture Fund—for those resulting from the efforts of DEA, the FBI, the U.S. Marshall's Service, the Immigration and Naturalization Service, as well as the U.S. Postal Service, the IRS, and the Bureau of Alcohol, Tobacco, and Firearms—or the Customs Forfeiture Fund—for U.S. Customs forfeitures (U.S. Bureau of Justice Statistics, 1992, p. 157).

Some of this federal forfeiture money is funneled to state and local law enforcement agencies, depending on their level of involvement in the seizure that resulted in the forfeiture. In federal fiscal year 1997, receipts into Justice and Customs's forfeiture funds exceeded of $500 million.

Despite the large dollar figures cited by proponents of this strategy or the news stories about millions of dollars being seized in drug raids, administrators need to consider several aspects when thinking about resorting to this practice to supplement traditional tax revenue for police operations. For one thing, while asset forfeiture targets may be frequent among investigations into high-level drug trafficking, most local police departments do not encounter such high-profile cases in the course of traditional police work. Most drug offenders that local police deal with have few assets other than what is in their pockets, on their backs, or in their veins. Federal agencies involved in interstate trafficking networks, local multijurisdictional drug enforcement task forces, or large urban departments are more likely to come across potential asset forfeiture cases. Most street-level sellers do not carry substantial amounts of cash, frequently are users working to obtain either drugs or money for drugs, and lack vital information that will link police to the distribution network where the large assets resulting from the drug trade reside (Johnson et al., 1990).

This point is evident when considering what types of police departments received money or property as the result of a drug asset forfeiture program. In 1990, more than 90% of local police departments serving a population over a quarter of a million people received money or property as the result of a drug asset forfeiture program. Less than one third of the agencies serving populations under 10,000 fell into this category (Reaves, 1992, p. 5). However, even among those large cities that received asset forfeiture proceeds, the total dollar amount was relatively small. For example, forfeited assets accounted for less than 1% of the 1993 total operating budgets in the New York City and Chicago Police Departments (Reaves and Smith, 1995). This observation does not imply that this influx is not helpful. For example, in 1990 the Chicago Police Department used $700,000 in forfeited funds to purchase fax machines and support computerization efforts (Recktenwald and Blau, 1990).

Another dimension of asset forfeiture that police leaders need to realize is that not all seized assets subsequently are forfeited. Seizure will not result in forfeiture if the suspect does not own the property, if the relationship between the property and illegal activity cannot be proven, or if innocent third parties own the property (U.S. Bureau of Justice Statistics, 1992, p. 156). Once assets are forfeited, the proceeds often are distributed among a number of different agencies and funds. For example, some state forfeiture laws require that a portion of the funds be allocated to drug treatment and prevention, while other states divide the money between the police department and the prosecutor's office that handled the case. Thus, depending on the distribution formula, the law enforcement agency making the seizure may not get all of the funds that result from the forfeiture of those assets.

The best way to look at asset forfeiture is that, while helpful, it alone cannot sustain police operations. Despite the public perception and isolated incidents reported in the media, asset forfeiture does not generate sufficient revenues to support a substantial portion of police operating costs. Furthermore, unlike property and sales tax receipts, this revenue is seldom a stable source of support for operating budgets, with wide fluctuations in year-to-year receipts (U.S. Advisory Commission on Intergovernmental Relations, 1993, p. 159). However, the proceeds from asset forfeiture can support specific programs of merit, which otherwise might not be provided. For example, some police departments have used asset forfeiture funds to procure equipment and other one-time expenses, such as training or support specific staff in drug enforcement or crime prevention positions.

CONCLUSION

Dramatic increases in police expenditures have occurred over the past few decades. However, they do not account for an appreciably larger share of total local government expenditures and, in many instances, have not keep pace with the increasing demands and expectations placed on police administrators. Part of this is due to the limited fiscal capacity of local units of government and intensive competition from other criminal justice and social service programs. As a result, many local governments, where the majority of law enforcement services are provided, have looked to state and federal governments for financial aid.

Although the infusion of federal funding has been around since the late 1960s, the types of federal grant programs, particularly those specifically geared toward policing, have changed considerably. The receipt of federal funds has been welcomed by many, but a profound question must be considered. Almost all federal criminal justice grant programs include requirements as to which programs should take priority and which types of offenders should be targeted. While these goals may be a top national priority, it does not necessarily mean that they are a local high priority. Therefore, "state and local elected officials may wish to consider whether the shift away from local control is worth the degree of funding relief provided" (U.S. Advisory Commission on Intergovernmental Relations, 1993, p. 168).

Even though the federal aid does not account for a substantial share of total state and local justice expenditures (less than 5% in 1994), the activities can have profound immediate and long-term ramifications. For example, hiring additional police officers through the federal COPS Program most likely will result in additional arrests, which must then be processed through the court and correctional systems with state or locally generated resources. In general, the majority of municipal government decisions to increase police budgets fail to consider whether increased police resources will be met with an increased demand for more court or correctional resources (U.S. Advisory Commission on Intergovernmental Relations, 1993, p. 141). The operational effectiveness of the entire system is compromised if police resources increase to the point where they overwhelm the courts, jails, or prisons. One has to look back only to the late 1980s and the "war on drugs" for an example of the impact this lack of planning can have. In addition, after the completion of the grant, it is up to the local unit of government to support program operations. This has been referred to by some policy analysts as the *multiplier effect* (Hudzik, 1984, p. 170). The result of the relatively small federal grant is a new program with costs local government must assume. With the COPS Program grants, each department will have to support the full costs of the additional officers after the year 2000.

The substantial amount of potential federal funding and the various means by which local law enforcement agencies can gain access to these resources—ranging from direct application and receipt to pass-through funds from state administrative agencies—have required local agencies to increase their capacity to identify funding sources and write and develop applications and proposals. Local police managers have to learn the processes their state administrative agency uses to identify areas of greatest need and allocate the federal funds it oversees. Most federal funds these state administrative agencies handle require the development of applications that identify the needs and intended uses of the federal funds within the particular state.

Local agencies, as well as statewide or regional police chief membership organizations, should seek ways to have their views and opinions heard by these state administrative agencies and included in the state applications for federal funds. Local law enforcement agencies seeking access to federal funds directly through some of the competitive programs administered by the U.S. Department of Justice's various bureaus should first contact those organizations to determine eligibility, funding levels, and requirements. Many of these organizations have Internet sites, which provide detailed information about grant programs as well as application forms to download. If the program involves a competitive process, agencies should determine what criteria will be used to select programs. At a minimum, proposals should include the following components:

- A clear and concise statement of the problem accompanied by data to substantiate the problem.
- Goal statements and specific, measurable objectives to be accomplished.
- A clear, logical, and detailed program strategy.
- Identification of performance indicators to gauge progress.
- A reasonable implementation schedule.
- A detailed budget and budget narrative.

In addition to support through state and federal grants, many departments have implemented various fees and fines to generate extra revenue for police activities. However, the police face considerable competition from other justice agencies eager to supplement their budgets with offender-generated revenues. There needs to be a balance between victim compensation or restitution and the costs associated with the collection and enforcement of the various fees and fines. Similarly, the push to extract funds through asset forfeiture should be approached from the perspective that it is not likely to result in a substantial, consistent cash flow. This is not to say, however, that the collection of fees, fines, and asset forfeiture proceeds cannot supplement police budgets and have profound impacts on specific police activities. Although these types of revenue sources do not account for large portions of police budgets, they do support programs that otherwise might not exist.

Police departments have no choice except to continue to rely on traditional tax revenues to support agency operations. If additional resources are going to come, particularly in light of the public climate toward tax rates and government inefficiency, police executives and policy makers are going to have to ensure effective management, planning, implementation, and evaluation of programs. Simply increasing resources will not reduce crime.

DISCUSSION QUESTIONS

1. Suppose you are examining the budgets of two municipal governments and discover that one city is spending more money per capita for police operations than the other. What factors, other than known crime rate, could explain this pattern?
2. Should federal assistance for law enforcement or other criminal justice activities be limited to specific issues identified by Congress or should this support be "unrestricted"? What benefits and weaknesses are derived from having federal support limited only to specific types of programs or activities?
3. Should assets seized from drug offenders be earmarked solely to support drug enforcement efforts or should these receipts be used to support any criminal justice system activity? Another possibility would be to deposit seized assets into the general fund of government units to support any government activity. What strengths or weaknesses are behind these possible alternatives?
4. What, if any, local police department expenses should be supported by the state or federal government? Why?
5. Should the private sector be involved in directly funding police activities, such as the support given to motor vehicle theft task forces by the insurance industry or local businesses "sponsoring" patrol cars?
6. Should the police impose fees, in addition to what already is paid in taxes, to high users of police services such as repeated false burglary or robbery alarms from private residences and business? Why or why not? If so, should these receipts be deposited into a special revenue fund and used only for police-related expenses or should the fees go into the general fund and used to support all government services?

REFERENCES

Benton, J. "Dimensions of public spending." *Policy Studies Journal* 12 (1983), pp. 233–246.

Dunworth, T., P. Haynes, and A. J. Saiger. (1997). *National Assessment of the Byrne Formula Grant Program.* Washington, DC: U.S. Department of Justice, 1997.

Dunworth, T., and A. J. Saiger. *State Strategic Planning Under the Drug Formula Grant Program.* Washington, DC: U.S. Department of Justice, 1992.

Fabricant, S. *The Trend of Government Activity in the United States Since 1900.* New York: National Bureau of Economic Research, 1952.

Gallagher, G. P. *Asset Forfeiture: The Management and Distribution of Seized Assets.* Washington, DC: U.S. Department of Justice, 1988.

Gold, S. D., and B. M. Erickson. *State Aid to Local Governments in the 1980s.* Denver: National Conference of State Legislatures, 1988.

Greenberg, D. F., R. C. Kessler, and C. H. Loftin. "The effect of police employment on crime rates and arrest rates." *Criminology* 21, no. 3 (1983), pp. 375–394.

Greenwood, M. J., and W. Wadycki. "Crime rates and public policy expenditures for police protection: Their interaction." *Review of Social Economy* 31 (1973), pp. 138–151.

Hanberry, J. L. *Distribution of Monies Collected from Criminal Fines and Fees.* Tallahassee: Florida Office of the Auditor General, 1992.

Hudzik, J. K. *Federal Aid to Criminal Justice: Rhetoric, Results, Lessons.* Washington, DC: The National Criminal Justice Association, 1984.

Illinois Criminal Justice Information Authority. *1997 Annual Report.* Chicago: Illinois Criminal Justice Information Authority, 1997.

Insurance Information Institute (1998). *Insurance Issues Update.* New York: Insurance Information Institute, 1998.

Johnson, B. D., T. Williams, K. A. Dei, and H. Sanabria. "Drug abuse in the inner city: Impact on hard-drug users and the community." In M. Tonry and J. Q. Wilson (eds.), *Drugs and Crime*, pp. 6–67. Chicago: University of Chicago Press, 1990.

Jones, T. "The impact of crime rate changes on police protection expenditures in American cities." *Criminology* 11, no. 4 (1974), pp. 516–524.

Kennedy, D. M. *The Strategic Management of Police Resources.* Washington, DC: U.S. Department of Justice, 1993.

Loftin, C., and D. McDowall. "The police, crime, and economic theory: An assessment." *American Sociological Review* 47, no. 3 (1982), pp. 393–401.

Maguire, K., and A. L. Pastore. *Sourcebook of Criminal Justice Statistics 1995.* Washington, DC: U.S. Government Printing Office, 1995.

_____. *Sourcebook of Criminal Justice Statistics 1997.* Washington, DC: U.S. Government Printing Office, 1998.

National Law Enforcement and Corrections Technology Center. *Police Share Creative Funding of Technology Experiences.* At http://rmlectc.dri.du.edu/DOCS/funding.html, 1995.

O'Connor, R. J., and B. Gilman. "The role of police in deterring crime." In J. A. Cramer (ed.), *Preventing Crime*, pp. 75–108. Beverly Hills, CA: Sage Publications, 1978.

Olson, D. E. "The impact of system generated revenue on the financing of Illinois' criminal justice system." Paper presented at the Criminal Justice Statistics Association's 1991 Annual Conference. Chicago.

Peak, K. J. *Justice Administration: Police, Courts, and Corrections Management*, 2nd ed. Englewood Cliffs, NJ: Prentice Hall, 1998.

Pilant, L. *Creative Funding.* Alexandria, VA: International Association of Chiefs of Police, 1998.

Reaves, B. A. *Drug Enforcement by Police and Sheriffs' Departments, 1990.* Washington, DC: U.S. Department of Justice, 1992.

_____. *Local Police Departments, 1993.* Washington, DC: U.S. Department of Justice, 1996.

_____ and P. Z. Smith. *Law Enforcement Management and Administrative Statistics, 1993: Data for Individual State and Local Agencies with 100 or More Officers.* Washington, DC: U.S. Department of Justice, 1995.

Recktenwald, W., and R. Blau. "Drugs funds to buy police high-tech aid." *Chicago Tribune* (March 12, 1990), section 1, p. 1.

Sadd, S., and R. M. Grinc. *Implementing Challenges in Community Policing: Innovative Neighborhood-Oriented Policing in Eight Cities.* Washington, DC: U.S. Department of Justice, 1996.

Solano, P. L., and M. R. Brams. "Budgeting." In J. R. Aronson and E. Schwartz (eds.), *Management Policies in Local Government Finance*, 3rd ed., pp. 118–157. Washington, DC: The International City Management Association, 1987.

Stellwagen, L. D., and K. A. Wylie. *Strategies for Supplementing the Police Budget.* Washington, DC: U.S. Department of Justice, 1985.

Uchida, C., and R. Goldberg. *Police Employment and Expenditure Trends.* Washington, DC: U.S. Bureau of Justice Statistics, 1986.

U.S. Advisory Commission on Intergovernmental Relations. *Safe Streets Reconsidered: The Block Grant Experience 1960–1975.* Washington, DC: U.S. Advisory Commission on Intergovernmental Relations, 1977.

_____. *The Role of General Government Elected Officials in Criminal Justice.* Washington, DC: U.S. Advisory Commission on Intergovernmental Relations, 1993.

U.S. Bureau of Justice Assistance. *Dedicated Funding for State and Local Anti-Drug Programs.* Washington, DC: U.S. Department of Justice, 1993.

_____. *FY 1998 Local Law Enforcement Block Grants Program.* Washington, DC: U.S. Department of Justice, 1998.

U.S. Bureau of Justice Statistics. *Justice Expenditure and Employment Extracts, 1980.* Washington, DC: U.S. Department of Justice, 1983.

_____. *Justice Expenditure and Employment Extracts, 1982.* Washington, DC: U.S. Department of Justice, 1984.

_____. *Report to the Nation on Crime and Justice.* Washington, DC: U.S. Department of Justice, 1988.

_____. *Drugs, Crime, and the Criminal Justice System.* Washington, DC: U.S. Department of Justice, 1992.

U.S. Department of Commerce. *State Payments to Local Governments.* Washington, DC: U.S. Department of Commerce, 1984.

_____. *Government Finances: Summary of Federal Government Finances.* At http:// www.census.gov/govs/fedfin/federal.txt, 1994.

_____. *U.S. State and Local Government Finances by Level of Government, 1994–1995.* At http:// www.census.gov/govs/estimate/95stlus.txt, 1997.

U.S. General Accounting Office. *State and Local Finances: Some Jurisdictions Confronted by Short- and Long-Term Problems.* Washington, DC: U.S. General Accounting Office, 1993.

_____. *Community Policing: Issues Related to the Design, Operation, and Management of the Grant Program.* Washington, DC: U.S. General Accounting Office, 1997.

Weimer, D. L., and A. R. Vining. *Policy Analysis: Concepts and Practice.* Englewood Cliffs, NJ: Prentice Hall, 1992.

Welch, S. "The impact of urban riots on urban expenditures." *American Journal of Political Science* 24, no. 4 (1975), pp. 741–760.

Wolpin, K. I. "Capital punishment and homicide in England: A summary of results." *American Economic Review* 68, no. 2 (1978), pp. 422–427.

Chapter 12

Policing in a Multicultural Society

Benjamin S. Wright, University of Baltimore

Since the 1980s, many large urban areas have undergone drastic changes in the demographic composition of the their populations. While these cities are becoming more diverse and multicultural, police leaders are realizing that their officers' training has been geared toward providing service in a unicultural society. Officers work the streets under the assumption that they still are dealing with immigrant groups striving to assimilate into the dominant culture. In the dominant culture, English is the primary way that police officers communicate with people with whom they have contact. However, many recent immigrant groups are slow to assimilate. They continue to use their native language as the primary means of communication. As a result, administrators are faced with the problem of training officers to move beyond the more comfortable unicultural policing approach to a multicultural policing approach if they are to be more effective in policing multicultural neighborhoods.

The prospect of multicultural policing presents several considerations for the police organization. First, there is no consensus on what the term *multicultural policing* means. Does multicultural policing denote a specific approach to law enforcement that takes cultural diversity into consideration? Or, is it a style of law enforcement that is intended to meet the needs of racial and ethnic minority-group members only? Second, if multicultural policing is a desirable goal, how does an agency put such a strategy into practice? Third, how does multicultural policing differ from the current, more traditional style of law enforcement? Finally, does a multicultural police strategy require police managers to incorporate various community diversity programs and strategies into their organizational policy?

UNICULTURALISM AND MULTICULTURALISM

Multiculturalism is a move away from the melting pot approach and cultural assimilation (Fowers and Richardson, 1996; Merelman, 1994). The *melting pot approach* to cultural assimilation maintains that diverse ethnic and racial groups eventually

229

learn how to blend or melt into the dominant culture. Proponents believe that immigrants shed their ethnic identity and view themselves as Americans after a generation or so.

Multiculturalism, on the other hand, assumes that society should be able to accommodate the uniqueness and differences associated with multiple cultures. Retaining a distinctive ethnic or racial identity becomes of paramount importance to immigrants. However, as society moves to embrace multiculturalism, it also must be prepared for tensions and conflicts to arise between dominant and subordinate cultural groups.

The melting pot notion offers a way to decrease conflict between different racial and ethnic groups that have very distinct cultural histories. A society that encourages assimilation is attempting to forge a single cultural bond for all the diverse cultural groups it encompasses. However, when multiculturalism enters the picture, there is no longer a common cultural history. For multiculturalism to work, people must be more tolerant and sensitive to differing views and approaches to the cultural, political, economic, educational, and justice system values espoused by a society that celebrates the existence of multiple cultures.

As multiculturalism becomes more the norm, it poses special problems for police administrators. For instance, how should the police meet the public safety needs of multiple cultures that do not agree on the legitimacy of the police authority? Will it be necessary for the police to address different safety needs for African-Americans, Koreans, Chinese, South American Hispanics, Cuban Hispanics? And what about the "old guard" immigrant groups who hail predominately from Western Europe? Immigrant groups from some Central American countries come from a background where the police are closely allied with "death squads." Administrators must realize that first-wave immigrant groups from Europe and Great Britain may feel isolated because the police are not consistently enforcing the laws that buttress or support the value system of an assimilated culture.

What follows in this chapter is an explanation and description of multicultural policing and the problems associated with a multicultural policing strategy. After that, we look at the various ways different police organizations have attempted to develop and implement a multicultural law enforcement approach. The final section of the investigation determines the degree to which police administrators have been successful in implementing genuine multicultural law enforcement practices and its level of acceptance by street-level officers.

WHAT IS MULTICULTURAL POLICING?

The literature that has arisen in the area of multicultural policing focuses on a myriad of topics. Some observers feel that having police officers attain foreign language competence is a pivotal achievement (Blair and Slick, 1990; Colvard, 1992; DiVasto, 1996; Youngs and Novas, 1995). Other commentators concentrate on instilling greater cultural awareness and sensitivity within patrol officers (Bennett, 1995; Bird, 1993; Cox, 1990; Hennessy, 1993; Lumb, 1995; Maddox, 1993; Merelman,

1994; Torres, 1992). Another group develops an agenda that addresses the increased need for sworn officers to attend cultural diversity training sessions (Barlow and Barlow, 1993; Bickham and Rossett, 1993; Blakemore, Barlow, and Padgett, 1995; Himelfarb, 1991; Hinkle, 1991; Hoffman, 1993; Pomerville, 1993; Scott, 1993). As you might begin to appreciate, this list could go on indefinitely.

Some common elements in the literature support the position that multicultural policing is a real phenomenon. For the current presentation, *multicultural policing* is defined as a specific organizational change in the style of policing in response to dramatic shifts in the demographic composition of a jurisdiction's population. These demographic changes toward new immigrant groups who are only partially assimi-lated into mainstream America forces police organizations to develop new policies and training guidelines that broaden the techniques officers use in the field. A multi-cultural policing approach requires officers to move away from unicultural policing that is more suited to a culturally assimilated society. Now, officers must receive specialized training that enables them to understand and meet the needs of racial or ethnic minority-group enclaves that exist on their patrol beats.

WHY MULTICULTURAL POLICING?

Perhaps the most astute observation this literature offers is the realization that many police organizations have yet to make the transition to multicultural policing. These agencies have no choice except to adjust because their neighborhoods are becoming more culturally diverse. Their constituency is changing. Many more neighborhoods are culturally diverse and, in some areas, residents might even regard English as a foreign language.

Take a peek at Los Angeles County in California. Block (1994, p. 24) explains that Los Angeles County is the "second largest Mexican, Armenian, Korean, Filipino, Salvadoran, and Guatemalan city in the world." This area, with a population close to 9 million people of diverse cultural backgrounds, is a prescription for many other urban areas in this country (Weaver, 1992). Similar population shifts are taking place throughout the rest of the country. Table 12–1 provides a good illustration of projected population growth among racial and ethnic minority groups in the United States through the year 2050. As was observed in Los Angeles County, the fastest population growth will occur among people of Hispanic origin. Based on the population projections found in Table 12–1, it is anticipated that Hispanic people will increase at such a rate that they will compose 24.5% of the United States's population by the middle of the 21st century. At the same rate, the traditional white population base will drop to only 52.8% of the population. As one might surmise, these rapid population shifts will demand special attention.

These changes in the traditional population base will produce urban areas that are more multicultural and more multinational. This tide also means that public services will have to adjust to embrace the diverse ethnic and racial groups that appear in their jurisdictions. Meeting the needs of a culturally diverse society

Table 12-1   Resident Population, by Hispanic or Non-Hispanic Origin, 1980–1996 and Projections for 1997–2050 (population figures are in thousands)

Year	Total	Hispanic Origin	Not of Hispanic Origin			
			White	Black	American Indian	Asian or Pacific Islander
Actual						
1980	226,546	14,609	180,906	26,142	1,326	3,563
1981	229,466	15,560	181,974	26,532	1,377	4,022
1982	231,664	16,240	182,782	26,856	1,420	4,367
1983	233,792	16,935	183,561	27,159	1,466	4,671
1984	235,825	17,640	184,243	27,444	1,512	4,986
1985	237,924	18,368	184,945	27,738	1,558	5,315
1986	240,133	19,154	185,678	28,040	1,606	5,655
1987	242,289	19,946	186,353	28,351	1,654	5,985
1988	244,499	20,786	187,012	28,669	1,703	6,329
1989	246,819	21,648	187,713	29,005	1,755	6,698
1990	248,718	22,354	188,306	29,275	1,796	6,988
1991	252,106	23,416	189,610	29,829	1,829	7,422
1992	255,011	24,349	190,693	30,317	1,856	7,796
1993	257,795	25,326	191,658	30,767	1,882	8,161
1994	260,372	26,300	192,496	31,183	1,907	8,486
1995	262,890	27,277	193,281	31,565	1,931	8,836
1996	265,284	28,269	193,978	31,912	1,954	9,171
Projected						
1997	267,645	28,680	195,091	32,396	1,980	9,497
1998	270,002	29,566	195,786	32,789	2,005	9,856
1999	272,330	30,461	196,441	33,180	2,029	10,219
2000	274,634	31,366	197,061	33,568	2,054	10,584
2010	297,716	41,139	202,390	37,466	2,320	14,402
2020	322,742	52,652	207,393	41,538	2,601	18,557
2030	346,899	65,570	209,998	45,448	2,891	22,993
2040	369,980	80,164	209,621	49,379	3,203	27,614
2050	393,931	96,508	207,901	53,555	3,534	32,432
Percent distribution						
2000	100.0	11.4	71.8	12.2	0.7	3.9
2010	100.0	13.8	68.0	12.6	0.8	4.8
2020	100.0	16.3	64.3	12.9	0.8	5.7
2030	100.0	18.9	60.5	13.1	0.8	6.6
2040	100.0	21.7	56.7	13.3	0.9	7.5
2050	100.0	24.5	52.8	13.6	0.9	8.2

Source: Adapted from U.S. Bureau of the Census, *Statistical Abstract of the United States—1997*, p. 19. Washington, DC: U.S. Government Printing Office, 1998.

requires more than just developing new rules and regulations. Attitudes have to change, not only among street-level officers but also among top-level administrators. Adopting a true multicultural approach to policing requires more than the use of cultural awareness training as a "quick fix" to negative police-citizen encounters (Maddox, 1993; Pitter, 1992; Weaver, 1992). The police organization must be committed to cross-cultural training as a long-term process that provides officers with the knowledge and skills to police culturally diverse neighborhoods. Police officers are able to fully incorporate various aspects of cultural diversity when they receive instruction over the span of several training sessions. The one-shot seminars developed more to please politicians than to actually educate officers about diverse population groups will not result in a team of culturally aware service providers.

Weaver (1992) found four primary factors associated with achieving a more culturally aware police organization. First, police officers need to understand how their own cultural background molds their values and behavioral patterns. Second, officers must understand that cultural assimilation no longer is the norm in the United States. Law enforcement officers must learn about the different ethnic and racial groups in the neighborhoods they patrol. Third, it is critical that officers understand the effective use of cross-cultural communication. Police officers who have a deeper insight into the beliefs, behaviors, and value orientations of various ethnic groups will rely less often on authority and force to resolve problematic situations. Finally, law enforcement officers must develop cross-cultural communicative, analytical, and interpretative skills. It is necessary for the officer to learn and experience various ethnic cultures beyond classroom walls. The ultimate goal is to allow police officers to become so familiar with an ethnic group that they instinctively know when to intervene in an intracultural group conflict and the best options for nonviolent police interventions.

Some researchers believe that, before law enforcement genuinely can police from a perspective of cultural diversity, the organization must examine its historical relationship with some of the most isolated racial and ethnic groups (Bennett, 1995; Carter, 1995; Murty, Roebuck, and Smith, 1990; Pitter, 1992; Poole and Pogrebin, 1990). One position consistently espoused is that police officers must strive to overcome the negative and hostile relations that currently characterize interchanges with some racial and ethnic minority groups in the United States. For example, Carter (1995) found that people, mostly African-Americans, who live in inner-city neighborhoods are deeply upset that their neighborhoods are underpoliced or not policed at all. These citizens take the position that poor, urban residents, even those who live in housing projects, mostly are law-abiding people. They would welcome strict enforcement of the criminal law on the streets where they live because it would improve their quality of life (Carter, 1995; Murty et al., 1990).

The police sometimes encounter cultural obstacles that make their jobs extremely difficult. For example, many Korean crime victims in one community did not fully understand how the American criminal justice system works. The victims insisted the police should arrest their assailants more quickly and incarcerate these criminals. When the police did not take some suspects into custody or when the legal system subsequently seemed unresponsive, many Korean immigrants became dissatisfied and no longer would call the police. Law enforcement in Korea is associated with a corrupt political system (Poole and Pogrebin, 1990). In that country, victims who report crimes to the Korean police often risk retaliation. Given this background, it is easy to understand why Korean immigrants distrust and avoid contact with the police in America.

The literature gives no clear and concise definition of the term *multicultural policing*. However, the concept is much more than merely a "politically correct" addition to the police administration terminology. There are clear indications that multicultural policing is not a euphemism to express a feeling or a court-ordered policy initiative. It is not an attempt by police administrators to save "face" or a public relations venture where the primary goal is image enhancement. The literature also is very clear that multicultural policing was not developed and implemented solely on the advice of any particular ethnic or racial minority group. Studies reveal that the demographic composition of the United States is changing steadily in ways that we never have seen before (Betsalel, 1990; Bracey, 1990; Cox, 1990; Dunham and Alpert, 1988; Hoffman, 1993; McCord and Wicker, 1990; Polk, 1995; Trojanowicz and Carter, 1990). As a result, police organizations are trying to respond to these population shifts by broadening their traditional strategies to reflect a need to patrol multicultural, nonassimilated neighborhoods. Just as a reminder, Table 12–1 is a good illustration of these shifts in current and projected population trends.

Some people feel that these new immigrants are not assimilating very easily into the dominant culture. It is not because these nonnatives intentionally choose to be segregated from the dominant culture. Rather, they have no choice (Dunham and Alpert, 1988; McCord and Wicker, 1990; Trojanowicz and Carter, 1990). Race and ethnicity play a major role in restricting new immigrants to partial assimilation. Since the late 1970s, over half the legal immigrants to the United States were either Chinese, Filipino, Indian, Korean, Vietnamese, or Cambodian. Another third came from Latin America to seek permanent residency (Trojanowicz and Carter, 1990). At the same time, only about 12% of legal immigrants to the United States arrived from Western European countries.

These new migration patterns mean that police departments now have to patrol poor inner-city neighborhoods where large numbers of recent immigrant groups cluster in well-defined geographical areas as a way to maintain their culture. The changing demographic composition of new immigrant groups, which are slow to assimilate into the dominant culture, requires corresponding changes in the way the law enforcement establishment communicates with non-English-speaking communities. Police departments face major decisions about how to allocate their limited resources to develop some type of bilingual component to supplement their patrol divisions.

Some agencies are making a conscious effort to recruit and select prospective officers who are bilingual. In addition, some agencies have initiated training incentives for officers who are interested in becoming bilingual. While much of this emphasis has concentrated on competence in Spanish, a few urban police departments with identifiable Chinatowns, Little Hanois, and Little Tokyos have branched out to attract patrol officers proficient in Asian language dialects.

A major benefit of foreign language competence is that patrol officers have an opportunity to become acculturated. Many training academies have designed foreign language courses to improve language speaking skills and familiarization with appropriate body language and facial expressions used to convey messages. Such courses help police officers understand body movements, personal space, and cultural nuances, like the meaning of touching, pushing, and prodding someone, as well as the Latin male reliance on "machismo" (Colvard, 1992).

Some scholars also view foreign language competence as a hedge against unnecessary civil litigation (Colvard, 1992; DiVasto, 1996; Youngs and Novas, 1995). Violent encounters can be diminished when the responding officer speaks the dominant language of a neighborhood and can communicate effectively. It also speeds up street contacts because street officers do not have to summon and wait for a translator. The patrol officer at the scene of the incident has the opportunity to defuse a potentially violent encounter by not allowing language to act as a barrier to his or her job performance. Most important, police officers who speak the dominant foreign language on their beat and understand certain types of nonverbal cultural cues demonstrate to the racial or ethnic minority group that their concerns will be heard with much less tension and confusion (DiVasto, 1996; Youngs and Novas, 1995). A patrol officer who can communicate with non-English-speaking residents in a culturally diverse neighborhood will engender more trust and empathy from the people who live there.

Another core component of the movement to embrace multicultural policing is that some departments require their officers display an enhanced cultural awareness and sensitivity to community diversity. A critical component of the literature on cultural awareness by police officers is that it is not grounded in the police community relations (PCR) literature of the 1960s. The cultural awareness and sensitivity literature does not seek to make African-Americans, Hispanics, and other racial and ethnic minority groups more tolerant of the police department's image in their communities. Instead, the current goal is to train and retool police officers to know and respect the diverse racial and ethnic groups for whom they provide law enforcement protection. The focus has shifted from police-community relations, which really amounted to nothing more than image enhancement, to policy mandates that require police personnel to become much better educated about the mostly poor, mostly urban neighborhoods that are home to a diverse mixture of racial and ethnic groups (Maddox, 1993).

Several scholars found that the police organization must become more aware of and educated about various cultural groups, with varying needs that sometime create intergroup conflict and violence (Bennett, 1995; Lumb, 1995; Maddox, 1993). These diverse cultural groups compete against each other for continually shrinking federal and state program dollars. And the law enforcement establishment ultimately must maintain order among them. To be perceived as providing fair and equal treatment to the older, mostly poor cultural groups (e.g., African-Americans and Mexican-Americans) and the new immigrant groups (e.g., from Asia and Latin America), police organizations need to continue to train and retrain officers on the subject of cultural awareness and sensitivity (Lumb, 1995).

Some researchers have found that it is virtually impossible to hire officers who are totally devoid of prejudicial attitudes (Lumb, 1995; Merelman, 1994). Seen in this light, police administrators must develop in-service training modules that assist officers in becoming more culturally literate. The most effective and successful cultural awareness education usually is fully integrated into the general police training curriculum (Lumb, 1995). The major objective of this training is to educate officers about different cultures and increase their understanding of the culturally diverse groups that rely on them for law enforcement protection. According to Lumb (1995), a former police chief himself, the most effective cultural sensitivity training curriculum delves into such core areas as race, culture, interethnic relations, and the causes and consequences of prejudice. The ultimate goal of this type of cultural awareness instruction is for officers to leave the classroom with useful skills and an enhanced understanding of how to deploy effective policing strategies.

THE NEED FOR MULTICULTURAL POLICE TRAINING

The final category of literature on the issue of multicultural policing focuses on the need for continuous police training in the area of cultural diversity. One important way to heighten cultural awareness skills is to train and retrain those officers so that training becomes a critical change agent (Blakemore et al., 1995; Lumb, 1995; Pomerville, 1993). Training is most effective when management provides clear and observable objectives to be achieved at the organizational and individual levels. Several researchers found that cultural diversity training has a much more lasting effect on officers if the instruction goes beyond the passive type of lecture presentation (Bennett, 1995; Himelfarb, 1991; Youngs and Novas, 1995). In general, cultural diversity training requires strong participant involvement. Based on that premise, cultural diversity training needs to be very action oriented. Officers should be ready to exchange perceptions with members of racial and ethnic minority groups, talk about their values and belief systems, and develop practical recommendations they can implement in multicultural neighborhoods. The most effective and successful cultural diversity training closely resembles other applied field training curriculums like pursuit driving, firearms familiarization, and CPR (Bickham and Rossett, 1993; Hennessy, 1993; Lumb, 1995).

The literature also provides guidelines as to what multicultural policing is not. On close inspection of the four primary themes that characterizes this literature, common elements emerge to support the position that multicultural policing is a real phenomenon. Therefore, for the purposes of the current presentation, *multicultural policing* is defined as a specific organizational change in the style of policing due to dramatic changes in the demographic composition of an area. The demographic changes note a shift in the department's more assimilated, traditional population base toward new immigrant groups from Asia and Central America that are only partially assimilated, which forces the police organization to develop new policies and training guidelines that broaden the types of policing techniques used in the field. So, a multicultural policing approach requires that police officers move away from the unicultural policing that is more suited to a culturally assimilated society and become better educated and trained to understand and meet the needs of the racial and ethnic minority enclaves on their patrol beat.

DIFFICULTIES OF POLICING IN A MULTICULTURAL SOCIETY

To fully embrace multicultural policing requires an acute awareness of the current dominant culture and the different cultural barriers that can impede successful realization of that goal. The police organization is a part of society. It recruits and hires the next generation of police officers from that society and must educate neophytes on the various ways the criminal code is used to protect that society. The challenge for law enforcement is to determine if the police leadership is fully committed to guiding it in a new direction that is dictated by rapid social change. In that regard, police administrators must confront the traditional way the police organization has used stereotypes. Police leaders must be proactive in telling and showing their subordinates that they need not rely on negative stereotypes of certain groups of people to be effective police officers. Another critical problem discussed in this section relates to the effective recruitment and selection of a new type of police officer, who is more adapted to policing in a multicultural community.

Defeating Stereotypes

A major problem that affects police agencies and their attempt to implement multicultural policing techniques is the way law enforcement officers rely on stereotypes when they police. According to Skolnick (1994, pp. 44–47), police use stereotypes as a shorthand technique to identify people who use certain types of language and dress in a flashy manner that experienced officers recognize as a potentially dangerous person. Police refer to these types of people as *symbolic assailants*, and they use the individual's appearance as a quick way to classify such encounters as more dangerous and violence prone. Whether or not these profiles are accurate is beside the point.

Weaver (1992) explains four faulty assumptions are made concerning the stereotyping of group behavior. First, many people mistakenly think that as the workforce and society become more diverse, group differences no longer are relevant. The reality is that sometimes cultural maltreatment and misunderstanding only make differences worse and increase the potential for intercultural conflict.

The second assumption is based on the idea of America as a melting pot. It dreamfully posits the notion that every one is equal and gets treated the same way. Nothing could be further from the truth.

The term *melting pot* is a prop or legitimization tool that outlived its usefulness. Originally, the melting pot was the preferred cultural model. It was shaped to accommodate immigrant groups who were much more likely to be white, Anglo-Saxon,

Protestant men. Groups who matched this cultural mold made substantial socioeconomic progress and gained access to opportunities for betterment. However, "people of color," such as African-Americans and the various American Indian tribes, were visibly different. As such, they could never be fully assimilated under the melting pot thesis (Mann, 1993).

The third faulty assumption about group behavior is that differences can be resolved easily through verbal communication. Consider, for a moment, that over 90% of the messages that people convey are not communicated verbally. Instead, their underlying meaning is transmitted by a person's posture, facial expression, and tone of voice (Mann, 1993; Weaver, 1992).

Police officers often interpret verbal disorder as an indicator of chaos or a breakdown in normal interaction. Whenever an officer handles a call for service, a high priority is assigned to maintaining respect and order (Sykes and Brent, 1980). Whenever the situation deteriorates, officers resort to a variety of techniques to control the flow or sequence of events. Should all else fail, officers will resort to coercion to settle the matter (Doerner, 1998, pp. 158–161). Given this backdrop, it is not difficult to envision how cultural differences in communication styles can get resolved through handcuffing.

The final barrier to cultural understanding is that conflict is conflict, regardless of with whom the officer is dealing in a situation. But the reality is that some cultural groups use inflammatory words and accelerated speech for verbal effect, with no intention of escalating the encounter to physical violence. While stereotyping may provide officers a handy group policing technique, it also reinforces negative images of racial and ethnic minority groups. Since a stereotype is an oversimplified image used to typify a specific cultural group's behavior, it ultimately becomes a caricature of group behavior. Of course, trying to predict individual behavior on the basis of group characteristics is fraught with difficulties. The typical stereotype in most urban areas in the United States indicates that most racial and ethnic minority group members (e.g., African-Americans and Hispanics) are presumed to be dangerous and violent. Therefore, officers who enter these encounters are likely to engage in a series of self-fulfilling behaviors.

Cultural barriers become even more ingrained because officers rely on these stereotypes when they initiate field encounters. These stereotypes fuel or reinforce "police suspicion" that such persons pose a danger to their safety and well-being (Mann, 1993). Relying on questionable stereotyped behaviors to target and interrogate people in multicultural neighborhoods only increases the hostility and resentment in these neighborhoods. The resulting self-fulfilling prophecy heightens these concerns for both the police and the policed. The self-fulfilling prophecy means that officers stereotype minority groups as dangerous or violent and behave toward them more aggressively and with less respect. Minority-group members, in turn, resent this unwarranted treatment and respond to this police behavior in kind. Ultimately, then, both sides contribute to a tumultuous situation in which each party perceives the other to be acting in a discriminatory and capricious way. This is exactly the cycle that multicultural policing attempts to circumvent in the first place.

Recruitment and Selection

Given the problems that cultural barriers create, many agencies experience difficulty when they try to recruit new members from racial or ethnic communities. Several obstacles impede the chances of having a police department that closely mirrors the composition of either the area's population or labor force (Lewis, 1989; Prince, 1982; Rafky, 1975). We can categorize them into societal, organizational, and individual factors.

There are a number of relevant factors at the societal level. For one thing, minority groups are not as defensive today about seeking police employment as they were in the 1970s and early 1980s. In fact, there is a great deal of competition in some urban areas for minority-group members who can meet the minimum entrance requirements. On the downside, urban minority applicants have a greater propensity to be disqualified from the hiring process because of the negative impact associated with living in large cities. The urban environment fosters such problematic conditions as lower educational attainment, heightened odds for an arrest history, and a lack of positive role models who can attract disadvantaged youths to police work (Kaminski, 1993; Rafky, 1975).

Also some organizational aspects should be considered. A number of police departments are much more inclusive in the way they recruit applicants from all walks of life. However, some mid-level police administrators remain whose attitudes are grounded in stereotypes. These influential mid-level managers strive to keep the police organization predominantly white and male.

Another organizational hurdle is that some local agencies artificially restrict the potential recruitment pool by imposing residential requirements on new police candidates. Many otherwise qualified applicants are lost because the department requires employees to live inside city boundaries. Perhaps an even bigger obstacle is the reliance on "word of mouth" to advertise vacancies. Since law enforcement remains mostly white and mostly male, there is a very good chance that such employment opportunities will not be disseminated widely among racial and ethnic minority-group members.

At the individual level, police departments face formidable impediments to hiring racial and ethnic minority-group members. A self-selection factor relates to the way public and private agencies compete for a small pool of talented, college-educated racial and ethnic minority-group members during each hiring cycle. Unless individuals already were committed to a law enforcement career prior to receiving their college degrees, they are quite likely to make other career choices. Such decisions are made for various reasons. However, the primary reasons usually are the low entry salary and limited career advancement opportunities that characterize law enforcement. For these reasons, an applicant's race matters when attempting to predict who would decline the offer of a sworn position (Ash, Slora, and Britton, 1990; Buzawa, 1981; Kaminski, 1993; Maghan, 1993).

African-American high school seniors are more likely to decline a police job offer for several reasons (Kaminiski, 1993). First, they perceive that African-American and white officers get along poorly on the job. Second, these young people think that police officers frequently treat racial or ethnic minority-group members unfairly. Third, graduating seniors acknowledge that people in their neighborhoods have very little respect for police officers. Finally, these students believe their parents would disapprove strongly if they decided to become police officers.

While it is hard enough for agencies to make the change from unicultural policing to a multicultural policing approach, these and other problems at the societal, organizational, and individual levels exacerbate the transition. It is apparent that the police leadership has very little, if any, control over the broad societal obstacles. However, the leadership is in a position to reduce some hindrances at the organizational and individual levels. The next section presents several techniques police administrators can invoke if they are genuinely interested in moving toward a multicultural policing approach.

CHANGE AGENTS AND MULTICULTURAL POLICING

The law enforcement world changes ever so slowly. In fact, Guyot (1979) remarks that attempting to institute any meaningful reform in policing is like trying to bend granite. The resistance to change is enormous. As a result, it often takes external mandates to force the law enforcement establishment to alter its infrastructure. The introduction of blacks and women into the rank and file are painful examples of this glacierlike pace.

Agencies are slowly, but steadily, incorporating various aspects of multicultural policing into their operations. Three major change agents account for much of this movement: affirmative action, community policing, and the inclusion of cultural diversity training requirements. As each of these reforms was implemented, it forced law enforcement to reexamine the traditional way it was delivering police services and alter those practices. We next look at these change agents and explore the impact they have had on the way some police departments are doing business in multicultural neighborhoods.

Affirmative Action

Although affirmative action mandates were imposed on the police, these efforts have been successful in guiding departments toward fair and open employment practices. Many police administrators initially opposed affirmative action because they feared that employment standards would be compromised. They resented the prospect of hiring less-than-qualified women and racial or ethnic minority-group members (Felkenes and Unsinger, 1992; Gaines, Costello, and Crabtree, 1989; Grant, Milne, and White, 1975; Martin, 1991; Moran, 1988). However, these fears have not materialized. Agencies have adjusted to the fact that they can hire qualified women and minority-group members who are capable of competing successfully with the traditional white male candidate pool. Despite some affirmative action litigation that questions job-related employment testing and merit system hiring, many police departments have come to accept affirmative action as a critical selection method to ensure gender and racial diversity within the ranks (Ermer, 1978; Evans, 1980; McCoy, 1984; Tafoya, 1991; Toffler and Toffler, 1990; Wright, 1996).

Affirmative action programs have provided a powerful mechanism for ensuring equal employment opportunity in police employment (Felkenes and Unsinger, 1992; Martin, 1991; McCoy, 1984; Moran, 1988). For example, Felkenes and Unsinger (1992) found that the Los Angeles Police Department (LAPD) made no substantial progress toward hiring women and minority-group members until after a consent decree (*Blake v. City of Los Angeles*, 1979) settled this matter. A *consent decree* is a federal court order that imposes hiring goals on agencies deemed deficient in their hiring of members from protected classes. While researchers attribute much of the credit for the growing racial and ethnic minority presence in law enforcement to affirmative action programs, ample room for improvement remains (Hochstedler, 1984; Hochstedler and Conley, 1986; Martin, 1991; Stalans, 1997; Stokes, 1997; Wright, 1996).

Although affirmative action is just one way to increase minority representation, these efforts have played a critical role in this area. While not a panacea, equal employment opportunity programs have altered the way that police departments make crucial hiring decisions. A more diverse roster adds legitimacy and credibility to the agency that serves multicultural neighborhoods. In short, affirmative action programs have been an important change agent for police organizations.

Community Policing

Community policing is another important change agent for multicultural policing. Community policing has forced the upper echelon to question whether the traditional emphasis on crime control and order maintenance is the most effective way to police. Advocates have found that the traditional police organizational structure was more suited to unicultural policing. As neighborhoods changed and grew more culturally diverse, law enforcement officials discovered that they were forced to deal with very complex social issues that were interrelated with criminal incidents. Responding time after time to calls by sending a radio-dispatched patrol car to the area was inefficient and ineffective. Starting in the early 1980s, many police administrators acknowledged that what they really needed was more direct contact with the people who lived in these rapidly changing neighborhoods. The realization dawned that it would take "a new breed of police officer" to work in these culturally diverse neighborhoods (Trojanowicz and Bucqueroux, 1990).

The basic principles of community policing are closely related to multicultural policing. Community policing calls for an organizational structure and strategy to provide police services at the neighborhood level (Lurigio and Rosenbaum, 1997). Embodied within community policing is the idea that law enforcement should shift its focus away from crime control to a more proactive style of neighborhood-level policing. It should seek to forge a partnership with citizens to solve community problems related to crime and neighborhood deterioration (Trojanowicz and Bucqueroux, 1990).

The goal of community policing is to get patrol officers out of patrol cars and into daily contact with the people who live on their beat. Increased interaction should improve rapport and trust between the police and the public. As Trojanowicz and Bucqueroux see it,

> community policing provides a new way for the police to provide decentralized and personalized police service that offers every law-abiding citizen an opportunity to become active in the police process. (1990, pp. 5–6)

This new breed of police officer would spend much more time interacting with people. While neighborhood-level policing is a major tenet of the community policing philosophy, officers also need to be trained to recognize and understand the culturally diverse geographic areas they are assigned to protect. Increased daily contact with the public creates opportunities for police officers to learn about many more potential criminal incidents. It also sidesteps the possible misinterpretation of a benign subcultural activity as a crime matter. In this regard, administrators have discovered that cultural diversity training plays a vital role in the way in which they prepare officers to work in local neighborhoods.

Cultural Diversity Training

Cultural diversity training is the third change agent that has propelled law enforcement away from unicultural policing and towards multicultural policing. The past few years have seen a new emphasis on developing training materials that familiarize police officers with the values and belief systems of different people. As Box 12–1 illustrates, some states have initiated this activity by adding statutory provisions to police officer certification requirements.

Most cultural diversity training programs were developed in larger urban areas because that was where the greatest need first became apparent. For example, Box 12–2 shows a broad policy developed by the Baltimore Police Department adminis-tration that addresses the interest and need to conduct cultural diversity training. Based on the statement "We Treat People with Respect and Sensitivity," the Baltimore Police Department mandates that all sworn and nonsworn personnel complete eight hours of in-service cultural diversity training per year. As you can see, agencies in urban areas most often are the ones who have had to carve out innovative ways to address the needs of socially complex multicultural neighborhoods. In one sense, then, police departments have adopted cultural diversity training programs in much the same way that many of them were given an "external push" to adopt affir-mative action and community policing approaches.

Most agencies adopted cultural diversity training curricula only in response to external pressures (Barlow and Barlow, 1993; Bennett, 1995; Blakemore et al., 1995; Lumb, 1995). These external pressures came primarily from community leaders who realized that their neighborhoods were becoming more diverse and that unicultural crime control techniques were inadequate. Blind adherence to unicultural policing

Box 12–1 Cultural Diversity Training Requirements for Florida Law Enforcement Officers

§943.1715 Basic Skills Training Relating to Diverse Populations.

The commission [Criminal Justice Standards and Training] shall establish and maintain standards for instruction of officers in the subject of interpersonal skills relating to diverse populations, with an emphasis on the awareness of cultural differences. Every basic skills course required in order for officers to obtain initial certification must include a minimum of 8 hours training in interpersonal skills with diverse populations.

§943.1716 Continued Employment Training Relating to Diverse Populations.

The commission [Criminal Justice Standards and Training] shall by rule require that each officer receive, as part of the 40 hours required instruction for continued employment or appointment as an officer, 8 hours of instruction in the subject of interpersonal skills relating to diverse populations, with an emphasis on the awareness of cultural differences.

§943.1758 Curriculum Revision for Diverse Populations; Skills Training.

1. The Criminal Justice Standards and Training Commission shall review its standards and training for basic recruits and its requirements for continued employment by integrating instructions on interpersonal skills relating to diverse populations into the criminal justice standards and training curriculum. The curriculum shall include standardized proficiency instruction relating to high-risk and critical tasks, which include but are not limited to, stops, use of force and domination, and other areas of interaction between officers and members of diverse populations.
2. The commission shall develop and implement, as part of its instructor training programs, standardized instruction in the subject of interpersonal skills relating to diverse populations.

Culturally sensitive lesson plans, up-to-date videotapes, and other demonstrative aids developed for use in diverse-population related training shall be used as instructional materials.

Source: Florida Statutes, Chapter 943 (1998).

Box 12–2   An Example of Agency Policy Regarding the Rationale for Cultural Diversity In-Service Training: The Values of the Baltimore Police Department

Late in 1991, a Task Force of Baltimore Citizens, government officials and police officers met in executive session to develop a statement of the mission of the Baltimore Police Department and values of policing that would reflect the expectations of the Baltimore community about how the community should be policed. The following statement of mission and values reflects the consensus reached from those meetings.

I. Policy
It is the policy of the Baltimore Police Department to ensure the policies and procedures written in this manual and the actions of its members are consistent with the values of this agency as explained in this Order.

II. The Statement of the Mission of the Department
The mission of the Baltimore Police Department, in partnership with the Baltimore community, is to protect and preserve life and protect property, to understand and serve the needs of the city's neighborhoods, and to improve the quality of life by building capacities to maintain order, recognize and resolve problems, and apprehend criminals in a manner consistent with the law and reflective of shared community values.

From this mission flows a set of values that lay the framework for the standards applied to policing in Baltimore over the coming years.

III. Standards of Performance/Values
That Guide Our Actions

Our Highest Commitment Is Protecting Life
We consider protecting life our highest priority. Our firearms policy reflects the commitment to protect life; we only use fatal force when it is absolutely necessary to save the life of a person or officer, or prevent serious bodily injury when no other options are available. . . .

We Treat People with Respect and Sensitivity
As policing professionals, we seek to ensure every person will be treated with dignity, fairness, and respect, without regard to race, religion, sex, sexual orientation, national origin, or handicapping condition. We will always protect individuals' constitutional rights. . . .

Source: Adapted from Baltimore [Maryland] Police Department, *Policy Manual.*

Box 12–3   Selected Internet Sites Pertaining to Multicultural Policing

Black Police Association of Nevada: http://www.bpan.tierrant.com

Catholic Peace Officers Association: http://www.cpoa.org

Fellowship of Christian Peace Officers—U.S.A.: http://www.fcpo.org

International Association of Women Police: http://www.iawp.org

Italian American Police Society of New Jersey: http://www.iapsnj.org

Latino Peace Officer's Association: http://www.amdahl.com

Miami Police Hispanic Officers Association: http://www.mphoa.com

National Organization of Black Law Enforcement Executives:
http://www.noblenatl.org

Texas Women in Law Enforcement: http://www.anet-dfw.com/~twlenfc

The National Center for Women and Policing: http://www.feminist.org/
police/ncwp.html

produced a skyrocketing number of citizen complaints about police brutality and similar civil lawsuits. Many police administrators, especially in the wake of the liability issues Professor Camp discloses in Chapter 7, determined that it was in their best interest to make some changes. Police executives were willing to educate and train their officers to be better prepared to provide police services to a culturally diverse population. As Box 12–3 shows, a growing number of readily available materials address these concerns.

Cultural diversity training sessions have to be more applied and situation oriented (Himelfarb, 1991; Lumb, 1995; Youngs and Novas, 1995). Lumb (1995) maintains that these training programs should provide officers with tools that improve their ability to manage multicultural police-citizen contacts. The objective is to help officers increase their knowledge of different cultural groups so they understand the diversity of the neighborhoods that they patrol. Furthermore, this training should be ongoing to ensure that police officers know how to use their cultural diversity skills. After all, agencies require officers to update their firearms training on a regular basis to make sure that those essential skills remain intact. Why should an agency settle for less durable human relations skills?

As you might imagine, there is a direct connection between a department's implementation of regular cultural diversity training and multicultural policing. More so than any other change agents we discuss, an organization's commitment to cultural diversity training also is a firm pledge to multicultural policing. Incorporating cultural diversity training into an agency's mission is a profound departure from past practices. Based on the changes implicit with the implementation of an ongoing cultural diversity training program, many police administrators have fully adopted all of the components of a multicultural policing approach. While some police managers are reluctant to leave behind unicultural policing, they recognize that multicultural policing gives them more flexibility in hiring personnel who can comfortably police at the neighborhood level and who are culturally knowledgeable about the diverse groups they will encounter.

CONCLUSION

The intention behind this chapter is to identify and discuss major issues associated with an agency's transition from unicultural policing to multicultural policing. Although the literature neglects to provide a solid working definition of *multicultural policing*, sufficient evidence suggests that such an approach does exist and is warranted. An examination of the police literature that focuses on such issues as policing in a diverse society, foreign language competency of police officers, and cultural diversity training provides evidence that many agencies are moving away from a unicultural policing approach. Many departments are attempting to adopt multicultural policing practices that require specific organizational changes in the style of policing to adjust to the dramatic changes in the demographic composition of their police jurisdiction. With a multicultural policing approach, the police administrator's primary motivation is to train and educate officers to meet the needs of the culturally diverse neighborhoods they are assigned to patrol.

Three change agents bear primary responsibility for this transition to multicultural policing. Whenever an agency brings affirmative action, community policing, and cultural diversity training into its organizational structure and mission, the way is paved for adopting a multicultural policing approach. In these places, multicultural policing becomes a broad-based commitment to hire officers who accurately reflect the community's racial and ethnic diversity. Multicultural policing also requires the delivery of police services at the neighborhood level by officers who continuously are trained to know and understand how to police multicultural neighborhoods.

Most of the available evidence indicates that multicultural policing techniques have been more fully utilized in urban police departments. This is primarily because urban areas and their police departments constantly are in a state of change. The issues that require police departments to rely on affirmative action, community policing, and cultural diversity training are well suited for urban police departments. Smaller, more rural police departments may never implement multicultural policing techniques if the population that they police view unicultural policing as the norm. Many rural police departments are not faced with major demographic changes in their traditional population base. And rural departments do not face the external and internal pressure to address the types of problems that usually are resolved through the use of such policing techniques as affirmative action, community policing, and ongoing cultural diversity training.

DISCUSSION QUESTIONS

1. Do you think police chiefs would be as interested in multicultural policing if cultural assimilation still was the norm in most of urban America?
2. What is multicultural policing and why do you think that some police chiefs view this concept as the policing approach of the future?
3. Do you agree that multicultural policing is the future for law enforcement in the United States or do you think that unicultural policing can be retained in its present form and still address the fundamental issues in law enforcement adequately?
4. If you were a police recruiter, how would you market multicultural policing so that you could convince the best and most qualified minority-group members to apply for sworn positions?
5. Assume you are a police recruiter who has enjoyed a great deal of success in recruiting racial and ethnic minority-group members to work in your police department. Obviously, you have developed a very effective presentation on the multicultural policing approach used in your department. Do you think the same presentation would be as effective in recruiting from a traditional pool of applicants? Explain your response.
6. Assume you are a police chief. How would multicultural policing play a role in satisfying the agency mission statement and goals?

REFERENCES

Ash, P., K. Slora, and C. Britton. "Police agency officer selection practices." *Journal of Police Science and Administration* 17, no. 4 (1990), pp. 258–269.

Barlow, D., and M. Barlow. "Cultural diversity training in criminal justice: A progressive or conservative reform?" *Social Justice* 20, nos. 3–4 (1993), pp. 69–84.

Bennett, B. "Incorporating diversity: Police response to multicultural changes in their communities." *FBI Law Enforcement Bulletin* 64, no. 12 (1995), pp. 1–6.

Betsalel, K. "Police leadership and the reconciliation of police minority relations." *American Journal of Police* 9, no. 2 (1990), pp. 63–77.

Bickham, T., and A. Rossett. "Diversity training: Are we doing the right thing right?" *Police Chief* 60, no. 11 (1993), pp. 43–47.

Bird, J. " Respecting individual and cultural differences: A prescription for effective supervision." *FBI Law Enforcement Bulletin* 62, no. 3 (1993), pp. 18–19.

Blair, G., and S. Slick. "Survival Spanish: Needed training for police." *Police Chief* 57, no. 1 (1990), pp. 42–47.

Blake v. City of Los Angeles, 595 F.2d 1367 (1979).

Blakemore, J., D. Barlow, and D. Padgett. "From the classroom to the community: Introducing process in police diversity training." *Police Studies* 18, no. 1 (1995), pp. 71–83.

Block, S. "Policing an increasingly diverse America: Notable speech." *FBI Law Enforcement Bulletin* 63, no. 6 (1994), pp. 24–26.

Bracey, D. "Preparing police leaders for the future." *Police Studies* 13, no. 4 (1990), pp. 178–183.

Buzawa, E. "The role of race in predicting job attitudes of patrol officers." *Journal of Criminal Justice* 9, no. 1 (1981), pp. 63–77.

Carter, R. "Improving minority relations." *FBI Law Enforcement Bulletin* 64, no. 12 (1995), pp. 14–17.

Colvard, A. "Foreign languages: A contemporary training requirement." *FBI Law Enforcement Bulletin* 61, no. 9 (1992), pp. 20–23.

Cox, S. "Policing into the 21st century." *Police Studies* 13, no. 4 (1990), pp. 168–177.

DiVasto, P. "Negotiating with foreign-language-speaking subjects." *FBI Law Enforcement Bulletin* 65, no. 6 (1996), pp. 11–15.

Doerner, W. G. *Introduction to Law Enforcement: An Insider's View.* Boston: Butterworth–Heinemann, 1998.

Dunham, R., and G. Alpert. "Neighborhood differences in attitudes toward policing: Evidence for a mixed-strategy model of policing in a multi-ethnic setting." *Journal of Criminal Law and Criminology* 79, no. 2 (1998), pp. 504–523.

Ermer, V. "Recruitment of female police officers in New York City." *Journal of Criminal Justice* 6, no. 3 (1978), pp. 233–246.

Evans, D. "Height, weight, and physical agility requirements—Title VII and public safety employment." *Journal of Police Science and Administration* 8, no. 4 (1980), pp. 414–436.

Felkenes, G., and P. Unsinger. *Diversity, Affirmative Action and Law Enforcement.* Springfield, IL: Charles C Thomas Publisher, 1992.

Fowers, B., and F. Richardson. "Why is multiculturalism good?" *American Psychologist* 51, no. 6 (1996), pp. 609–621.

Gaines, L., P. Costello, and A. Crabtree. "Police selection testing: Balancing legal requirements and employer needs." *American Journal of Police* 8, no. 1 (1989), pp. 137–152.

Grant, R., R. Milne, and K. White. "Minority recruiting: The Tucson police experience." *Journal of Police Science and Administration* 3, no. 2 (1975), pp. 197–202.

Guyot, D. "Bending granite: Attempts to change the rank structure of American police departments." *Journal of Police Science and Administration* 7, no. 2 (1979), pp. 253–284.

Hennessy, S. "Achieving cultural competence." *Police Chief* 60, no. 8 (1993), pp. 46–48.

Himelfarb, F. "A training strategy for policing in a multicultural society." *Police Chief* 58, no. 11 (1991), pp. 53–55.

Hinkle, D. "Language barriers and the police." *Law and Order* 39, no. 3 (1991), pp. 38–42.

Hochstedler, E. "Impediments to hiring minorities in public police agencies." *Journal of Police Science and Administration* 12, no. 2 (1984), pp. 227–240.

_____ and J. Conley. "Explaining underrepresentation of black officers in city police agencies." *Journal of Criminal Justice* 14, no. 4 (1986), pp. 319–328.

Hoffman, V. "Role of police in the process of societal change: Korean and American examples." *Police Studies* 16, no. 3 (1993), pp. 84–89.

Kaminski, R. "Police minority recruitment: Predicting who will say yes to an offer for a job as a cop." *Journal of Criminal Justice* 21, no. 4 (1993), pp. 395–409.

Lewis, W. "Toward representative bureaucracy: Blacks in city police organizations, 1975–1985." *Public Administration Review* 49, no. 3 (1989), pp. 257–268.

Lumb, R. "Policing culturally diverse groups: Continuing professional development programs for police." *Police Studies* 18, no. 1 (1995), pp. 23–43.

Lurigio, A. J., and D. P. Rosenbaum. "Community policing: Major issues and unanswered questions." In M. L. Dantzker (ed.), *Contemporary Policing: Personnel, Issues, and Trends*, pp. 195–216. Boston: Butterworth–Heinemann, 1997.

Maddox, J. "Community sensitivity." *FBI Law Enforcement Bulletin* 62, no. 2 (1993), pp. 10–12.

Maghan, J. "The changing face of the police officer: Occupational socialization of minority police recruits." In R. Dunham and G. Alpert (eds.), *Critical Issues in Policing: Contemporary Readings*, pp. 348–360. Prospect, IL: Waveland Press, 1993.

Mann, C. *Unequal Justice: A Question of Color*. Bloomington: Indiana University Press, 1993.

Martin, S. "The effectiveness of affirmative action: The case of women in policing." *Justice Quarterly* 8, no. 4 (1991), pp. 489–504.

McCord, R., and E. Wicker. "Tomorrow's America: Law enforcement's coming challenge." *FBI Law Enforcement Bulletin* 59, no. 1 (1990), pp. 28–32.

McCoy, C. "Affirmative action in police organizations—Checklists for supporting a compelling state interests." *Criminal Law Bulletin* 20, no. 3 (1984), pp. 245–254.

Merelman, R. "Racial conflict and cultural politics in the United States." *Journal of Politics* 56, no. 1 (1994), pp. 1–20.

Moran, T. "Pathways toward a nondiscriminatory recruitment policy." *Journal of Police Science and Administration* 16, no. 4 (1998), pp. 274–287.

Murty, K., J. Roebuck, and J. Smith. "The image of the police in black Atlanta communities." *Journal of Police Science and Administration* 17, no. 4 (1990), pp. 250–257.

Pitter, G. "Policing cultural celebrations." *FBI Law Enforcement Bulletin* 61, no. 9 (1992), pp. 10–14.

Polk, O. E. "The effects of ethnicity on career paths of advanced/specialized law enforcement officers." *Police Studies* 18, no. 1 (1995), pp. 1–21.

Pomerville, P. "Popular myths about cultural awareness training." *Police Chief* 60, no. 11 (1993), pp. 30–31, 40–42.

Poole, E., and M. Pogrebin. "Crime and law enforcement policy in the Korean American community." *Police Studies* 13, no. 2 (1990), pp. 57–66.

Prince, J. "A pilot study to select and prepare underprivileged minorities and women for employment in law enforcement." *Journal of Police Science and Administration* 10, no. 3 (1982), pp. 350–356.

Rafky, D. "Racial discrimination in urban police departments." *Crime and Delinquency* 21, no. 3 (1975), pp. 233–242.

Scott, E. "Cultural awareness training." *Police Chief* 60, no. 11 (1993), pp. 26–28.

Skolnick, J. H. *Justice without Trial: Law Enforcement in a Democratic* Society, 3rd ed. New York: Macmillan College Publishing Company, 1994.

Stalans, L. "Police officers: A gender perspective." In M. L. Dantzker (ed.), *Contemporary Policing: Personnel, Issues, and Trends*, pp. 1–29. Boston: Butterworth–Heinemann, 1997.

Stokes, L. D. "Minority groups in law enforcement." In M. L. Dantzker (ed.), *Contemporary Policing: Personnel, Issues, and Trends*, pp. 31–51. Boston: Butterworth–Heinemann, 1997.

Sykes, R. E., and E. E. Brent. "The regulation of interaction by police: A systems view of taking charge." *Criminology* 18, no. 2 (1980), pp. 182–197.

Tafoya, W. "The future of policing." *FBI Law Enforcement Bulletin* 59, no. 1 (1991), pp. 13–17.

Toffler, A., and H. Toffler. "The future of law enforcement: Dangerous and different." *FBI Law Enforcement Bulletin* 59, no. 1 (1990), pp. 2–5.

Torres, J. "Making sensitivity training work." *Police Chief* 59, no. 8 (1992), pp. 32–33.

Trojanowicz, R., and B. Bucqueroux. *Community Policing: A Contemporary Perspective*. Cincinnati: Anderson Publishing Company, 1990.

Trojanowicz, R., and D. Carter. "The changing face of America." *FBI Law Enforcement Bulletin* 59, no. 1 (1990), pp. 6–12.

U.S. Bureau of the Census. *Statistical Abstract of the United States—1997.* Washington, DC: U.S. Government Printing Office, 1998.

Weaver, G. "Law enforcement in a culturally diverse society." *FBI Law Enforcement Bulletin* 61, no. 9 (1992), pp. 1–7.

Wright, B. "An examination of the current status of affirmative action in law enforcement." Unpublished manuscript, 1996.

Youngs, A., and A. Novas. "Accelerated learning: A new approach to cross-cultural training." *FBI Law Enforcement Bulletin* 64, no. 3 (1995), pp. 14–16.

Index

251

core values of, 41
crime rates and, 101
crime reporting by, 96
discrimination in, 239
domino effect in, 29
employment disputes in, 129
entrance standards of, 148
evaluation of, 108, 109–110
expectations of, 78–79
fitness programs in, 150–151
fitness standards in, 144, 149–150
funding for, 11, 208–209
humanistic, 184
language training in, 234–235
litigation against, 116, 122
litigation's impact on, 137–138
organizational charts for, 5, 6
private-sector support of, 220–221
professionalization of, 7–8, 187
rank structure in, 3–4
resource allocation for, 213–214
responsiveness of, 68
special, 2
standards for, 190
state accreditation of, 199–201, 202
structure of, 4–8
tobacco use in, 152
urban *vs.* rural, 246
wage issues in, 134
Law Enforcement Assistance Administration (LEAA), 92, 168
Law Enforcement Command College, 25
Law Enforcement Education Program (LEEP), 92
laws. *See also* common law; federal law; ordinances; state law; statutes; torts
asset forfeiture, 222
for constitutional violations, 125
for emergency vehicles, 123
fair employment, 118, 128, 129
in policy development, 81
protection by, 159
understanding, 137–138
lawsuits. *See* litigation
layoffs, in public sector, 166
LEAA. *See* Law Enforcement Assistance Administration
leaders
as change agents, 57–58

defined, 54
development of, 25
ethical duties of, 59
expectations of, 16
organizational impact of, 58–59
performance assessment of, 108
roles for (*See* roles, leader)
skills of, 55–56
values of, 56–57, 61, 69
leadership
characteristics of, 21–23
concept of, 16, 48
continuity in, 198
credo for, 85
defined, 54
development of, 24
by example, 59
future of, 25–26
maxim for, 9
mentor's obligation to, 40
in patrol operations, 45
quality of, 16–18
skills in, 32
style of, 23–24, 86
training facilities for, 25
traits for, 47–48
visionary, 25–26, 54, 58, 85
vs. management, 15, 53
Leadership Lessons, Goodwin's Ten, 55
leadership role
basis for assuming, 29
expectations for, 16
for managers, 19
preparation for, 17
for supervisors, 47
lead worker, 45, 46
LEEP (Law Enforcement Education Program), 92
legal services, of unions, 183
leniency, in performance evaluation, 103
levels of compliance, 190
Lewis, D. A., 96
Lewis, John L., 164–165
liability. *See* civil liability; executive liability
libel, 121
lieutenants. *See also* police officers
collective bargaining by, 174
in organizational chart, 6
in rank structure, 3

278   *Contemporary Police Organization and Management*

Southwestern Law Enforcement Institute, 25
sovereign immunity, 135
Spanish language training, 234
span of control
    defined, 6, 30
    policy guidelines for, 7
specialized assignments, 40–41
specialized training, 44
special revenue fund
    defined, 208–209
    for forfeited assets, 221
speech, freedom of, 133
Sprague, J., 98–99
SSPBA. *See* Southern States Police Benevolent Association
staff functions, 5
staffing, in patrols, 45
stamina, tests for, 149
standardization, of promotion process, 31, 32–33
standards, accreditation
    number of, 200–201
    parts of, 190–191
    policy derived from, 201
standard statement, 190
state administrative agencies (SAAs)
    block grant distribution to, 215–217
    federal funding via, 224
state government. *See also* government
    budget cycle of, 207
    expenditures of, 209–210, 211, 212–213
    federal support for, 214–217
    funding from, 223
    local-level support by, 218
state law enforcement agencies
    accredited, 194–195
    asset forfeiture funds for, 221
    capital costs in, 211–212
    federal funding for, 214–217
    function of, 2
    resource allocation for, 213–214
state laws. *See also* torts
    civil liability under, 119
    for emergency vehicles, 123
    for employment issues, 129
    for forfeited assets, 222
    protective, 159
state militias, 164
state peace officer associations

Internet sites for, 169
    nonunion, 171
states
    accreditation programs of, 188, 199–201, 202
    civil service systems in, 160
    fee systems of, 220
    fiscal capacity of, 206
    grants from, 216
    sovereign immunity in, 135
statute of limitations, in litigation, 116
statutes
    C/As in, 117
    for collective bargaining, 174
    for cultural training, 243
    fair employment, 128
    for forfeited assets, 221
statutory torts, 119
stereotypes, 237–238
stewardship
    importance of, 9
    supervisor's role in, 47
Stiebel, D., 76
Stone, A. R., 110
S-T-O-P Violence Against Women Act
    Formula Grant Program, 216
strategic planning, 58
strength testing, 149
stress
    alcohol use and, 153
    factors increasing, 10
    lifestyle changes and, 143
    management of, 145, 154–155, 156
    mortality due to, 144
    physical fitness and, 145
    in political environment, 60
    reactions to, 153
    tobacco use and, 152
    types of, 154
strictness, in performance evaluation, 103
strikes
    Boston police, 166–167, 172
    prohibition of, 165
    railway, 164
    right to, 179–180
    San Francisco police, 181
stroke
    alcohol-related, 152
    qi gong and, 146

local, 171–172
national, 172
power of, 42
private- *vs.* public-sector, 181
recruitment by, 166
structure of, 172
traditional, 174, 175, 178
union steward mentality, 49
United Auto Workers, 165
United States National Commission on Law
Observance and Enforcement, 91
Universal Hiring Program, 217
University of North Florida, 25
University of Virginia, 25
"unreasonable interference," 120
unrestricted intergovernment aid, 207–208
Unsinger, P., 241

V
values
accountability for, 69–70
appropriate, 72–73
change in, 78
communication of, 65, 67
in community policing, 107
culture and, 233
demonstrating, 71
disagreements over, 76
of ethical leaders, 56–57, 61
humanistic, 48
implicit *vs.* explicit, 71, 73
importance of, 68
leadership credo for, 85
multicultural sharing of, 236
organizational, 41, 71–72
policy for, 59, 80, 81
promoting, 9, 60
values-driven guidelines, 80
value system
for community support, 72–73
defined, 71
importance of, 68
multicultural, 230
Van Maanen, J., 33
Vaughn, J. B., 92
Vaughn, M. S., 126
verbal abuse
defense training for, 79
stress and, 153

verbal communication, 238. *See also*
communication
vicarious liability, 115
violence
factors leading to, 153
job-related, 147
Violent Crime control and Law Enforcement
Act (1994), 217
VISAR, in change process, 75
vision
accountability for, 69–70
in change process, 75, 78
communication of, 55, 61, 65
credo for, 85
described, 25
developing, 70–71
ethics and, 58
importance of, 68
in leadership, 54
in mission statement, 90
policy for, 80
preserving, 4
vision statement
development of, 71
promotion of, 9
Vollmer, August, 91

W
Wadycki, W., 210
wages. *See* salaries
Wagner Act (1935), 165
Walker, J. T., 110
Walker v. Darby, 133
"walking the talk"
concept of, 54
demonstrating, 58
importance of, 9, 61
Walsh, W. F., 98
warrants, search and seizure, 133
Waterman, R., 71
Watson, E. M., 110
Weaver, G., 237
Wegener, W. F., 103, 104
weight control, 143
wellness. *See also* health
approach for, 153–154
continuum for, 156
defined, 143
fitness programs for, 146, 148